FINANCIAL INTEGRATION IN EUROPE

FINANCIAL AND MONETARY POLICY STUDIES

Volume 24

The titles published in this series are listed at the end of this volume.

FINANCIAL INTEGRATION IN EUROPE

by

HARALD A. BENINK

Assistant Professor of Finance,
University of Limburg, Maastricht, The Netherlands, and
Adviser of the Banking and Financial Services Group
of Moret Ernst & Young

ERNST & YOUNG

SPRINGER SCIENCE+BUSINESS MEDIA, B.V.

Library of Congress Cataloging-in-Publication Data

Benink, H. A.
[Financiële integratie in Europa 1993. English]
Financial integration in Europe / by H.A.Benink.
p. cm. -- (Financial and monetary policy studies ; 24)
Rev. translation of: Financiële integratie in Europa 1993.
ISBN 978-94-010-4811-8 ISBN 978-94-011-1838-5 (eBook)
DOI 10.1007/978-94-011-1838-5
1. Monetary policy--European Economic Community countries.
2. Finance--European Economic Community countries. I. Title.
II. Series.
HG930.5.B4613 1992
332.4'566'094--dc20 92-16497

ISBN 978-94-010-4811-8

Printed on acid-free paper

TABLE OF CONTENTS

FOREWORD

One of the key issues relating to the performance of national economies is the efficiency of the financial system which stands at the heart of the capital-allocation process. There are two aspects which define efficiency.

Static efficiency involves the all-in difference between rates of return provided to ultimate savers and the cost of funds to users. This 'gap', or spread, reflects the direct costs of production (operating and administrative costs, cost of capital, etc.). It also reflects losses incurred in the financial process, as well as any monopoly profits earned and liquidity premiums. Financial processes that are considered 'statically inefficient' are usually characterised by high 'spreads' due to high overhead costs, high losses, barriers to entry, and the like.

Dynamic efficiency is characterised by high rates of financial product and process innovation through time. Successful product and process innovation broadens the menu of financial products available to ultimate issuers, ultimate savers, or other agents along the various financial process channels described above. Probably the most powerful catalyst affecting the competitive dynamics of the financial services industry has been technological change.

In recent years global financial markets for foreign exchange, debt and to a lesser extent equity have developed various degrees of 'seamlessness'. Indeed, it is arguable that the most advanced western financial markets are approaching a theoretical, 'complete' optimum where there are sufficient financial instruments and markets to span the whole spectrum of risk and return outcomes. Financial systems that are deemed inefficient or incomplete are characterised by a limited range of financial services and obsolescent financial processes.

Both static and dynamic efficiency are obviously important from the standpoint of national and global resource allocation, not only within the financial services industry itself but also as it affects users of financial services. That is, since financial services can be viewed as 'inputs' to the overall real production process, along with labor and capital, the level of national output and income - as well as its rate of economic growth - are directly affected. A 'retarded' financial services sector can represent a serious impediment to a nation's overall real economic performance. One major reason for progressive deregulation in many countries during the 1980s was an attempt to capture, for the countries involved, static and dynamic efficiency gains - and at the same time to capture the added value generated in the financial services industry itself.

In this volume Harald Benink has done an admirable job of chronicling the reconfiguration of the European Community financial structure - its origins in the Treaty of Rome, the progressive liberalisation of capital movements among members, and the creation of a comparatively level playing field for credit institutions, securities firms, insurance companies and institutional investors. All of this is accomplished in a coherent analytical framework.

The author traces liberalisation of intra-EC banking activities to the 1977 first banking directive, which allowed banks based anywhere in the EC to establish branches or subsidiaries in any other member country (freedom of establishment) on the condition that banking regulations in the host country were fully observed. It also required member states to establish a licensing system for credit institutions, including minimum 'fit and proper' criteria for authorisation to do business.

Under the 1989 second banking directive, a single EC banking license allowed credit institutions (authorised to do business in any single member state) to have full access to other national markets for all credit services without separate authorisation. This includes deposit-taking, wholesale and retail lending, leasing, portfolio advice and management, as well as trading in securities. In line with the broader dictates of the Basle Concordat of 1983, prudential control over all banks authorised to do business in the EC is exercised by home countries, including subsidiaries (which come under a separate 1983 EC directive on consolidated supervision).

Non-banking securities firms are to be covered by the Commission's 1989 draft investment services directive (ISD) and draft insurance directives, scheduled to go into effect sometime after

December 31, 1992. Again, home-country agencies - public authorities or professional self-regulatory organisations (SROs) appointed by public authorities - will retain the power of licensing, supervising and regulating investment firms. Institutions duly registered and supervised by EC home countries are essentially free to establish a commercial presence and to supply securities services in any member country without separate authorisation. Investment firms holding membership in stock exchanges in their home countries will likewise be free to apply for full trading privileges on all EC stock, options and futures exchanges. Close collaboration is envisaged between the EC Commission, the authorities responsible for securities markets and institutions, and banking and insurance authorities. Some insurance can already be bought freely cross-border, but final definition of the playing field in the insurance sector may well lag well behind the banking and securities industries.

Foreign financial institutions are treated in accordance with the principle of 'reciprocal national treatment' and, once certified by a member country, notionally fall under the same 'single passport' rules as EC financial institutions as long as their home countries are not found to discriminate against EC-based institutions. However, 'reciprocal national treatment' needs to be understood in the context of the procedural requirements of the second banking directive, which limit the possible misuse of reciprocity. The absence of such restraints in U.S. legislation could lead to their removal in Europe, with the danger of reciprocity showdowns about relative details of regulation. The benefit of the single passport is only available to EC subsidiaries of foreign financial institutions. Branches are not eligible and cannot be 'certified'. This is a major point, because of the capital cost of putting significant operations into subsidiaries. The same issue comes up in U.S. banking law - certain agencies, such as the SEC, are aggressively in favour of forcing use of subsidiaries, which raises a reciprocity threat against U.S. branches in Europe. Requirements to use subsidiaries rather than branches arguably constitute significant barriers to competition.

Another point of contention involves the capital-to-assets ratio required of banks and securities firms which impacts directly on their funding costs, as well as their ability to execute transactions, and hence their ability to offer competitive financing to clients. The move towards international agreement on regulatory capital achieved momentum with an Anglo-American initiative announced in January 1987 to strengthen the international banking community and create a level playing field among competing banks globally - as agreed in the 1988 Basle Accord - intended to promote a level playing field for credit institutions regardless of where they are home-based, and at the same time making further harmonisation of capital standards for credit institutions largely superfluous.

Comparable initiatives have been under active discussion within the EC with respect to the securities industry in the form of the capital adequacy directive (CAD), with respect both to securities firms and the securities activities of banks. The alternatives range from matching capital against position (market) risks, to minimum levels of firm capital covering all eventualities, along with EC-wide enforcement of maximum exposure limits.

Whatever capitalisation requirements emerge will also have to be aligned as between banks and non-banks doing securities business, in order to achieve regulatory parity, not least because the banking and securities activities are heavily integrated in most EC countries under universal banking structures. This is likely to become even more so in the future. Indeed, implementation of the draft ISD in the absence of an EC capital adequacy directive bearing on non-bank securities firms could lead to significant competitive dislocations among such firms, and between independent securities firms and banks. The debate is whether it makes sense to enact the CAD in the absence of the ISD or whether both must be enacted simultaneously.

Whereas the EC 'single passport' for banks and securities firms will be under the control of home country authorities, conduct-of-business rules regarding EC financial markets themselves will be the exclusive responsibility of host-country authorities. As it stands, under existing EC membership financial institutions will have to deal with 13 different sets of rules (including the Eurobond market), plus those of non-member countries. This will increase regulatory confusion and leave open the possibility of rule-based protectionism against non-domestic firms. It seems likely, however, that EC rules will gradually converge towards a consensus on minimum acceptable conduct-of-business standards, which will seek to optimise the balance between market efficiency and regulatory soundness.

Areas of particular interest with respect to conduct-of-business rules include insider trading and information disclosure. For example, the view that insider trading is a crime, rather than a professional indiscretion, is new in most of Europe - nobody in the EC has ever been jailed for insider trading, and in several member countries it is not a criminal offense. With regard to information disclosure in securities new issues, there has been consistent opposition to efforts at standardising the content and distribution of prospectuses covering equity, bond and Eurobond issues for sale to individuals and institutions in the member countries. An EC disclosure directive that was put forward in late 1988 for application in 1992 (involving a common prospectus but exempting Euro-securities not sold to the general public) was initially defeated, but two prospectus directives have since been adopted.

The regulatory environments of national bond and stock markets have certainly changed dramatically over the years. Starting in 1975 with the U.S. introduction of negotiated securities commission rates on 'Mayday' and working through assorted deregulation in the 1986 'Big Bang' reforms in London, as well as significant reforms in Tokyo, Toronto, and Paris, restrictive pricing conventions have been eliminated and business practices liberalised. Regulatory convergence has thus come some distance.

Finally, an EC directive governing the operation and sale of mutual funds - Undertakings for the Collective Investment of Transferable Securities (UCITS) - came into force on October 1, 1989 after 15 years of negotiation. It specifies general rules for the kinds of investments that are appropriate for mutual funds and how they should be sold. The regulatory requirements for fund management and certification are left to the home country of the firm, while specific rules for adequacy of disclosure and selling practices are left to the respective host countries.

Consequently, funds duly established and monitored in any EC member state and that are in compliance with UCITS can be sold without restriction to investors in local markets Community-wide, and promoted and advertised through local selling networks and direct mail, as long as selling requirements applicable in each country are satisfied. Permissible investment vehicles include high-performance 'synthetic' funds, based on futures and options, not previously permitted in some financial centers such as London. Under UCITS, (a) 90% of assets must be invested in publicly traded companies; (b) no more than 5% of the outstanding stock of any company may be owned by a fund; and (c) there are limits on investment funds' borrowing rights. Real estate funds, commodity funds and money market funds are excluded from UCITS.

The direction of EC regulation of credit institutions, securities firms, and investment vehicles - and the alignment of non-EC European markets to these standards - is of great importance for the future shape and volume of financial market activity. Financial markets regulation imposes both benefits and costs on participants, and it is *optimum* rather than *minimum* regulation that will attract transactions-flows to particular markets. Symmetry of regulation and creation of a level playing field, especially as between banks and non-bank financial institutions and investment vehicles will represent an important determinant of the composition of market participants and the structure of transactions flows. Europe seems well on its way toward creating such a playing field, one that will be highly competitive and fully capable of competing with markets elsewhere in the world.

Assuming no regulatory and protectionist backsliding, the European financial market environment is likely to be of a kind that will allow various players to compete in each-others' markets geographically, cross-client, and cross-product, including insurance, real estate and various areas of commerce. The European regulatory setting should thus continue to evolve along the lines of the universal banking model, without significant geographic constraints, and provide a relatively level playing field for all kinds of financial institutions to compete for business across the entire financial intermediation spectrum. This could provide a platform for some European institutions to mount a serious challenge in North American and Asian financial markets.

In its outstanding coverage of these complex issues in a straightforward, rigorous and understandable way, the author has created a volume of great importance to students of international finance, practitioners as well as regulators.

Ingo Walter

New York University
and
INSEAD

PREFACE

The subject of this publication is the planned completion of the internal market for financial institutions on January 1, 1993. At this date, or at a later time in the 1990s, there will be freedom of capital movements, freedom to provide financial services, and freedom of establishment by financial institutions in the Europe of the twelve European Community (EC) member states.

This financial integration process is being achieved through coordination and harmonisation at the Community level of the national legislation of the EC member states. The coordination of regulations in Europe is a process characterised by a huge amount of information in different forms (decisions, regulations, directives, recommendations and opinions) at various stages of consideration. While current developments are debated in the influential media, the latter do not always offer a coherent overview of EC coordination efforts as a whole, nor of relationships with other regulations produced, as for example in the framework of the Bank for International Settlements (BIS). Such an overview is essential in order to have a proper understanding of the consequences for the various countries.

This publication aims to provide this overview by discussing in a systematic way the regulations created since the Treaty of Rome. Attention will be paid to the regulations concerning the liberalisation of capital movements, credit institutions and investment firms, securities markets and undertakings for collective investment in transferable securities, insurance companies, and pension funds. The overview covers EC and BIS regulations in so far as they had been published in the Official Journal of the European Communities (OJEC) and in official BIS documents up to April 1, 1992.

I should like to take this opportunity to acknowledge the support I have received from the following people.

First, I should like to thank Jaco G.I.M. Reijrink, chairman of the Ernst & Young International Banking and Financial Services Committee, for arranging the sponsoring of this publication by Ernst & Young. This has resulted in fruitful cooperation between academics and commercial professionals.

Secondly, my gratitude is directed to Professor Jacques J. Sijben, who lectures at the Department of Monetary Economics at Tilburg University, Tilburg, the Netherlands and at the post-graduate School of Financial Economics of the Tilburg Institute of Advanced Studies. His unabating enthusiasm in critically reading and guiding this study, has stimulated me enormously.

Harald A. Benink,
Maastricht, June 1992

I. INTRODUCTION, SUMMARY AND CONSEQUENCES

1.1 The birth of the European Communities (EC)

The idea of European unity goes back far into the past. However, for centuries the impetus of the nation state with its absolute sovereignty predominated. In the twentieth century this tendency has changed. The period between the world wars, with its chaos in economic and monetary areas, was already characterised by a strengthening of the idea of a united Europe. After the Second World war and the resulting division of Europe into an eastern and a western part, the motives were strong enough. The countries of Western Europe decided to unite in a number of international regional organisations. An important reason for this was the bad experience with the protectionism of the 1930s as well as the necessity of economic recovery after the destruction that had been caused by the war. Furthermore, the desire of the Western European states to eliminate war forever (the relationship between West Germany and France) and the need to combine forces against the danger from the communist world (the Cold War) played an important role.

After the war, Winston Churchill was the first to publicise the idea of European unification. On September 19, 1946 he suggested in a speech at the University of Zurich the necessity of constructing a kind of 'United States of Europe'. He saw the improvement of relations between France and West Germany as a first step in this direction. Some years later the idea was taken up by the French Minister of Foreign Affairs Robert Schuman. On May 9, 1950 he presented the so-called Schuman Plan. The spiritual father of this plan was Jean Monnet, at that time head of the French Planning Bureau. Schuman suggested that the entire Franco-German production of coal and steel be placed under a single common High Authority. The organisation would be open to other countries and could form the foundation for a European federation. The High Authority would have a supranational character. This meant that it would have to consist of individuals appointed jointly by the governments, who could take decisions that would be binding on France, West Germany and other participating countries (partial renunciation of national sovereignty).

The Schuman Plan was accepted by France, West Germany, Italy and the Benelux countries (Belgium, the Netherlands and Luxembourg). However, the British government rejected the plan since it was not favourably disposed towards a supranational High Authority or a future European Federation. On April 18, 1951 the treaty for the foundation of the European Coal and Steel Community (ECSC) was signed. The ECSC treaty came into force on July 25, 1952.

Jean Monnet became the first president of the High Authority. The treaty represented the creation of a common market for coal and steel. Within this market article 4 of the treaty prohibits (1) the imposition of import or export duties or levies with a similar effect and quantitative restrictions on the movement of goods, (2) the imposition of measures or practices that involve discrimination between producers, between buyers or between consumers, as well as measures and practices that restrict the buyer in the free choice of his supplier, (3) the provision by the states of subsidies or aid or the imposition by the states of particular duties, in any form, (4) the imposition of restrictive practices resulting in division or exploitation of markets.

The Schuman declaration on May 9, 1950 heralded the start of a period of ambitious attempts to shape European unification in several other fields according to this example. Two of these attempts reached the detailed wording stage: the treaty for a European Defense Community (EDC) and the draft treaty for a European Political Community (EPC). Particularly in France there was much opposition to the far-reaching consequences that acceptance of the EDC would have. When, in 1954, it finally proved impossible for the EDC treaty to come into force, the founding treaty for a European Political Commission was also dropped. In May, 1955 the Benelux countries introduced a new initiative. In a memorandum to the ECSC partners they argued that a new impetus for European integration would have to come initially from the economic area. Political integration would accordingly have to be preceded by economic integration.

The Benelux countries suggested the convening of a conference in order to produce the text of a treaty that would embody far-reaching cooperation (the creation of new communities), in areas including the development of peaceful uses of nuclear energy and the establishment of a common market. On June 1 and 2, 1955 the Foreign Ministers of the ECSC countries gathered in Messina to discuss the Benelux memorandum. It was accepted in broad outline. A Committee of Government Representatives led by Spaak, the Belgian Minister of Foreign Affairs, was appointed to make a preparatory study. The Spaak Report was completed in April 1956. During a conference in Venice on May 29 and 30, 1956 the ministers accepted this report as the basis for negotiations to draft the necessary treaties. After long negotiations, the treaty for the establishment of the European Economic Community and the treaty for the establishment of the European Community for Nuclear Energy (ECA, EURATOM) were signed in Rome on March 25, 1957. The ratification procedure proceeded rapidly, so that both treaties came into force on January 1, 1958.

The above has been a brief description of the origin of the three European Communities. In view of the subject of this study particular attention will be paid in the following sections to the European Economic Community (EEC).

1.2 The EEC Treaty

The Treaty regulates the substantive law of the EEC and encompasses rules relating to the free movement of goods, persons, services and capital, competition, the harmonisation of legislation and trade policies, the coordination of economic and social policies and a common policy in the agriculture and transportation sectors. A number of important articles are discussed below.

Article 1
This article states that the higher authorities concluded the Treaty in order to establish a European Economic Community.

Article 2
Article 2 lists the objectives and means of the Community.
These objectives are:

- a harmonious development of economic activity throughout the Community;
- continued and balanced expansion;
- increased stability;
- increasing improvement of the standard of living;
- closer relations between the member states of the Community.

The establishment of a common market and the progressive approximation of the economic policies of the member states are indicated as the means to achieve these objectives.

The common market referred to above is a form of cooperation more advanced than a free-trade area or a customs union. Both the latter imply the free movement of goods among the member states as a result of the abolition at internal frontiers of import duties and other obstacles to free trade such as quantitative restrictions. In a customs union a common customs tariff is also used in trading with third countries. In addition to a customs union in which goods can circulate freely, a common market also entails free movement of the factors of production (persons, services and capital), rules to safeguard fair competition (cartels, subsidies) and amendment of legislation to the extent necessary to guarantee such free circulation and movement. Amendment of legislation may for example include harmonisation of tax systems in the participating states.

In summary, it can be stated that a common market is a market in which every participant is free, under conditions of fair competition, to invest, produce, buy or sell, or to provide or obtain services, wherever the economic conditions are most favourable. A genuine common market is similar in nature to the domestic market of a single state.

In addition to the establishment of a common market, the coordination of economic policy is indicated as a means to realise the objectives of the EEC Treaty. However, both means are very closely related. The achievement of free movement of goods, persons, services and capital results in the member states being forced to coordinate their domestic economic policies. This is due on the one hand to the fact that liberalisation has made national economies more sensitive to developments in other member states as a result of a decline in the effectiveness of national policy instruments. On the other hand, excessive divergence of economic development in the member states may endanger the liberalisation achieved, as a result of states taking restrictive measures in order, for instance, to avoid disequilibrium in their balance of payments.

Article 3

The detailed content of the means discussed in article 2 are given in article 3. They consist of:

- a The abolition between the member states of customs duties and quantitative restrictions on the import and export of goods, as well as of all other measures having a similar effect.
- b The introduction of a single common customs tariff and of a single common trade policy with regard to third states.
- c The removal of obstacles to the free movement of persons, services and capital between the member states.
- d The creation of a common agricultural policy.
- e The creation of a common transportation policy.
- f The introduction of a regime guaranteeing fair competition within the common market.
- g The use of procedures to enable the coordination of the economic policies of the member states and to counteract disturbances in their balance of payments.
- h Further approximation of national legislation to the extent necessary for the operation of the common market.
- i The formation of a European Social Fund, in order to improve job opportunities for employees and to contribute to the improvement of their standard of living.
- j The establishment of a European Investment Bank, in order to facilitate the economic growth of the Community by tapping new resources.
- k Association with overseas countries and territories, in order to expand trade and jointly to promote economic and social development.

The subjects mentioned in article 3 are developed into legal regulations in the various chapters of the Treaty (articles 9-136). These legal regulations regarding the separate elements are preceded by three fundamental principles (articles 5, 6 and 7), while article 8 sets the pace for the development of the common market. It emerges from this structure that each individual provision of the Treaty must be interpreted in the light of the objectives and means mentioned in articles 2 and 3 in conjunction with the fundamental principles of articles 5, 6 and 7.

Article 4

Article 4 indicates the four institutions responsible for execution of the tasks entrusted to the Community.

- *The Commission*
The Commission is the permanent executive body of the Community, responsible for the initiation and coordination of Community policies and the supervision of their implementation and for the guardianship of the treaties.

- *The Council of Ministers*
The Council is the most important legislative body in the Community and responsible for the coordination of the general policies of the member states.

- *The European Parliament*
The European Parliament is the representative body of the Community and has a limited legislative task. It exercises the political control over the Commission, with which it shares powers of decision as regards the EC budget.

- *The Court of Justice*
The Court represents the judicial powers of the Community.

Together with the EEC Treaty and the Euratom Treaty the Agreement for Common Institutions entered into force on January 1, 1958.

Under this Agreement the three European Communities (ECSC, EEC and Euratom) have one Parliament and one Court of Justice. Since the entry into force of the Fusion Treaty on July 1, 1967 the High Authority of the ECSC and the Commissions of the EEC and Euratom have been replaced by a single Commission, while the Special Council of Ministers of the ECSC and the Councils of the EEC and Euratom have been replaced by one Council of Ministers.

Furthermore, article 4 provides that the Council and the Commission will be assisted by an Economic and Social Committee with an advisory function.

Article 5
Article 5 is the first of three articles indicating the general obligations of the member states. These fundamental principles are defined in articles 5, 6 and 7. In article 5 the member states are instructed to take all general or special steps appropriate to assuring the fulfilment of the obligations arising out of the Treaty or out of the actions of the institutions. They must also facilitate the fulfilment of the Commission's task. In addition to these positive obligations, member states must refrain from behaving in a manner that might endanger the achievement of the objectives of the Treaty. In view of the above, article 5 is also referred to as the principle of community allegiance.

Article 5 implies that the implementation of the Treaty is a matter not only for the institutions of the EC, but also for the member states, which must give their full cooperation in good faith. The following statement by Schuman can be quoted in this context: 'Europe will not be made all at once or according to a single general plan. It will be built through concrete achievements, which create a de facto solidarity'.

Article 6
Article 6 imposes on member states the obligation to coordinate their economic policies. This coordination should take place in close collaboration with the community institutions and to the extent necessary to achieve the objectives of the Treaty.

Article 7
Article 7 entails a prohibition of discrimination on grounds of nationality. This means that subjects of other member states must be treated in the same way as nationals.

Article 8
This article provides that the common market will be gradually realised over a transitional period of twelve years. This transitional period ended on December 31, 1969. However, the common market has still not been completed. The date for its final completion has been set by the Single European Act of February 1986 at December 31, 1992. The Single European Act will be discussed later. Articles 1-8, discussed above, form the first part of the EEC Treaty and are described as the principles of this treaty. The second part contains the foundation of the Community. The latter comprises on the one hand the principles with respect to agriculture and transportation and on the other hand the principles regarding the free movement of goods, persons, services and capital. The free movement of persons is divided into the free movement of employees and the freedom of establishment.

Free movement of goods

The provisions regarding the free movement of goods are included in articles 9-37 of the EEC Treaty.

These administrative provisions provide for the abolition of all obstacles to inter-state trade of a financial nature, such as customs tariffs and taxes, and of a quantitative nature (e.g. quotas), as well as the establishment of a customs union. The provisions concerning the free movement of goods apply not only to goods originating in the member states, but also to goods from third countries in free circulation in the member states. The latter goods are products for which import formalities have been completed and for which the due customs duties and taxes of the same effect have been paid and for which no complete or partial refunds have been allowed.

Free movement of workers

The provisions regarding the free movement of workers can be found in articles 48-51 of the EEC Treaty.

The free movement of workers entails the elimination of any discrimination, on the basis of nationality, between workers of the member states, with respect both to job opportunities and to remuneration and other conditions of employment.

Freedom of establishment

The provisions concerning the freedom of establishment are laid down in articles 52-58 of the EEC Treaty.

This relates to the free exercise of a non-salaried commercial activity, in the context of a permanent establishment in another member state by establishing agencies or branch offices, or by having more than one centre of activity.

Freedom to provide services

The provisions concerning the free exchange of services are included in articles 59-66 of the EEC Treaty.

This relates to the freedom to undertake commercial activities of a subject living in a member state other than the member state of the recipient, whether or not this involves temporary relocation of the recipient or the supplier of the service.

Both the freedom of establishment and the freedom of provision of services are jointly referred to as the freedom of employment and business performance.

Free movement of capital

Articles 67-73 contain the provisions concerning the free movement of capital. The free movement of capital between the member states comprises the abolition of restrictions on the movement of capital belonging to persons residing or established in the member states, as well as a ban on discriminative treatment on grounds of nationality, place of establishment or area of investment. An important aspect in this respect is that article 67 prescribes a liberalisation of capital movements only to the extent necessary to ensure the proper functioning of the common market.

The EEC Treaty is mainly a 'traité-cadre' (framework treaty) or a 'traité de procédure' (procedure treaty). This means that the Treaty contains objectives and principles, but that their elaboration into concrete measures is left to the institutions of the Community. Apparently there was insufficient time and consensus to include a detailed regulation in the Treaty.

With a view to such concrete measures, the Council and the Commission draft regulations and directives, and issue decisions, recommendations and opinions.

A *regulation* is general in application. It is binding in all its parts and directly applicable in every member state. The general application implies that it has a normative character and contains rules for an unknown number of persons and cases. The binding character in all its parts indicates that the regulation, as opposed to the directive, comprises binding rules. As such it creates rights and duties not only for the community institutions and national governments, but also for individuals. From the direct applicability in every member state it emerges that the regulation is valid as a community regulation throughout the Community, without the member states having to take action to implement such regulation in their national laws. We refer to this as the autonomous validity of the regulation. The direct applicability and autonomous validity of the regulation mean that regulations have priority over preceding and later incompatible national provisions. From the moment that the Community uses its regulating authority, the member states lose the authority themselves to legislate, unless the regulation determines otherwise.

A *directive* is directed at one or more member states and imposes on them the obligation to create in its or their legal order the legal position as defined by the directive. In contrast to the regulation, the directive is only binding with regard to the obligation laid down in it. The purpose of the directive is thus not to create uniform rules that apply to the entire Community, as is the purpose of regulations, but to adapt national laws to each other according to the purposes of the Community. The member states to which the directive is addressed, are free to choose the form in which and means with which they wish to implement the directive in their own laws. Depending on the circumstances they may choose the legal instrument and the procedure available within the national legislation for the subject to which the directive applies. The non-implementation of a directive in national law constitutes a violation of the Treaty.

A *decision* is an act in which on the basis of a general rule of Community law, a decision is made for an individual case. In contrast to a regulation a decision is only binding in all its parts on those to whom it is addressed. Decisions may be addressed to member states as well as to individuals. As with directives, decisions addressed to the member states have to be implemented by the national authorities in order to acquire the force of law. This is not the case with decisions addressed to individuals.

Recommendations and opinions have no binding force.

On the basis of article 8, paragraph 7 the common market should have been completed by January 1, 1970. This has not been achieved. It took until the 1980s before the idea of the creation of a common market was discussed with new élan. The White Paper of June 1985 and the Single European Act of February 1986 indicate December 31, 1992 as the latest date for its accomplishment. The slow pace of European integration was caused by the tension that existed between the requirements of the accomplishment and maintenance of the common market on the one hand and the national policies of the individual member states on the other. Two factors played a major role in this.

1 Insufficient coordination of negative (market) integration and positive (policy) integration.

Article 2 of the EEC treaty names on the one hand the completion of a common market, and on the other hand the coordination of economic policy as the means of accomplishing the objectives of this treaty. The common market results from permanent legal constraints on the use of national policy instruments that stand in the way of the functioning of a free market in the Community (negative integration). Community-instigated harmonisation or coordination of legislation and policy and the transfer of major national powers to the Community are referred to as positive integration. The designers of the EEC treaty expected that market integration would automatically lead to policy integration. Policy integration did not therefore have a high priority. This lack of attention to policy integration, however, has had a highly negative effect on the realisation of the common market: on the one hand there was a tendency to restrict the use of national policy instruments that restricted the effect of the free market, on the other hand, with the rise of the welfare state, national governments adopted interventionist policies to correct imperfections in the market economy. Such interventionist policies themselves do not necessarily have a negative impact on European integration, but the problem is that they were uncoordinated and unharmonised. There was a lack of coordination between the national policy interventions. Negative integration has to be accompanied by positive integration. A lack of positive integration also causes the negative integration to fail. In the process of achievement of integration between mixed economies, the two forms of integration are inextricably connected. Unfortunately, the EEC Treaty proved inadequate for the creation of the necessary cohesion between both forms of integration. This flaw in the EEC Treaty resulted in a lack of integration which had a delaying effect on the realisation of the common market.

2 Over the course of time a number of developments have impeded coordination of positive and negative integration and so increased the integration gap. These are discussed below.
   - Positive integration is only possible if there is adequate decision-making capacity at the Community level. This was lacking from the very beginning. It was even further restricted by the Agreement of Luxembourg and the expansion of the Community.

     The Agreement of Luxembourg of January 28 and 29, 1966 was connected with the fact that on January 1, 1966 a new stage in the transitional period up to January 1, 1970 became effective. During this new phase the Council was able to decide by qualified majority instead of the formerly required unanimity. This also applied to the proposals for the financing of agriculture that the Commission had presented to the Council in 1965. France, which in contrast to the other member states, was unable to agree with the proposals, was afraid of being overruled by a qualified majority. At the end of 1965 the French caused a crisis by boycotting the Council sessions. The Agreement of Luxembourg put an end to this crisis. The Agreement contained the following: when, in the case of decisions that can be made by a majority of votes there are very important (vital) interests at stake, the members of the Council will attempt, within a reasonable period of time, to produce solutions acceptable to all the members of the Council. With regard to the interpretation of the concept of a 'reasonable period of time' the French delegation considered that, where important interests are concerned, the discussion should be continued until general agreement is reached. Although the Agreement of Luxembourg did not introduce a formal right of veto, the

Agreement did create the political scope for recognising more or less vital national interests whenever they are threatened. This impaired the Council's decision-making ability including its ability to take decisions on positive integration.

- Expansion of the Community (United Kingdom, Ireland and Denmark on January 1, 1973, Greece on January 1, 1981 and Spain and Portugal on January 1, 1986) resulted in greater differences of opinion concerning the position of government in relation to the market. This complicated the achievement of the consensus required for positive integration.
- The stagnating economic growth since the early 1970s restricted the tangible scope for positive integration at the Community level. At the national level this stagnation also led to more government intervention, which was uncoordinated and consequently disruptive to the common market.

In conclusion it can be said that the abolition of the existing lack of coordination is necessary for effective completion of the common market. This means restoration of coordination between negative and positive integration. In this context the White Paper of 1985 and the Single European Act of 1986 play a significant role.

1.3 The White Paper and the Single European Act

'Completing the internal market' is the title of the White Paper presented by the European Commission to the European Council at the European Summit of June 28 and 29, 1985 in Milan. The White Paper names as its objective the completion of the internal (not the common) market on December 31, 1992. For this purpose a detailed timetable is presented with approximately 300 proposals to be implemented before January 1, 1993. The completion of the internal market was elevated to the status of a Treaty commitment as a result of the signing of the Single European Act in February 1986, which came into effect on July 1, 1987. The Single European Act is a treaty and contains provisions that entail modifications of the three EC treaties (ECSC, EEC and Euratom). With respect to the achievement of the internal market the Single European Act adds articles 8a, 8b and 8c to article 8 (transitional period until January 1970) of the EEC treaty. Article 8a stipulates that the internal market has to be completed by December 31, 1992. In addition, the internal market is defined in this article as an area free of internal frontiers, in which the free movement of goods, persons, services and capital is guaranteed. This definition is narrower than that of a 'common market'. Article 8b provides for the Commission to report to the Council on the progress of the activities with respect to the completion of the internal market, prior to December 31, 1988 and prior to December 31, 1990. Based on proposals by the Commission the Council will determine by qualified majority of votes the necessary policies and conditions to ensure balanced progress in all the sectors concerned. Under article 8c the Commission must take into account differences in economic development, which may lead to temporary deviation but must cause the least possible disturbance to the operation of the internal market. This provided a legal basis for the phenomenon of integration at two or more speeds. The possibility of voting by qualified majority mentioned in article 8b is further elaborated in the new article 100a. Under the latter article, as far as harmonisation of laws, regulations and administrative provisions relating to the creation and operation of the internal market are concerned, the unanimity of votes of article 100 is replaced by a qualified majority. The relaxation in the voting procedure does not, however, apply to tax provisions, to provisions relating to the free exchange of goods and persons or to the rights and interests of workers.

Under article 100b the Commission must during 1992 draw up a report on the rules which have not yet been the subject of harmonisation. The Council can then resolve by a qualified majority of the votes to deem the rules in force in a member state as equivalent to those in force in another member state. This is the principle of mutual recognition. The replacement of the principle of complete harmonisation by the principle of partial harmonisation supplemented by mutual recognition of rules not yet harmonised was already suggested in the White Paper. This included the following remark: 'In the first twenty five years harmonisation policy has been the cornerstone of the Community's actions and has produced unparalleled results in the establishment of common Community-wide regulations. Over the years however, a number of shortcomings have appeared and it is clear that a genuine common market cannot be completed by 1992 if the Community has to rely solely on article 100 of the EEC Treaty. In the future a clear distinction will have to be made in respect of initiatives for the internal market, between *items that must unconditionally be harmonised and those for which mutual recognition of national rules is sufficient.*

The realisation of the White Paper and the Single European Act represent a break with the preceding period in which the European integration process was on the back burner. An increasing consensus had developed within the EC on the need to realise an internal market as a defence against increasing competition on the world market. The globalisation of products and markets means that European businesses must produce on a scale equal to that of American and Japanese businesses. In this connection it is important to have a large homogeneous home market of some 350 million consumers. The resulting economies of scale can reduce unit production costs. The report 'The Economics of 1992' by the Steering Committee of the 'Costs of non-Europe' project, presided over by the Italian Paolo Cecchini and published in March 1988, deals with the extensive positive growth effects that will be generated by the internal market. The Cecchini report argues that these growth effects will occur through four main channels:

1 Cost savings through the economies of scale of a large homogeneous market.
2 The free internal market will increase competition between businesses, resulting in improved efficiency.
3 In a free internal market with increased competition the member states will concentrate on the production of those products in which they have a comparative advantage. This means more efficient production on a Community scale.
4 The free internal market will be characterised by great dynamism, as a result of which new and better products will be produced by innovation.

In summary it can be stated that the free internal market will exhibit great efficiency, flexibility and dynamism. This supply-side strengthening will generate a permanent increase in the level of production, consumption and investment.

1.4 The internal market for financial institutions

In the context of this study the globalisation of financial markets is of particular interest. It is the integration of financial markets on a global scale that has increased the need for a free internal market for financial institutions. This globalisation means that, since the 1970s, there has been increasing integration between the international financial markets (particularly the Euromarkets) and between the national financial markets, a trend which accelerated in the 1980s. The expansion of the markets for international bonds (namely eurobonds), for euronotes and for euro commercial paper has strongly increased the possibilities of holding both international capital assets and taking up international credits.

The consequence of this is that the character of the intermediation process of saving and investing has acquired an increasingly international character and takes place relatively less through national money and capital markets. This process of globalisation is particularly apparent in the increased use of new financial products such as note issuance facilities (NIFs), swaps and forward rate agreements (FRAs), which have strongly increased the volume of international financial transactions. The causes of this globalisation of the financial markets are to be found primarily in the financial innovation process that has taken place since the late 1970s. In order to demonstrate clearly the position of this globalisation within the financial innovation process, the causes of financial innovation will be discussed below. A distinction will be made between demand-driven and supply-driven causes of financial innovation. An explanation will be given on the one hand of why a demand has arisen on the part of economic agents for new instruments to perform certain financial functions. On the other hand an explanation will be given of why and how financial institutions have been willing and able to act as the counterparty for the above-mentioned economic agents.

The demand-driven causes of financial innovations

The need for new instruments that fulfil certain functions originates from the interplay of market forces in the financial markets and in the world economy. Government policy in the areas of macro-economics and financial regulation also plays an important part. This process is known as the demand-driven view of the innovation process.

On the basis of the function of such new instruments, we can distinguish the following four demand-driven innovations:

a risk-transferring innovations;
b liquidity-increasing innovations;
c credit-generating innovations;
d equity-generating innovations.

A risk-transferring innovations

The *risk-transferring innovations* make it possible to transfer the risks connected with certain financial positions to other economic agents in the financial system. This relates both to the transfer of market and price risks and to the transfer of credit risks. Market and price risks arise from fluctuations in asset prices. This has a negative influence on the value of a financial position. The credit risk is the risk of a debtor being unable to fulfil his obligations.

The demand for price-risk-transferring innovations originated as a result of the increased vulnerability of financial positions to changes in asset prices. This was connected with the greater mobility and especially the unpredictability of interest rates and exchange rates. The rise of inflation in the 1970s was the cause of these increasing fluctuations. The abolition by many countries of interest rate ceilings and the transition to a system of flexible exchange rates made such fluctuations possible. The acceptance of monetary aggregates rather than price variables (short-term interest and long-term interest) as intermediary target variables of monetary policy (in October 1979 the Federal Reserve of the US switched to a policy of controlling growth in the money supply in order to curb inflation) also strongly increased fluctuations in interest rates and exchange rates. This increased mobility or volatility created a demand for new financial instruments to provide protection against the resulting interest and exchange rate risks.

The demand for credit-risk-transferring innovations is directly connected with an increased vulnerability of existing financial positions to deterioration of the solvency of debtors. A recent example of such a deterioration of solvency is the international debt crisis. The outbreak of this crisis in August 1982 resulted in the banks being suddenly confronted with a deterioration of the quality of their international loans (increasing credit risks). In this period relatively high amounts were outstanding in countries with a high credit risk or low creditworthiness. This caused a demand for new products to reduce these risks to a more acceptable level.

B liquidity-increasing innovations

The *liquidity-increasing innovations* relate either to new instruments or techniques that increase the liquidity or marketability of existing financial instruments, or to new instruments with greater liquidity.

These innovations are the result of a general increase in the demand for liquidity. This increased demand can be attributed to several factors. One of the most important was the increase in interest rates at the end of the 1970s and at the beginning of the 1980s. As a result the more interest-conscious public began to exercise a demand for interest-bearing money substitutes (optimum cash management). The increased concern of the public regarding the liquidity of the banks as a result of the international debt crisis also played a part. As a result, the public became more likely to invest directly in the financial markets rather than depositing their money in banks. However, investment in financial markets is less liquid than short-term bank deposits. This loss of liquidity created a demand for liquidity-generating products. The increased use of loan capital, by businesses as well as by individuals, also led to liquidity-increasing innovations. This, coupled with decreasing inflation led to a higher perceived (real) indebtedness, which increased the demand for precautionary liquidity. The increased demand for such precautionary liquidity serves, in this context, as compensation for the risks connected with the fixed interest and repayment obligations on borrowed capital.

C credit-generating innovations

The *credit-generating innovations* increase the economic agents' access to the credit supply. This can be achieved by an increase in the overall volume of credit on the one hand, or by substitution between credit forms (e.g. from short-term bank credit to long-term loans), on the other.

The demand for an increase in the credit volume was caused by three factors. The most important is the increased need for finance on the part of national governments, especially the American government. This increase resulted in the other players being crowded out of the market, thereby creating a need for credit-generating instruments for such players. In addition to this crowding out, the demographic factor of the baby boom played a part. The baby boom relates to a comparatively large group of people born after World War II, reaching the age of independency in the 1970s and the 1980s and causing an increased demand for mortgages and personal credit. Trade and industry were also in need of greater credit. This was caused by the (real or perceived) undervaluation of listed American corporations by the financial markets; since it led to mergers and takeovers, which were financed with borrowed capital. Consequently, this potential threat of hostile takeovers resulted in a higher need for credit. To prevent such takeovers many companies started buying their own shares. This, in turn, was financed with more borrowed capital.

In addition to the need for an increased volume of credit, there was also a need for the substitution of one form of credit with another. The latter factor is closely related to the shift in worldwide balances of payment, and thus to the geographical shift of the world's financial flows. In 1982 the current account surplus of the OPEC countries changed into a deficit. In turn, the United States was confronted with large current account deficits and became a net importer of capital in 1983. Japan experienced a further increase in its current account surplus and became the biggest world creditor in 1984. The deficits of the non-oil-exporting developing countries declined at the outbreak of the debt crisis as a result of reorganisation programmes. In addition, the banks became much less willing to grant more credit to such countries. The above-mentioned shift resulted in a change in the structure of international financing flows. This resulted in a need for new forms of intermediation. In the 1970s the surpluses of the OPEC countries were mainly passed on to the developing countries in the form of credits from the international banks (recycling of petrodollars). This is connected with the fact that the OPEC surplus countries had a substantial preference for investing their dollars in bank deposits in the eurodollar market. In the 1980s however, Japan took over the OPEC countries' function as the provider of dollars. However, Japanese institutional investors did not lend these dollars to the European banking system (whose creditworthiness had declined as a result of the debt crisis), but invested the dollars directly in American shares and government paper.

The shift in worldwide balances of payment was not the only reason for the demand for substitution between forms of credit. The unequal pace of the process of financial liberalisation and deregulation in the various countries was also a cause. This created new arbitrage possibilities, while new financial instruments also ensured that such arbitrage possibilities could also be exploited in practice. The result was that debtors were able take up credit at a lower price.

D equity-generating innovations

The *equity-generating innovations* increase access to the market for equity capital for those seeking such capital.

The need for these innovations was prompted by the stricter solvency requirements imposed on the banks. These requirements are closely related to the lower creditworthiness and the higher risks in the banking business. This led to an increased demand for equity capital (own funds in EC terms) and hence to equity-generating innovations. Two examples of such innovations are variable-dividend preference share capital and perpetual floating rate notes.

The supply-driven causes of financial innovations

Four factors play a part in the increased willingness of financial institutions to meet the demand for innovative instruments:

a technology;
b higher solvency requirements;
c increased competition in the financial system;
d historical dynamics of the innovation process.

A technology

The rapid developments in telecommunications technology, combined with a reduction in the cost of performing financial transactions, have led to the creation of a financial market on a worldwide scale. The associated higher turnover potential stimulated financial institutions to act as market maker in new instruments. In addition, the improvements in the process of information gathering and information processing enabled market makers to quote even complex financial instruments on a continuing base. Finally, technological progress provided faster and improved information flows, thereby reducing the cost of finding the cheapest means of finance. As a result of this it became increasingly easy for economic agents to compare prices offered by various financial institutions and to play one institution off against another. The resulting increased competition led to a fall in profit margins on traditional financial products. These developments in turn stimulated financial institutions to introduce new and innovative products geared to the wishes of clients. These products yield high profit margins in the initial stage (premium rates as long as there are still few if any competitors).

B higher solvency requirements

The higher solvency requirements connected with the lower creditworthiness of the banks entail a greater need for equity capital (own funds). However, precisely because of the lower credit rating the costs of equity capital had increased (higher risk premium). This encouraged the banks to undertake a substitution process from on-balance-sheet activities to off-balance-sheet activities. As a result of such substitution a greater part of the banks' profit is made in activities that do not reflect on the balance sheet and are thus also not subject to solvency requirements.

C increased competition in the financial system

Computerisation, telecommunications, worldwide deregulation and liberalisation of financial markets have contributed to increased competition in the financial system. As mentioned before, this has caused financial institutions to be more willing to respond to the demand for new instruments on conditions favourable to clients.

D historical dynamics of the innovation process

New innovations are often improvements of earlier innovations. In this respect existing products are given a facelift. If there is a demand for this type of development, the financial institutions will be happy to respond.

In summary it can be stated that the above-mentioned globalisation is closely connected with the financial innovation process which began at the end of the 1970s. In addition, particularly the deregulation and liberalisation measures and the technological innovations (24-hour market) have created the framework within which the increasing need for international financial transactions has been able to crystallise. The need for an internal market for financial institutions in 1993 therefore arises from the above-mentioned developments in financial markets worldwide.

1.5 Three freedoms

The internal market for financial institutions in 1993 is to be achieved by means of three freedoms, namely the freedom of establishment, the freedom of provision of services and the freedom of capital movement. In order to achieve this, Community legislation for these areas is to be established and implemented.

With regard to legislation on the liberalisation of the movement of capital, the Council directive of June 24, 1988 stipulates that freedom of movement of capital should in principle exist by July 1, 1990. Only Spain, Portugal, Greece and Ireland may apply derogation provisions for a number of years.

The above-mentioned freedom of movement of capital entails freedom of banking capital, of securities capital and of insurance capital. A free internal banking market in 1993 will be achieved not only through liberalised movements of banking capital, but also through freedom of establishment of banks and of provision of banking services. In this study the discussed legislation with regard to establishment and provision of services is divided into a number of categories. First of all attention is given to the category 'establishment and provision of services in the narrow sense'. This concerns the EEC rules that have to ensure the abolition of restrictions on the freedom of establishment and of the provision of services. Another important aspect is the first coordination directive of 1977. The aim of the latter is to facilitate the effective possibility of establishment and of provision of services across the borders of the member states by means of coordination of banking laws. The directive should be seen as a first step towards effective coordination. This is because it is restricted to a number of provisions of a general nature, which lay down the basis for more detailed coordination regulations in directives to be adopted or proposed at a later stage. The main provisions concern the concept of 'credit institution', the adoption of a system of authorisation, solvency and liquidity ratios and collaboration between the competent national authorities.

Subsequently, attention is given to more detailed coordination rules in directives adopted or proposed at a later stage. The following categories are dealt with: consolidated supervision, annual accounts and consolidated accounts, publication of annual reports, own funds and solvency, large exposures, deposit guarantee schemes, reorganisation and winding-up, consumer credit and mortgage loans. However, the cornerstone of all Commission initiatives for banking in the framework of the completion of the internal market in 1992 is formed by the second coordination directive adopted in December 1989. The aim of this directive is to remove the remaining restrictions on the freedom of establishment in the banking business and to ensure complete freedom of provision of services. The key element in this directive is the requirement for a single, universal banking authorisation (licence). On the basis of this single banking licence, authorised institutions may operate in all twelve EEC countries, both in commercial banking and in investment banking. The universal licence applies to the permitted services listed in the annex to the directive.

In addition to the above-mentioned liberalisation of equity capital, the free internal market for securities in 1993 also requires freedom of establishment and of the provision of services by investment firms. To this end a draft directive on the provision of services in the field of securities investment is circulating in Brussels. This draft directive can be regarded as the counterpart of the adopted second coordination directive for banking credit institutions. The Commission's aim is to make both directives effective with effect from January 1, 1993. In this way distortion of competition between the securities departments of credit institutions (covered by the second coordination directive) and the investment firms (covered by the directive for investment firms) will be avoided.

Attention is then given to a number of adopted or proposed directives concerning the following categories: the admission of securities to official stock exchange listing, the public offer prospectus, the information to be published when a qualifying holding of the capital of an undertaking listed on a stock exchange is acquired or disposed of, insider trading, a European code of conduct for transactions in securities, and undertakings for collective investment in transferable securities.

In the context of the insurance market in 1993 the regulations concerning a number of types of insurance, such as non-life insurance (divided into a number of sub-categories such as motor vehicle liability insurance, credit and suretyship insurance, legal expenses insurance etc.) and life assurance are discussed.

The coordination of freedom of establishment has been achieved by the first coordination directive on non-life insurance of July 24, 1973 and by the first coordination directive on life assurance of March 5, 1979. The two coordination directives make admission to the insurance business subject to granting of authorisation. In addition to extensive regulations concerning the conditions of admission, the two directives introduce regulations concerning the conditions governing the pursuit of the business. This relates to supervision of the financial situation of admitted insurers. Three concepts play a part in this connection, namely the technical reserves, the solvency margin, and the minimum guarantee fund. Insurers must create a technical reserve for the purpose of fulfilling commitments that they have made. The solvency margin is the free capital required to withstand the uncertainties of the business. The purpose of the minimum guarantee fund is to ensure that, at the time of their establishment, insurance companies already have sufficient resources and to prevent the solvency margin from falling below the minimum safety margin during the performance of the business. With regard to the freedom of provision of services, the second coordination directive for direct insurance other than life assurance was adopted on June 22, 1988. The Council adopted the second life assurance directive on November 8, 1990. Complete liberalisation in the field of establishment and provision of services by insurance companies is to be created by the third non-life insurance directive (amended proposal of February 24, 1992) and the third life assurance directive (proposal of February 25, 1991).

1.6 Strategies in 1993

As of January 1, 1993 the second coordination directive for credit institutions and the directive concerning the provision of services in the field of investments in securities for investment firms will enter into force. On the basis of a universal banking authorisation the institutions concerned can operate in all twelve EC member states, both in the field of commercial banking and in the field of investment banking. The universal authorisation applies to the permitted services listed in the annexes of both directives. The abolition of the distinction between commercial banking and investment banking will have significant consequences for countries in which banks may not undertake securities business or may only undertake such business on a restricted basis (Belgium, France, Greece, Italy, Spain and Portugal, inter alia). These are countries with highly protected and regulated markets. Countries such as Germany, Luxembourg, the Netherlands and the United Kingdom already have a more or less universal banking system. In the latter countries the consequences will therefore be less significant.

The question now arises whether, in view of the internal market with effect from January 1, 1993, financial institutions should review their strategies. Financial institutions will then have the possibility of serving a home market of some 350 million residents. The thinking in this respect is that if financial institutions start to operate on a wider European scale, this could result in economies of scale. However, this line of thinking is not undisputed. American research by the Federal Reserve Bank of New York into the optimal size of financial institutions reveals that initially average costs decrease with an expansion in the level of activity. However, from a certain level onwards economies of scale are outweighed by diseconomies of scale, this being reflected in an increase in average costs. Whether this also applies to Europe will be discussed later.

The above-mentioned study concludes that an optimal size for American banks is between 15 and 37 billion dollars in total assets. For purposes of comparison: the total assets of Citicorp amount to approximately 200 billion dollars. It appears that for many American banks efficiency is more important than the size. This means that a reduction in average costs is more likely to be achievable by means of an increase in efficiency than an increase in size. In other words: 'Don't get bigger, get fitter'.

If this conclusion were also to be valid for European financial institutions, the financial institutions concerned would not have many problems in determining their strategic policy in the light of 1993. The problem is, however, that the twelve EC member states together have a population almost one and a half times larger than that of the United States, while the geographical area of the EC countries together is just less than half the size of the United States. This makes it easier for economies of scale to occur. In view of this and given the fact that the European internal market will be characterised by a high degree of competition, the motto for financial institutions in the territory of the EC should rather be: 'In any case get fitter, and if necessary get bigger'.

The increase in the size of individual financial institutions can occur in four ways:

1 The provision of services from the country of origin.
  This strategy only works for certain financial products, such as credit cards and shares in investment funds. For the majority of financial products a physical presence is required in the country where the services are offered.
2 Establishment or expansion of the institution's own office network abroad.
  This is an effective strategy when dealing with only an expansion by means of a few offices in other EC countries. It will however, not be possible to operate on a European scale in the retail market, but on the other hand the business sector can be serviced everywhere while the inconveniences of a large unwieldy organisation can be avoided. If an organisation really wants

to establish a European branch network, the strategy becomes very expensive and time consuming. Citicorp, for instance, tried to establish such a branch network in the United Kingdom, through which it intended to sell mortgages. However, the costs were very high and there was fierce competition.

3 Joint operations.
This means that financial institutions in Europe enter into a collaboration agreement in the form of a holding company or a similar joint operation. An advantage of this strategy is the relatively low demands made on solvency. This is in contrast to takeovers (to be discussed below), in which one financial institution buys another. Examples are the proposed partial share exchange between the French Credit Lyonnais and the German Commerzbank and the proposed partial exchange of shares between the Dutch AMRO bank and the Belgian Societé Générale de Banque, which has since been cancelled. The intention of the latter share exchange was that it would have culminated in a full merger of the two banks into one new bank.

4 Takeovers.
This strategy means that a financial institution takes over another such institution, or allows itself to be taken over by financial institutions. Examples are the takeover of the Banca d'America d'Italia by the Deutsche Bank, the takeover of Nederlandse Credietbank by the Credit Lyonnais Bank Nederland and the wave of takeovers in the Spanish banking sector. Such takeovers however, require considerable amounts of money, which many financial institutions do not possess.

In summary it can be stated that, depending on the current starting position (substantial or insubstantial financial resources, nationally or internationally oriented) and on the individual perception concerning the possibilities and consequences of the internal market, financial institutions will chose a size that is optimal for their individual situation. Besides European banks there will continue to be a place for regional (nationally oriented) banks and for banks that have specialised in one of the niches of the internal market (niche banking).

The individual perceptions referred to are surrounded with considerable uncertainty, since it is not sure how the 350 million EC residents will respond to the new possibilities that the internal market will offer them. In this context the following statement of a banker can be quoted: 'What really matters is not knowing what will happen, but what most people think will happen'.

The internal market for financial institutions offers many possibilities, but the realisation thereof is clearly a reflection of developments in the globalised financial markets in a worldwide context: '1993 is not about European competitiveness, it is about global competitiveness for European companies'.

1.7 Europe in 1993, the consequences for governments

The principles of minimal harmonisation, mutual recognition and home country control, anchored in the White Paper and the Single European Act, will lead to convergence of national regulations in individual member states with respect to the supervision of financial institutions.

The Commission intends, for example, to establish minimum solvency rules. However, each member state is free to define more stringent solvency control. On the basis of the principle of mutual recognition, however, the more stringent regulations in country A are equivalent to the minimum regulations of country B. If banks from country B open a branch office in country A, then, by virtue of the principle of home country control, they fall under the relatively flexible supervision of country B. As a result, these branches can compete strongly with the local banks in country A, since, because of their lower solvency requirements, they can supply their products on more favourable terms. The local banks will see their market share drop and will put pressure on their supervisors to adjust the solvency requirements towards the minimum EC requirements. This will lead to convergence.

Another question is the supervision of financial institutions whose head office is established outside the EC. On the basis of the directives for credit and financial institutions, subsidiaries may claim entitlement to the universal banking authorisation and will come under the supervision of the EC member state in which they are established. These subsidiary banks are a legally independent part of the non-EC parent bank and are established according to the laws of one of the EC member states. Branch offices of non-EC financial institutions form a legally dependent part of the parent bank, while such parent bank is not established according to EC laws and does not fall under the supervision of one of the EC member states. For this reason under European regulations branch offices will be subject to supervision by the authorities of the country in which they operate. For instance, a branch office of a Japanese bank in the Netherlands will be subject to supervision by De Nederlandse Bank (the Dutch central bank) and a branch office of the same bank in Germany to that of the Bundesbank. To be eligible for a universal banking licence, the Japanese bank concerned would have to establish a subsidiary in one of the twelve EC member states and place its branch offices under that subsidiary.

The entire European network of this Japanese bank would then be subject to supervision by one EC member state. However there is an objection to this. Formerly, with respect to solvency, the branch offices formed part of the Japanese parent bank, and in the new situation they form part of the subsidiary. The establishment of a legally independent subsidiary means that independent own funds (equity capital) must be created.

Closely related to the above is the question of the extent to which non-EC financial institutions may have access to the European internal market. The Commission's legislation is based on the principle of reciprocity. The interpretation of the principle of reciprocity is limited to national treatment. This means that in a third (non-EC) country financial institutions from the Community must receive national treatment offering the same opportunities to compete as those offered to local institutions. In addition, efforts are being directed towards effective market access comparable to that granted by the Commission to financial institutions from non-member countries.

European financial integration will also have consequences for national tax systems. At the moment there are still substantial differences in regulations concerning interest and dividend income, securities transactions and capital gains. Spanish deposit-holders for example cannot escape taxation on their deposits by virtue of a 20% withholding tax. In France there is no withholding tax but the banks have to report the interest they pay to the fiscal authorities. By diverting to Luxembourg, such depositors can gain fiscal advantages, since Luxembourg has neither a withholding tax, nor a requirement for banks to report to national or foreign fiscal authorities. (banking secrecy). Fiscal harmonisation will therefore have to be achieved in order to eliminate these divergences in net returns. In the absence of such harmonisation, savings and investment flows will become concentrated in certain financial centres.

1.8 Europe in 1993, the consequences for financial institutions

The internal market for financial institutions, to be completed on January 1, 1993, will enable such institutions to expand their area of activity. The present position of a financial institution influences the strategies that it will follow. A number of factors that determine the initial position are discussed below:

a Home market
Financial institutions with a large home market are in a stronger position to start operating internationally. This advantage is even greater if the home market concerned is liberalised, since in that case financial institutions are accustomed to operating in a competitive environment.

b Equity base
A strong equity base offers the possibility of financing foreign expansion.

c Access to the capital market
Financial institutions quoted on stock exchanges have better access to the market for equity capital than unlisted undertakings. The equity base can be considerably reinforced via the capital market.

d Profitability
Financial institutions with high profitability have the possibility of financing their expansion themselves. In addition, as a result of their profitability, they have more favourable access to the share capital market.

e Nature of the activities
The internal market enables banks to operate as universal banks in the EC of the Twelve. In this respect, banks that have traditionally operated both as commercial banks and as investment banks have a comparative advantage.

f Management
The competitive and international market of 1993 places heavy demands on management. Financial institutions that already have highly qualified management are in a favourable starting position.

g Technology
Computerisation, telecommunications and information technology and automation play an important part in cost reduction.

h Cost structure
Financial institutions with an excessively large branch network, too many staff and an inadequate level of automation have an unfavourable cost structure. In the light of 1993 they will have to streamline their operations.

i International character
Financial institutions that already have long international experience will be more able to handle the challenges of the internal market than nationally oriented banks.

In addition to making appropriate use of their own starting position, financial institutions need to develop a vision with regard to the possibilities that the internal market will create. A recent study by Price Waterhouse can be of assistance in this respect. The study makes an estimate of the potential price reductions that financial services will undergo as a result of the completion of the internal market. The largest potential price reductions and, thus, the greatest profit achievable in the short-term are to be found in the southern EC countries, such as Spain and Italy. Financial markets in the northern EC countries are less protected, more competitive and therefore charge less for their financial services. For the financial institutions in the latter countries this creates favourable possibilities for developing activities in the southern countries.

It does not make much difference whether the internal market is completed in 1992 or later. Depending on their starting position and of their perception with regard to the possibilities of the internal market, financial institutions are already adopting a specific positioning with a view to the post-1992 internal market.

1.9 The road beyond 1992

If 'Europe 1993' is completely successful it will mean the advent by December 31, 1992 of an internal market in the Europe of the Twelve. The realisation of an economic and monetary union and the establishment of a European central bank are regarded as the next logical steps.

This follow-up integration process is discussed in this section. First of all, some theoretical and practical aspects related to European economic and monetary union (EMU) are discussed. Then follows a short history of the development of the central banks as we know them and their position in relation to government. The current system of central banks in Europe is also discussed. Subsequently, the establishment of a European central bank as part of a European monetary union is discussed.

European economic and monetary union

An economic and monetary union (EMU) comprises the most far-reaching form of collaboration. From an economic point of view, a union constitutes a zone in which goods, persons, services and capital can move freely without distortions in competition, within which regional and structural imbalances are avoided as much as possible. From a monetary point of view, a union is an area in which exchange rates are irrevocably fixed and where there is full convertibility. Replacement of national currencies by a common currency is then merely a technical, monetary step.

Other characteristics of a union will also include the organisation of the central banks at the Community level and the transfer of the required decision-making authority in respect of economic policy to the Community level.

An EMU has a number of benefits and drawbacks. The benefits are:

- enhanced effectiveness of money as a medium of exchange;
- simplification of the function of money as a store of value;
- greater effectiveness of money as a unit of account for the comparison of prices;
- restriction of internal speculative capital movements within the Community;
- elimination of the drawbacks of limited integration:
  - lower cost of capital as a result of the elimination of capital restrictions;
  - limitation of the consequences of exchange rate fluctuations;
- macro-economic benefits, such as:
  - reduced dependence on the dollar;
  - tighter control over policy instruments such as interest rates and money supply;
  - better possibilities for coordinating a policy of stabilisation.

The drawbacks are:

- loss of national sovereignty;
- a possible conflict between the role of the national central bank as guardian of the value of a country's own currency and its role within a supranational body;
- disappearance of instruments for resolving internal and external regional imbalances.

Comparison of the pros and cons does not lead to clear conclusions. The benefits are frequently not straightforward: some occur at the macro-economic level, others at the micro-economic level. Some are certain to occur, others are no more than expectations. The benefits are sometimes difficult to quantify, while a number of drawbacks are tangible.

The literature on the realisation of an EMU describes various approaches, which often have their followers within certain national boundaries in the EC. German economists for instance, place particular emphasis on the convertibility of currencies and the freedom of movement of capital, while the British and the Italians emphasise regional problems, the effects of strictly fixed parity ratios in regions with high rates of inflation and structural problems. The French for their part emphasise above all the international implications of such an EMU.

A distinction is made between federalists and neo-functionalists. To the federalists, the apportionment of power between central and regional institutions is of primary concern; their approach to the process of integration is based on the ultimate goal, i.e. the federal state (cf. the United States). Progress in this context means transfer of power to the central authorities at the expense of national sovereignty. The neo-functionalists want to force integration through the creation of international institutions that deal with cross-border technical matters; collaboration in a particular field then necessarily results in collaboration in others.

Four strategies for the accomplishment of the EMU may be identified:
- unification of exchange rates: immutably fixed parity ratios between member states require codes of conduct for surplus and deficit countries with regard to intervention in the exchange markets and the establishment of an exchange rate stabilisation fund;
- harmonisation and coordination of economic policy with the object of eliminating differences in economic structure between the member states in order to prevent disparities in exchange rate movements;
- conversion of national currencies into a European currency unit;
- unification of national policies with regard to capital markets.

Attempts to create a EMU go back many years. After the establishment of an EMU was agreed at the European summit meeting in the Hague in 1969, many reports were published describing the conditions required for the establishment of an EMU. Important reports in this context were the Werner report (1970) and the All Saints' Day Manifesto (1975).

In the Werner report the most important features of an EMU were set out and a number of institutional reforms were proposed. The features concerned were:
- total convertibility of currencies without fluctuation bands and at fixed parities;
- the responsibility for monetary policy in respect of non-member countries rests with the Community;
- uniform capital market policy in all member states;
- structural and regional policy at the Community level;
- dialogue between government, management and the trade unions at the Community level.

The institutional reforms comprise:
- a decision-making centre for economic policy purposes;
- a Community system of central banks.

The far-reaching political implications of this report delayed the implementation of the proposals.

The Federal Trust report of 1972 shifted the emphasis to the creation of a new currency, the Europa, alongside existing currencies, and the creation of a European Bank with regulatory powers. The All Saints' Day Manifesto of 1975 proposed the launch of a new European currency with constant purchasing power, available to residents of Europe by exchanging national currencies at a variable rate of exchange.

The European Monetary System (EMS) came into effect in 1979. It is a system of exchange rates with a number of new elements, such as the use of the European Currency Unit (ECU), credit mechanisms and a plan to proceed to an institutional phase of the EMS.

The ECU is a composite 'basket' unit of account in which each Community currency has a certain percentage and hence absolute participation. Within the EMS the central banks must intervene on exchange markets whenever excessive exchange rate variations occur. Credit mechanisms, expressed in ECU make this possible. An EMS was to have been finally institutionalised in 1981. However, not much of this institutional phase was achieved, despite satisfaction with regard to the functioning of the system. Realisation of the Europe of 1993 (an internal market with free movement of capital) coupled to the objective of the EMS (establishing a zone of monetary stability), requires coordination of the monetary and budgetary policies of member states and the adoption of a common external policy.

In 1985 the chairman of the European Commission, Jacques Delors, proposed the transfer of the monetary powers of national governments and central banks to the European level, and specifically to the Council of Ministers. He did not speak of a transfer to a European Central Bank. This would represent a fundamental change for countries in which central banks have enjoyed great autonomy in matters concerning monetary policy (Germany and the Netherlands).

The role of the central banks

In the past many large, leading banks used to issue their own bank notes. They were called banks of issue. In the course of the last century it became clear, however, that for a country to have different bank notes circulating side by side was detrimental to economic development, so that banks of issue were subjected to legal regulations. Issuing rights were granted to one bank of issue, which developed into a central bank.

The relationship between central banks and the government can take a number of forms. Two extreme views can be distinguished in this context.

The first view is that the central bank is an extension of the Minister of Finance and cannot be independent of the government. The second view is that the power to issue money (the government) and the power to create money (the central bank) must be segregated. In between these two concepts there are many intermediate forms and views. Arguments advanced in favour of an independent central bank include, in particular, avoidance of the danger of inflation that would result from politically expedient objectives financed by the government via a dependent central bank. Counter-arguments include the view that whereas monetary policy would thus escape democratic controls, budgetary policy would not.

In the 1930s and 1940s government influence on the central banks increased as a result of:

- the adverse effects of the worldwide recession, resulting in the desire for increased government control over the economy;
- the departure from the gold standard, resulting in a greater need for monetary management;
- greater government control over the economy during World War II;
- the trend towards a welfare state.

Western economies have no truly independent central banks; rather they are independent within the government. Generally speaking, central banks nowadays have the following tasks:

- regulating the money supply;
- banker and agent to the government;
- management of the cash reserves of the commercial banks;
- management of a country's foreign currency reserves;
- provision of credit facilities to commercial banks;
- acting as lender of last resort;
- clearing of transfers between commercial banks;
- looking after foreign exchange transactions;
- control over credit for the purpose of implementing monetary policy.

These tasks are usually described in a banking law.

Differences in the working methods of central banks are often apparent from their memorandum and articles of association. In some countries maintenance of the value of the domestic currency has the priority (Germany and the Netherlands), while tasks sometimes also focus on general economic policy.

In most countries the government owns the shares in the capital of the central bank; in the United States, Switzerland, Italy and Greece this is not the case. Particularly in countries with a federal tradition, such as Germany, Switzerland and the United States, the call for an independent central bank is loudest. *The Banker* of October 1979 published the following summary:

	1	2	3	4	5	6	7	8	9
Australia	•		•				•		•
Austria	•						•		
Belgium	•	•							
Canada	•		•			•	•	•	•
Denmark	•								•
France	•			•			•		•
Germany	•		•		•	•	•		•
Italy	•	•		•			•		
Japan	•		•				•	•	
The Netherlands	•		•				•		•
Norway	•	•							•
South Africa	•		•				•	•	
Sweden	•	•		•					•
Switzerland	•		•		•				
United Kingdom	•	•		•			•		•
United States	•				•		•	•	

1 = central bank is the chief executant of the current economic policy in the monetary field
2 = central bank has no statutory duty to pursue stated economic objectives
3 = central bank has general duty to promote country's welfare or government policy
4 = central bank is subject to general directions of government in pursuing objectives
5 = central bank is largely independent of government in pursuit of statutory duties
6 = central bank has openly acted contrary to government's economic objectives
7 = interchange of staff takes place between government and central bank
8 = central bank is directly accountable to parliament
9 = the stock of the central bank is wholly-owned by the state

Within the EC the German Bundesbank plays a major role; the policy of the central banks in other EC member states is often aligned with that of the Bundesbank. It is also the most independent central bank in the EC: the German Finance Minister is not entitled to give directions.

The European central bank and European economic and monetary union

We have discussed earlier the EMS and the concept of a central bank in the EC. If such a central bank exists, the national central banks will become the executive bodies of its policy. Integration of monetary policy would then be a prerequisite however.

The independence of such a European central bank, in relation to both the member states and the other EC bodies, is emphasised by Germany and the Netherlands in particular.

In fact, the Community's central banks have already been collaborating within the EMS for ten years. Their presidents meet monthly with a representative of the European Commission. Once a year developments in the ECU-market are subjected to close scrutiny. Board members of the central banks meet monthly in Brussels in the context of the Community's Monetary Committee, together with ministry of finance representatives. Groups of experts from the central banks regularly prepare technical policy recommendations on monetary policy and the EMS. Collaboration between the central banks is therefore already institutionalised.

However, the current phase is regarded as a transitional period during which the monetary policy of EMS participants is being coordinated while national sovereignty is retained.

At the European summit held in Hannover in June 1988 government leaders agreed to set up a committee to be headed by Jacques Delors, the current chairman of the European Commission, who was given the remit to study the concrete steps that would lead to economic and monetary union (EMU). A year later the result of the study, 'Report on economic and monetary union in the European Community', was discussed at the European summit in Madrid. The first phase of the proposed EMU involves the liberalisation of capital movements by July 1, 1990. An intergovernmental conference, which began its deliberations in December 1990, had the task of deciding on the treaty changes required for the next phase of EMU. Progress in the form of agreement on a treaty on EMU was made at the European summit held in Maastricht in December 1991. The treaty contains the following key points:

- Effective January 1, 1994, no restrictions will be permitted on the free movement of capital. This also applies to Spain, Portugal, Greece and Ireland, which did not have to comply with the obligations on free capital movements of July 1, 1990.
- The second phase of EMU is also due to start on January 1, 1994. In this phase, there will be closer matching of the economic and monetary policies of member states, excessive budget deficits will be avoided and all national central banks will have to become independent.

  The European Monetary Institute (EMI), to be founded early in the second phase, will supervise coordination of monetary policy and prepare for the formation of the European Central Bank (ECB).
- Not later than December 31, 1996, the European Council is to decide by qualified majority whether a majority of the member states have complied with the conditions (adequate convergence of economic and monetary policy) for the transition to a single currency and, if this is the case, set a date for such transition (beginning of the third phase).

  If these conditions have not been met, and no date has been set for the beginning of the third phase by the end of 1997, this third phase will begin on January 1, 1999. On or before July 1, 1998, the European Council is to decide by qualified majority which of the member states comply with the conditions. Such member states then no longer have to constitute a majority of the member states.
- Member states which do not comply with the conditions will be given exemption. The position of such member states is to be reviewed every two years.
- The European Central Bank is to be formed by July 1, 1998 at the latest.
- At the start of the third phase, the member states which have not been exempted are to decide unanimously on immutable parity ratios between their domestic currencies and the ECU. The ECU is to become an autonomous currency.

II. LIBERALISATION OF CAPITAL MOVEMENTS

2.1 Freedom of capital movements in 1993

This chapter will give an overview of the development of capital movements since the establishment of the EEC.

The final result of this development should be a free internal market in which banking capital, investment capital and insurance capital can move freely from one member state to another in 1993 (for eight EC member states even by July 1, 1990).

The freedom of movement of capital is detailed in articles 67-73 of the EEC Treaty. This freedom comprises both the abolition of restrictions on the movement of capital belonging to persons living or established in the member states as well as a prohibition on discriminatory treatment on the basis of nationality or of the place of establishment of the parties or on the basis of the area where the capital is invested. The EEC Treaty is principally a conceptual framework. This means that the Treaty contains objectives and principles, leaving it to the institutions of the Community to work out the practical measures needed to effectuate them. The directives with which the Community institutions have given concrete form to the objectives and principles of the Treaty are surveyed below.

2.2 Pre-1986 directives

I FIRST DIRECTIVE OF MAY 11, 1960 FOR THE IMPLEMENTATION OF ARTICLE 67 OF THE TREATY
(OJEC 921/60 12.7.1960)

This first directive relates to the liberalisation of a number of categories of capital movement. These categories are included in lists A, B and C of annex I of the directive. They are introduced in articles 1-3. There is also a list D with no liberalisation obligation. Annex II contains a nomenclature of capital movements. The annexes were later changed substantially by directives to be discussed below. By including the categories of capital movement in different lists it is possible to apply any restrictive measures or different exchange rates individually per list.

Lists A and B are to be unconditionally liberalised although the stipulations on exchange rates applicable to list A are more stringent than those for list B. Exchange rates applicable to list A are those that also apply to current transactions, while, for the transfers in list B, member states will endeavour to have them effected at rates 'not significantly and permanently at variance with rates applicable to current transactions', if they are effected on foreign exchange markets in which rate fluctuations are not subject to official limits. For list C there is a conditional liberalisation obligation, while the categories mentioned in list D are not subject to any liberalisation obligation.

Article 1 stipulates that the member states must grant all foreign exchange authorisations required for the conclusion or performance of transactions or for transfers between residents of member states in respect of the capital movements set out in list A of annex I.

The following categories of capital movements are concerned:

- Direct investments.
  Excluding purely financial investments made with a view only to giving the persons providing the capital indirect access to the money or capital market of another country, through the creation of an undertaking or participation in an existing undertaking in that country.

- Liquidation of direct investments.
- Investments in real property.
- Capital movements of a personal nature.

The following categories are mentioned:
° Endowments and gifts;
° Dowries;
° Inheritances;
° Settlements of debts in their country of origin by immigrants;
° Transfers of capital belonging to residents who emigrate;
° Transfers of capital belonging to emigrants returning to their country of origin.
  - Granting and repayment of credits relating to commercial transactions in which a resident is participating.
    This relates exclusively to short-term transactions (less than one year), or medium-term transactions (from one to five years).
  - Sureties, other guarantees, rights of pledge and related transfers in respect of:
° Short- and medium-term credit, to finance commercial transactions in which a resident is participating;
° Long-term loans, with a view to establishing or maintaining lasting economic links.
  - Transfers in performance of insurance contracts.
    As and when freedom of movement in respect of services is extended to those contracts in implementation of articles 59-66 of the Treaty.

Article 2 liberalises the categories of capital movement named in list B of annex I:
- Acquisition by non-residents of domestic securities dealt in on a stock exchange (excluding units of trust funds) and the repatriation of the proceeds of liquidation thereof.
- Acquisition by residents of foreign securities dealt in on a stock exchange and the use of the proceeds of liquidation thereof.
  There are two exceptions. The first exception concerns the acquisition of bonds issued abroad and denominated in national currency. The second exception concerns units of unit trusts.
- Physical import and export of the above-mentioned securities.

Subject to the provisions of paragraph 2, the member states shall, on the basis of article 3, paragraph 1, grant general authorisation required for the conclusion or performance of transactions or for transfers between residents of member states, in respect of the capital movements set out in list C of annex I. In list C the following categories of capital movement are mentioned:
- Issue and placing of securities of a domestic undertaking on a foreign capital market.
- Issue and placing of securities of a foreign undertaking on the domestic capital market.
- Acquisition by non-residents of domestic securities not dealt in on a stock exchange and repatriation of the proceeds of liquidation thereof (compare list B).
- Acquisition by residents of foreign securities not dealt in on a stock exchange and use of the proceeds of liquidation thereof (compare list B).
- Acquisition by non-residents of units in domestic unit trusts dealt in on a stock exchange and the repatriation of the proceeds of liquidation hereof (compare list B).
- Acquisition by residents of units in foreign issued unit trusts dealt in on a stock exchange and use of the proceeds of liquidation thereof (compare list B).
- Acquisition by residents of foreign bonds dealt in on a stock exchange, issued on a foreign market and denominated in national currency (compare list B).
- Physical import or export of the above-mentioned securities.
- Granting and repayment of credits related to commercial transactions in which a resident is participating.

In contrast to the short- and medium-term transactions mentioned in article 1, this relates exclusively to long-term credits (five years or more).

- Granting and repayment of credits related to commercial transactions in which no resident is participating.
  This relates solely to medium- and long-term transactions.
- Granting and repayment of loans and credits not related to commercial transactions.
  Here too this relates to medium- and long-term transactions.
- Sureties, other guarantees, and rights of pledge, and related transfers in respect of:
  - ° Long-term credit in respect of commercial transactions in which a resident is participating (compare article 1);
  - ° Medium-and long-term credits in respect of commercial transactions in which no resident is participating;
  - ° Medium- and long-term loans and credits not related to commercial transactions.

It must be noted that a number of the categories of capital movement named in article 3 are complementary to the categories mentioned in articles 1 and 2. There is nevertheless a reason for dealing with them in a separate article. The categories mentioned in article 3 are covered by the derogation provision mentioned in paragraph 2 of this article. Paragraph 2 states that if liberalisation obstructs the achievement of the objectives of the economic policy of a member state, such state may maintain or reintroduce the exchange restrictions on the involved categories of capital movement which were in effect on the date of entry into force of this directive. In this context the member states often had recourse to articles 108 and 109 of the EEC Treaty. Under these articles the member states may take restrictive measures in the case of balance of payments problems. A sound balance of payments can be considered as one of the objectives of the economic policy as mentioned in paragraph 2. Furthermore, article 73 of the EEC Treaty enables the member states to take safeguard measures in the field of capital movements if capital movements result in disturbance of the operation of the capital market.

List D of annex I mentions the following categories of capital movements:

- Short-term investments in Treasury bills and other securities normally dealt in on the money market.
- Opening and placing of funds on current and deposit accounts with credit institutions; repatriation or use of the balances on these accounts.
- Granting and repayment of credits related to commercial transactions in which no resident is participating.
  This relates exclusively to short-term transactions (compare list C).
- Granting and repayment of loans and credits not related to business transactions.
  Here too this relates exclusively to short-term transactions (compare list C).
- Capital movements of a personal nature.
  In article 4 this relates solely to loans (compare list A).
- Sureties, other guarantees and rights of pledge and related transfers in respect of:
  - ° Short-term credits granted in respect of commercial transactions in which no resident is participating (compare list C);
  - ° Short-term loans and credit not connected with commercial transactions (compare list C);
  - ° Loans of a personal nature.
- Physical import and export of financial assets.
- Other capital movements.

From the above summary it is clear that a number of categories of capital movement in article 4 are complementary to the categories listed in articles 1 and 3.

Article 67 of the EEC Treaty prescribes a liberalisation of capital movements only to the extent necessary to ensure proper functioning of the Common Market. For that reason article 5, paragraph 3 of the directive stipulates that restrictions on capital movement under the rules for establishment in a member state shall be abolished only in so far as it is incumbent upon the member states to grant freedom of establishment in implementation of articles 52 to 58 of the EEC Treaty.

The implementation of this directive by the member states will be discussed later in this chapter.

II SECOND COUNCIL DIRECTIVE OF DECEMBER 18, 1962 ADDING TO AND AMENDING THE FIRST DIRECTIVE FOR THE IMPLEMENTATION OF ARTICLE 67 OF THE TREATY

(OJEC 62/63 22.1.1963, directive 63/21/EEC)

Article 2 of this second directive contains a number of additions and amendments to the annexes I and II of the first directive.

The following categories of capital movements have been added to list A of annex I:

- Transfers of workers' savings during their period of stay (personal capital movements).
- Transfers by instalments of funds belonging to non-residents, by the holders of such funds in case of special hardship (personal capital movements).
- Annual transfers of blocked funds to another member state by a non-resident account holder up to an amount or percentage of the total balance, fixed uniformly by the member state concerned for all applicants (personal capital movements).
- Transfers of minor amounts abroad (personal capital movements).
- Death duties.
- Damages and interests (where these can be considered as capital).
- Refunds in case of cancellation of contracts and refunds of uncalled-for payments (where these can be considered as capital).
- Authors' royalties, patents, designs, trade-marks and inventions (assignments and transfers arising out of such assignments).
- Transfers of the money required for the provision of services.

Furthermore, in lists A, C and D the term 'commercial transactions' is complemented with the addition 'or the provision of services'. List B remains unaltered. In list D the item 'remaining forms of capital movements' is replaced by 'remaining forms of capital movements: miscellaneous'.

The above modifications are carried over into the nomenclature incorporated in annex II.

III COUNCIL DIRECTIVE OF MAY 31, 1963 FOR THE ABOLITION OF ALL PROHIBITIONS ON, OR OBSTACLES TO PAYMENTS FOR SERVICES

(OJEC 1609/63 10.6.1963, directive 63/340/EEC)

This directive can be considered as a logical result of the general programme for the abolition of the obstacles to the free provision of services of 1962 (OJEC 32/62 15.1.1962).
Under this directive the member states must grant any exchange permit required for the transfers of payments for provided services.

The member states did not have to change their national laws to implement this directive.

IV COUNCIL DIRECTIVE OF JULY 30, 1963 LIBERALISING TRANSFERS IN RESPECT OF INVISIBLE TRANSACTIONS NOT RELATED TO THE MOVEMENTS OF GOODS, SERVICES, CAPITAL AND PERSONS
(OJEC 2240/63 17.8.1963, directive 63/474/EEC)

Under article 1 the member states must grant all exchange permits required for transfers between residents in connection with the invisible transactions listed in the annex of this directive.

This relates to the following invisible transactions:

- Bank costs.
- Representation costs.
- Participation by branch offices etc. in the general expenses of their foreign head office and vice versa.
- Additional payments, sureties and deposits relating to the business in futures of goods, performed in accordance with existing commercial customs.
- Contributions to associations, except contributions in payment of services and amounts transferred to government or private institutions for social security.
- Public expenditures (official representations in foreign countries, contributions to international bodies).
- Taxes and duties (except death duties, since they are already part of list A of the directive discussed under II), legal expenses, registration costs for patents and trademarks.
- Compensation, in so far as it is not a capital transaction.
- Refunds in case of cancellation of contracts and refunds of uncalled-for payments (in so far as these do not represent capital transactions).
- Fines.
- Periodic payments by mail, telegraph and telephone services, as well as by public transport companies.
- Consular receipts.
- Legal alimony and financial support in cases of hardship.
- Documentation costs of any nature, incurred on account of acknowledged foreign exchange banks and offices.
- Premiums of sportsmen and proceeds of competitions (excluding those obtained by professional sportsmen).

There was no need to implement the above directive in the national laws of the original six member states, since their national laws did not contain regulations that were incompatible with the provisions of this directive. The same applied to the member states that joined on January 1, 1973 (United Kingdom, Ireland and Denmark). At the moment the Commission is investigating whether Greece, which joined on January 1, 1981, has abolished its restrictions.

Spain and Portugal, who joined in January 1, 1986, enjoy a number of transitional regulations, laid down in their accession treaties. With regard to the liberalisation of the movement of capital, the transitional period applicable to Spain and Portugal is seven years from the date of accession (January 1, 1986). This means that both countries must, in principle, have freedom of movement of capital by January 1, 1993. This matches exactly the picture of a free internal market in 1993.

V COUNCIL DIRECTIVE OF DECEMBER 20, 1985 AMENDING THE DIRECTIVE OF MAY 11, 1960 FOR THE IMPLEMENTATION OF ARTICLE 67 OF THE TREATY

(OJEC L 372 31.12.1985, directive 85/583/EEC)

This directive represents a second amendment of the directive of May 11, 1960 (the first amendment has been discussed under II). The subject of the directive is securities transactions relating to units of unit trusts. In the original directive of May 11, 1960 these transactions were incorporated in list B and C, as follows:

List B

- Acquisition by non-residents of domestic securities dealt in *on a stock exchange (excluding units of unit trusts),* and repatriation of the proceeds of liquidation thereof.
- Acquisition by residents of foreign securities dealt in *on a stock exchange* and the use of the proceeds of liquidation thereof
  - excluding the acquisition of bonds issued abroad and denominated in national currency;
  - *excluding units of unit trusts.*
- The physical import and export of the above securities.

List C

- Acquisition by non-residents of units of domestic unit trusts dealt in on *a stock exchange* and repatriation of the proceeds of liquidation thereof.
- Acquisition by residents of units of foreign unit trusts dealt in *on a stock exchange* and the use of the proceeds of liquidation thereof.
- The import and export of the above securities.

In summary it can be stated that in the original directive of May 11, 1960 transactions in units of unit trusts were excluded from list B and were only given a place on list C (subject to the derogation provision of article 3, paragraph 2). In addition, this related solely to securities dealt in on a stock exchange. The explanation for these restrictions has to be sought in the major differences in the national laws relating to unit trusts in 1960. This made it impossible to offer investors equivalent protection in all the member states and to give investment funds equal opportunities to compete in all member states. The Council directive of December 20, 1985 amending and relaxing the directive of May 11, 1960, to be discussed below, was made possible by the adoption by the Council on the same date (December 20, 1985) of directive 85/611 EEC. The purpose of the latter directive is the coordination of the laws, regulations and administrative provisions concerning certain undertakings for collective investments in transferable securities (UCITS). An important factor with respect to the issue in question is that this directive established coordination with regard to the conditions under which undertakings for collective investments in transferable securities (previously referred to as unit trusts) can operate. As a result it was possible to relax the stringent conditions of 1960 with regard to capital movements arising from UCITS. In the amended directive, transactions in units in UCITS covered by directive 85/611/EEC are placed in list C, whether they are dealt in on a stock exchange or not. Transactions in units in UCITS not covered by directive 85/611 EEC, are included in list C.
The latter group can therefore be covered by the derogation provisions of article 3, paragraph 2.

In summary the new lists B and C are as follows:

List B

a Securities dealt in on a stock exchange

- Acquisition by non-residents of domestic securities and repatriation of the proceeds of liquidation thereof
  - excluding units in unit trusts that are not covered by directive 85/611/EEC.
- Acquisition by residents of foreign securities and the use of the proceeds of liquidation thereof
  - excluding bonds issued abroad and denominated in national currency;
  - excluding units in unit trusts that are not covered by directive 85/611/EEC.

b Securities not dealt in on a stock exchange

- Acquisition by non-residents of units in domestic undertakings for collective investment in transferable securities covered by directive 85/611/EEC and repatriation of the proceeds of liquidation thereof.
- Acquisition by residents of units in foreign undertakings for collective investment in transferable securities covered by directive 85/611/EEC and the use of the proceeds of liquidation thereof.

c Physical import and export of securities mentioned under a and b

List C (with respect to transactions in securities)

a Securities dealt in on a stock exchange

- Acquisition by non-residents of units in domestic undertakings for collective investment not covered by directive 85/611/EEC and repatriation of the proceeds of liquidation thereof.
- Acquisition by residents of units of foreign unit trusts not covered by directive 85/611/EEC and the use of the proceeds of liquidation thereof.
- Acquisition by residents of bonds issued abroad and denominated in national currency.

b Securities not dealt in on a stock exchange

- Acquisition by non-residents of domestic securities and repatriation of the proceeds of liquidation thereof
  - excluding units in domestic undertakings for collective investment in transferable securities covered by directive 85/611/EEC.
- Acquisition by residents of foreign securities and the use of the proceeds of liquidation thereof
  - excluding units of foreign undertakings for collective investment in transferable securities covered by directive 85/611/EEC.

c Physical import and export of securities mentioned under a and b

The notes to the nomenclature in annex I of the directive of May 11, 1960 are supplemented by a definition of the concept 'undertakings for collective investments in transferable securities' (UCITS). UCITS are undertakings:

- the sole object of which is the collective investment in transferable securities of capital raised from the public and which operate on the principle of risk-spreading, and
- the units of which are, at the request of the holders, repurchased or redeemed, directly or indirectly, out of those undertakings' assets. Action taken by a UCITS to ensure that the stock exchange value of its units does not significantly vary from their net asset value shall be regarded as equivalent to such repurchase or redemption.

The undertakings referred to above may be constituted according to law, either under the law of contract (as common funds managed by management companies) or trust law (as unit trusts) or under statute (as investment companies).

Under article 3 of the directive the member states must enact the measures necessary to comply with this directive, not later than October 1989. Portugal is permitted to delay the liberalisation of transactions concerning the acquisition by residents of units of foreign undertakings for collective investments, as defined in directive 85/611/EEC, until December 31, 1990.

2.3 The situation at the beginning of 1986

Until 1986 little progress had been made with regard to implementation of article 67 of the Treaty (liberalisation of capital movements). Through the safeguard clauses (articles 108, 109 and 73 of the Treaty) the member states were able, to a significant extent, to avoid implementation of the directives discussed under I and II, while the directive of December 20, 1985 (discussed under V) amending the directive of May 11, 1960 for the implementation of article 67 of the Treaty was subject to a transitional period until October 1989.

In order to revive the liberalisation of capital movements, the Commission on May 23, 1989 presented to the Council a programme for the liberalisation of capital movements in the Community. This 'Communication from the Commission to the Council' was published as COM (86) 292. In this programme the liberalisation of capital movements is proclaimed as one of the top priorities of the Community.

In the above-mentioned document the part of the liberalisation process still to be implemented is divided in two phases:

Phase 1

In the first phase the derogations that are still effective in a number of countries on the basis of articles 108, 109 and 73 must be terminated. In December 1984 the Commission reviewed a number of derogation decisions that applied for France, Ireland and Italy. These reviews meant that the derogations could remain in force until the end of 1986 for France and until the end of 1987 for Ireland and Italy. In December 1985 Greece had been allowed to maintain certain derogations until the end of 1988. The Spanish and Portuguese accession acts include temporary derogations. Spain benefits until the end of 1990 and Portugal until the end of 1992. Furthermore, in the first phase an expansion of the categories of capital movement mentioned in lists A and B is to take place. List A and list B are subject to an unconditional liberalisation obligation. The ultimate objective of the first phase is that the categories of capital movements most needed for the adequate functioning of the internal market and for the linking of the national financial markets should have been unconditionally liberalised. For this purpose the remaining restrictions on long-term capital movements will be removed. The following categories were added to lists A and B:

- long-term commercial credits;
- securities transactions whether or not listed;
- admission of securities to the capital market.

The necessary expansion of the categories of capital movement named in lists A and B was achieved on November 17, 1986, when the Council adopted a directive amending the first directive of May 11, 1960 for the implementation of article 67.

This directive concludes the first phase of the programme for liberalisation of capital movements. It will be discussed under VI below.

Phase 2

Phase 2 is to bring about the complete liberalisation of capital movements. For this purpose any remaining obstacles to short-term capital movements must be removed. The following categories will have to be liberalised:
- Transactions involving securities normally dealt in on the money market;
- Transactions on current and deposit accounts with financial institutions;
- Financial loans and credits.

In this connection the Council adopted a directive for the implementation of article 67 of the Treaty on June 24, 1988. This directive will be discussed under VII.

2.4 Directives since 1986

VI COUNCIL DIRECTIVE OF NOVEMBER 17, 1986 AMENDING THE FIRST DIRECTIVE OF MAY 11, 1960 FOR THE IMPLEMENTATION OF ARTICLE 67 OF THE TREATY

(OJEC L 332 26.11.1986, directive 86/566/EEC)

The directive of November 17, 1986 amends the first directive of May 11, 1960 for the implementation of article 67 of the Treaty for the third time. The first amendment took place on December 18, 1962 (discussed under II) and the second on December 20, 1985 (discussed under V).

This directive provides for an expansion of the categories of capital movements named in lists A and B. The expansion relates to the following categories: long-term commercial credits, securities transactions, whether listed or unlisted securities and admission of securities to the capital market.

Both lists are to be unconditionally liberalised. However, article 1 of the directive of May 11, 1960, relating to list A, introduces more stringent regulations for the exchange rates used for transfers concerning the categories of capital movements named in list A.

This article must be compared with article 2 of the directive of May 11, 1960, relating to the capital movements of list B. Under article 1, paragraph 2, the member states guarantee the transfer of the capital amounts mentioned in list A on the basis of exchange rates applicable to payments relating to current transactions. Article 2, paragraph 2, however, is less stringent: 'Where such transfers of capital are made on a foreign exchange market on which the fluctuations of exchange rates are not officially restricted, member states shall endeavour to ensure that transfers are made at rates which do not show appreciable and lasting differences from those ruling for payments relating to current transactions'.

The directive of November 17, 1986 combines the two unconditionally liberalising lists A and B into one new list A. This new list A is covered by article 1 of the directive of May 11, 1960 and so by the stringent regulations on exchange rates for capital movements. Article 2, with the regulations concerning the no longer existing list B, is deleted. List C is renamed list B and list D is renamed list C.

An overview is given below of the new lists A, B, and C, classified according to financial activity (investment, granting of credits, funding and payment transactions in general).

For each category of capital movement, the origin is indicated. This may be the first directive of May 11, 1960, but also an amendment to this first directive based on the directives of December 18, 1962, December 20, 1985 and November 17, 1986. The latter directive may also introduce new categories. The following categories are concerned: long-term commercial credits, securities transactions, whether listed r unlisted securities, and the admission of securities to the capital market. Certain items, indicated with ( ), will be explained in the footnotes.

Activity	Category	Directive
Investment	• real estate	• Nov. 17, 1986, list A (May 11, 1960, list A)
	• shares and other securities of a participating nature, listed or unlisted, held by a resident or non-resident* (1)	• Nov. 17, 1986, list A (May 11, 1960, lists B, C) (Dec. 20, 1985, lists B, C)
	• bonds, listed or unlisted, held by a resident or non-resident* (2)	• Nov. 17, 1986, list A (May 11, 1960, lists B, C) (Dec. 20, 1986, lists B, C)
	• units of undertakings for collective investment:	
	- dealt in on a stock exchange*(3)	• Nov. 17, 1986, list A (May 11, 1960, lists B, C) (Dec. 20, 1985, lists B, C)
	- not dealt in on a stock exchange:* (4)	
	• in undertakings for collective investment in transferable securities covered by directive 85/611/EEC*	• Nov. 17, 1986, list A (Dec. 20, 1985, lists B, C)
	• in other undertakings for collective investment the sole purpose of which is investment in securities or other assets*	• Nov. 17, 1986, list A (Dec. 20, 1985, lists B, C)
	- in undertakings not covered by directive 85/611/EEC the sole purpose of which is not investment in securities and other assets*	• Nov. 17, 1986, list B (Dec. 20, 1985, list C)
	• short-term investments in Treasury bills and other securities, normally dealt in on the money market*	• Nov. 17, 1986, list C (May 11, 1960, list D)

* = including the physical import and export of stock

Activity	Category	Directive
Granting of credits	• granting of credits related to commercial transactions or the provision of services in which a resident is participating (long, medium and short-term) (5)	• Nov. 17, 1986, list A (May 11, 1960, lists A, C) (Dec. 18, 1962, lists A, C)
	• granting of short-term credits related to commercial transactions or the provision of services in which no resident is participating	• Nov. 17, 1986, list C (May 11, 1960, list D) (Dec.18, 1962, list D)
	• granting of medium and long-term credits related to commercial transactions or the provision of services in which no resident is participating	• Nov. 17, 1986, list B (May 11, 1960, list C) (Dec. 18, 1962, list C)
	• sureties, other guarantees and rights of pledge and related transfers in respect of credits in connection with commercial transactions or the provision of services in which a resident is participating (6)	• Nov. 17, 1986, list A (May 11, 1960, lists A, C) (Dec. 18, 1962, lists A, C)
	• sureties, other guarantees, and rights of pledge and related transfers in respect of credits in connection with commercial transactions or the provision of services in which no resident is participating (6)	• Nov. 17, 1986, lists B,C (May 11, 1960, lists C, D) (Dec. 18, 1962, lists C, D)
	• granting of short-term credits not related to commercial transactions or the provision of services	• Nov. 17, 1986, list C (May 11, 1960, list D) (Dec. 18, 1962, list D)
	• granting of medium and long-term credits not related to commercial transactions or the provision of services	• Nov. 17, 1986, list B (May 11, 1960, list C) (Dec. 18, 1962, list C)
	• sureties, other guarantees and rights of pledge related to long-term loans with a view to establishing and maintaining lasting economic links	• Nov. 17, 1986, list A (May 11, 1960, list A)

Activity	Category	Directive
Granting of credits	• sureties, other guarantees, rights of pledge and transfers related to them for loans not related to commercial transactions or the provision of services	• Nov. 17, 1986, lists B,C (May 11, 1960, lists C, D) (Dec. 18, 1962, lists C, D)
Funding	• opening, and placing funds on current or deposit accounts, repatriation or use of balances on current or deposit accounts	• Nov. 17, 1986, list C (May 11, 1960, list D)
	• admission of an undertakings' securities to the capital market:	
	- shares and other securities with a participating nature, dealt in on, or in the process of introduction to a stock exchange in a member state*	• Nov. 17, 1986, list A
	- bonds, dealt in on, or in the process of introduction to, a stock exchange of a member state*	• Nov. 17, 1986, list A
	- units of undertakings for collective investment in transferable securities covered by directive 85/611/EEC*	• Nov. 17, 1986, list A
	• admission of an undertaking's securities to the capital market:	
	- shares and other securities of a participating nature, not dealt in on, or in the process of introduction to, a stock exchange in a member state *	• Nov. 17, 1986, list B
	- bonds, not dealt in on, or in the process of introduction to a stock exchange in a member state*	• Nov. 17, 1986, list B
	- units of undertakings for collective investment not covered by directive 85/611/EEC*	• Nov. 17, 1986, list B

* = including the physical import and export of stock

Activity	Category	Directive
Payment transactions, general	• personal capital movement, general (various categories)	• Nov. 17, 1986, list A (May 11, 1960, list A) (Dec. 18, 1962, list A)
	• transfers in performance of insurance contracts	• Nov. 17, 1986, list A (May 11, 1960, list A)
	• personal capital movements concerning loans, including sureties, other guarantees rights of pledge and related transfers	• Nov. 17, 1986, list C (May 11, 1960, list D)
	• capital movements related to direct investment and liquidation, excluding purely financial investments	• Nov. 17, 1986, list A (May 11, 1960, list A)
	• other capital movements	• Nov. 17, 1986, lists A,C (May 11, 1960, list D) (Dec. 18, 1962, lists A,D)
	• physical import and export of financial assets	• Nov. 17, 1986, list C (May 11, 1960, list D)

* = including the physical import and export of stock

Footnotes to lists A, B, and C

1 The difference between securities dealt in on a stock exchange and securities not dealt in on a stock exchange, from the directives of 1960 and 1985, disappears with regard to bonds, shares and other securities with the character of a participation. It remains with respect to units of undertakings for collective investments in transferable securities. The above results from one of the new categories ('securities transactions, whether listed or unlisted securities') which are introduced by the directive of 1986.

2 See (1).
The conditional liberalisation obligation for bonds issued abroad and denominated in national currency (old list C) has been converted into an unconditional liberalisation obligation (new list A).

3 In the case of units of undertakings for collective investment dealt in on a stock exchange, it no longer matters whether such units are covered by directive 85/611/EEC or not. They are now always covered by the unconditional liberalisation obligation.
In the directive of 1985 this obligation only applied to units covered by directive 85/611/EEC.

4 In the case of units of undertakings for collective investments not dealt in on a stock exchange, they are covered by the unconditional liberalisation obligation in the following two cases:
- units of undertakings for collective investment covered by directive 85/611/EEC.

- units of other undertakings for collective investment the sole purpose of which is investment in securities or other assets the acquisition of which has been liberalised.

Only in the case of units of undertakings for collective investment not dealt in on a stock exchange and not covered by directive 85/611/EEC, and whose sole purpose is *not* investment in securities or other assets the acquisition of which has been liberalised, does a conditional liberalisation obligation apply (new list B).

In the directive of 1985 the unconditional liberalisation obligation applied only to the category of institutions referred to in directive 85/611/EEC.

5 This relates to the granting and repayment of short-term, medium-term or long-term credits. Long-term is a new category added by the directive of 1986 to those of 1960 and 1962 ('long-term commercial credits').

The directive of 1962 provides that credits may relate not only to commercial transactions, but also to the provision of services.

6 This relates to sureties, other guarantees, rights of pledge and related transfers in respect of short-term, medium-term and long-term credits. Here too, long-term is a new category added by the directive of 1986 to those of 1960 and 1962 ('long-term commercial credits').

The directive of 1962 states that credits may be used not only to finance commercial transactions but also to finance the provision of services.

All member states, except Spain and Portugal, were to take the measures necessary to implement the directive of November 17, 1986 not later than February 28, 1987. Spain and Portugal can make use of transitional arrangements until December 31, 1990 (Spain) and December 31, 1992 (Portugal).

VII COUNCIL DIRECTIVE OF JUNE 24, 1988 ON THE IMPLEMENTATION OF ARTICLE 67 OF THE TREATY

(OJEC L 178 8.7.1988, directive 88/361/EEC)

The purpose of this directive is the implementation of article 67 of the Treaty. This means that the objective is complete liberalisation of the movement of capital. Article 1 expresses this by stating that the member states are to remove all obstacles to capital movements between residents of the member states. In order to facilitate the application of the directive, the various categories of capital movement are classified according to the nomenclature of annex I. In this nomenclature capital movements are classified according to the economic nature of the balances and commitments to which they relate, denominated in national or foreign currencies. The capital movements summarised in the nomenclature include:

- all activities necessary for the realisation of capital movements: conclusion and performance of the transactions and relevant transfers; in general the transactions take place between residents of different member states; however, it does occur that certain capital transfers are made by one person for his or her account (e.g. transfers of funds by emigrants);
- activities performed by natural or legal persons, including activities relating to balances or commitments of the member states or other statutory services and institutions, subject to the provisions of article 68, section 3 of the Treaty;
- access to all financial techniques available on the market used for the realisation of the activities. The acquisition of securities for example, relates not only to cash activities, but all available trading techniques: futures transactions, activities with options or warrants, exchange for other assets etc. Thus, activities in current and deposit accounts with financial institutions include not only the opening of and placing of funds in the accounts, but also forward foreign exchange transactions, regardless of whether their purpose is to cover an exchange rate risk or to take up an open currency position;

- the liquidation or transfer of financial assets, repatriation of the proceeds of such liquidation or the local use of these proceeds within the limits of community commitments;
- the repayment of credits or loans.

The nomenclature does not constitute an exhaustive description of the concept of capital movement. A category XIII.F 'other capital movement - various' has therefore been included. The nomenclature may therefore not be interpreted as a limitation of the scope of the principle of complete realisation of capital movements as set out in article 1 of the directive in question.

The nomenclature is as follows:

I DIRECT INVESTMENTS

1 Establishment of new and extension of existing branches or undertakings belonging solely to the capital provider; complete acquisition of existing undertakings.
2 Participation in new or existing undertakings with a view to establishing or maintaining lasting economic links.
3 Granting of long-term loans with a view to establishing or maintaining lasting economic links.
4 Reinvestment of revenues with a view to establishing or maintaining lasting economic links.

A Direct investments on national territory by non-residents.
B Direct investments abroad by residents.

II INVESTMENTS IN REAL ESTATE
(not covered by category I)

A Investments in real estate on national territory by non-residents.
B Investments in real estate abroad by residents.

III OPERATIONS IN SECURITIES NORMALLY DEALT IN ON THE CAPITAL MARKET
(not covered by categories I, IV and V)

a Shares and other securities of a participating nature.
b Bonds.

A Transactions in capital market securities

1 Acquisition by non-residents of domestic securities dealt in on a stock exchange.
2 Acquisition by residents of foreign securities dealt in on a stock exchange.
3 Acquisition by non-residents of domestic securities not dealt in on a stock exchange.
4 Acquisition by residents of foreign securities not dealt in on a stock exchange.

B Admission of securities to the capital market

i Introduction on a stock exchange.
ii Issue and placing on a capital market.
 1 Admission of domestic securities to a foreign capital market.
 2 Admission of foreign securities to the domestic capital market.

IV OPERATIONS IN UNITS OF UNDERTAKINGS FOR COLLECTIVE INVESTMENT

a Units of undertakings for collective investment in transferable securities normally dealt in on the capital market (shares, other certificates of participation and bonds).
b Units of undertakings for collective investment in transferable securities normally dealt in on the money market.
c Units of undertakings for collective investment in other assets.

A Transactions in units of undertakings for collective investment

1 Acquisition by non-residents of units of domestic undertakings dealt in on a stock exchange.
2 Acquisition by residents of units of foreign undertakings dealt in on a stock exchange.
3 Acquisition by non-residents of units in domestic undertakings not dealt in on a stock exchange.
4 Acquisition by residents of units in foreign undertakings not dealt in on a stock exchange.

B Admission of units of undertakings for collective investment to the capital market

i Introduction on the stock exchange.
ii Issue and placing on a capital market.
  1 Admission of units of undertakings for collective investment to a foreign capital market.
  2 Admission of units of foreign undertakings for collective investment to the domestic capital market.

V OPERATIONS IN SECURITIES AND OTHER INSTRUMENTS THAT ARE NORMALLY DEALT IN ON THE MONEY MARKET

A Transactions in securities and other instruments of the money market

1 Acquisition by non-residents of domestic securities or instruments of the money market.
2 Acquisition by residents of foreign securities or instruments of the money market.

B Admission of securities and other instruments to the money market

i Introduction on an officially recognised money market.
ii Issue and placing on an officially recognised money market.
  1 Admission of domestic securities to a foreign money market.
  2 Admission of foreign securities to the national money market.

VI OPERATIONS ON CURRENT AND DEPOSIT ACCOUNTS WITH FINANCIAL INSTITUTIONS

A Operations performed by non-residents with domestic financial institutions.
B Operations performed by residents with foreign financial institutions.

VII CREDITS RELATED TO COMMERCIAL TRANSACTIONS OR THE PROVISION OF SERVICES IN WHICH A RESIDENT IS PARTICIPATING

1 Short-term (shorter than one year).
2 Medium-term (from one to five years).
3 Long-term (five years and longer).

A Credits granted by non-residents to residents.
B Credits granted by residents to non-residents.

VIII FINANCIAL LOANS AND CREDITS
(not covered by categories I, VII and XI)

1 Short-term (shorter than one year).
2 Medium-term (from one to five years).
3 Long-term (five years and longer).

A Loans and credits granted by non-residents to residents.
B Loans and credits granted by residents to non-residents.

IX SURETIES, OTHER GUARANTEES AND RIGHTS OF PLEDGE

A Granted by non-residents to residents.
B Granted by residents to non-residents.

X TRANSFERS IN PERFORMANCE OF INSURANCE CONTRACTS

A Premiums and contributions in respect of life assurance contracts

1 Contracts concluded between domestic life insurance companies and non-residents.
2 Contracts concluded between foreign life insurance companies and residents.

B Premiums and contributions in respect of credit insurance contracts

1 Contracts concluded between domestic credit insurance companies and non-residents.
2 Contracts concluded between foreign credit insurance companies and residents.

C Other transfers of capital in respect of insurance contracts

XI PERSONAL CAPITAL MOVEMENTS

A Loans.
B Gifts and endowments.
C Dowries.
D Inheritances.
E Settlement of debts in their country of origin by immigrants.
F Transfers of capital belonging to residents who emigrate, at the time of their establishment or during their stay abroad.
G Transfers of savings by immigrants, during their stay, to their country of origin.

XII IMPORT AND EXPORT OF FINANCIAL ASSETS

A Securities

B Means of payment of any kind

XIII OTHER CAPITAL MOVEMENTS

A Death duties.
B Damages and interests (where these can be considered as capital).
C Refunds in case of cancellation of contracts or uncalled-for payments (where these can be considered capital).
D Authors' royalties, patents, designs, trade marks and inventions (assignments and transfers resulting out of such assignments).
E Transfer of the moneys required for the provision of services (not included under category VI).
F Miscellaneous.

EXPLANATORY NOTES

For the purpose of this nomenclature and exclusively for the purpose of this directive the following definitions are given:

Direct investments

Investments of all kinds by natural persons or commercial, industrial or financial undertakings and which serve to establish or to maintain lasting and direct links between the capital provider and the entrepreneur or undertaking to which the capital is made available in order to carry on an economic activity. This term must therefore be understood in its broadest sense.

The undertakings mentioned under point I.1 of the nomenclature include legally independent undertakings (wholly-owned subsidiaries) and branches.

As regards those undertakings mentioned under 2 which have the status of companies limited by shares, participation in the nature of direct investment exists where the block of shares held by a natural person or any other undertaking or any other holder enables the shareholder, either pursuant to the provisions of national laws relating to companies limited by shares or otherwise, to participate effectively in the management of the company or in its control.

Long-term loans of a participating nature, mentioned under I.3 of the nomenclature, mean loans for a period of more than five years which are made for the purpose of establishing or maintaining lasting economic links. The main examples which may be cited are loans granted by a company to its subsidiaries or to companies in which it has a share, and loans linked with a profit-sharing arrangement. Loans granted by financial institutions with a view to establishing or maintaining lasting economic links are also included under this heading.

Investments in real estate

Purchases of buildings and land, as well as the construction of buildings by private persons for gain or personal use. This category also includes rights of usufruct, rights of easements and building and planting rights.

Introduction on a stock exchange or on an officially recognised money market

The admission of securities and other negotiable instruments, in accordance with a specified procedure, to the dealings of a stock exchange, or department of the money market, whether controlled officially or unofficially.

Securities dealt in on a stock exchange (quoted or unquoted)

Securities the dealings in which are controlled by regulations, the prices for which are published according to fixed rules, either by official stock exchanges (quoted securities) or by other bodies attached to a stock exchange, e.g. committees of banks (unquoted securities).

Issue of securities and other negotiable instruments

By means of a public offer.

Placing of securities and other negotiable instruments

The direct sale of securities by the issuer, or by the consortium acting on the instructions of the issuer, other than by means of a public offer.

Domestic or foreign securities and other negotiable instruments

Securities according to the country in which the issuer has its principal place of business. The acquisition by residents of domestic securities issued on a foreign market is regarded as equivalent to the acquisition of foreign securities.

Shares and other securities of a participating nature

Include rights to subscribe for new issues of shares.

Bonds

Negotiable securities with a period of two years or more when issued, of which the interest rate and the way of repayment of the principal and the payment of interest is declared at issue.

Undertakings for collective investment in transferable securities

Undertakings,
- the sole subject of which is the collective investment in transferable securities of capital raised from the public and which operate on the principle of risk-spreading, and
- the units of which are, at the request of the holders, repurchased or redeemed, directly or indirectly, out of those undertakings' assets. Action taken by a UCITS to ensure that the stock exchange value of its units does not significantly vary from their net asset value shall be regarded as equivalent to such re-purchase or redemption.

Such undertakings may be constituted according to law, either under the law of contract (as common funds managed by management companies) or trust law (as unit trusts) or under statute (as investment companies).

For the purposes of this directive 'common funds' shall also include unit trusts.

Securities and other instruments normally dealt in on the money market

Treasury bonds and other negotiable treasury bills, deposit certificates, bank acceptances, commercial paper and equivalent instruments.

Credits related to commercial transactions or the provision of services

Contractual commercial credits (advances or payments by instalment for orders, assignments or the execution of work and extension of payment, whether accompanied by the signing of commercial paper or not) as well as the financing of this by credits provided by credit institutions. This category includes factoring.

Financial loans and credits

Means of finance of any nature, granted by financial institutions including those relating to commercial transactions or the provision of services in which no resident participates.

This category also includes mortgage loans, consumer credit, finance leasing as well as back-up facilities and other note issuance facilities.

Residents or non-residents

Natural or legal persons according to the definitions laid down in the exchange control regulations in force in each member state.

Proceeds of liquidation (of investments, securities etc.)

The proceeds of sale, including any added value, amounts of repayments, proceeds of execution of judgements etc.

Natural or legal persons

As defined by national laws.

Financial institutions

Banks, saving banks and institutions specialising in the provision of short, medium or long-term credit, and insurance companies, building societies, investment companies and equivalent institutions.

Credit institutions

Banks, saving banks and institutions specialising in the provision of short, medium or long-term credit.

The general formulation of the liberalisation obligation in article 1 serves to exclude any misunderstanding about the scope of the directive. Specifically the directive liberalises a number of short-term capital movements that were not previously liberalised. The following categories are concerned:

- Operations related to securities normally dealt in on the money market.
  Examples are Treasury bonds and other negotiable Treasury bills, certificates of deposit, bank acceptances, commercial paper and equivalent instruments.
- Operations on current and deposit accounts with financial institutions.
- Financial loans and credits.
  This relates to means of finance of any nature, provided by financial institutions, including those related to commercial transactions or the provision of services in which no resident participates.

This category includes mortgages, consumer credit and finance leasing as well as back-up facilities and other note issuance facilities.

Furthermore, article 1 provides that transfers relating to capital movements must take place on the same exchange rate conditions as those that apply to payments with respect to current transactions.

Article 3 introduces a special *safeguard clause*. This article provides as follows: 'When short-term capital movements of extraordinary proportions cause severe tensions on the currency markets and are severely hampering the monetary and currency policies of a member state, (reflected in significant domestic liquidity fluctuations), the Commission can, after consulting the Monetary Committee and the Committee of Presidents of the central banks, authorise this state to take measures to safeguard the categories in question. Conditions and method of application are determined by the Commission. In emergency cases the member state itself can take such measures, if necessary. However, the Commission and the other member states must be notified of the measures, not later than at the time such measures come into effect. After consulting the Monetary Committee and the Committee of Presidents of the central banks, the Commission decides if the involved member state may continue to enforce the measures or whether it must amend or withdraw them'. The decisions made by the Commission can be withdrawn or amended by the Council by qualified majority of votes. The measures in question are to last for a maximum period of six months.

The reasons why a separate safeguard clause is included in the directive instead of applying the safeguard clauses mentioned in articles 73, 108 and 109 of the EEC treaty, are as follows:
- Articles 108 and 109 require that the member states be experiencing balance of payments difficulties. However, disturbing short-term capital movements are very likely to occur, for example under the influence of exchange rate expectations, without a balance of payments crisis existing. The safeguard clause in the directive meets this need. Article 73 is meant to apply to disruptions in the operation of the capital market. Disruptions caused by short-term transactions are not covered.
- Since the measures to be taken will influence short-term and monetary transactions, the Committee of Presidents of the central banks must be consulted. The safeguard clauses included in the EEC Treaty do not provide for this.
- It is desirable to make the operation of the safeguard measures subject to a short time limit. The clause in the directive sets a maximum period of six months. The clauses in the EEC Treaty do not provide for such a short maximum period.

Annex II lists the following categories of capital movement for which safeguard measures may be taken:
- Operations related to securities that are normally dealt in on the money market;
- Operations on current and deposit accounts with financial institutions;
- Operations related to units of undertakings for collective investment
  - undertakings for collective investment in securities or instruments normally dealt in on the money market;
- Financial loans and credits
  - short-term (shorter than one year);
- Personal capital movements
  - loans;
- Import and export of financial assets
  - securities normally dealt in on the money market;
  - means of payment;

- Other capital movement: various
  - short-term operations that can be regarded as equivalent to those above.

The restrictions that the member states may apply to the above capital activities must be defined and applied in such a way as to cause the least possible disturbance to the free movement of persons, goods and services.

Article 5 indicates that the provisions of the Accession Act of 1985 of Spain and Portugal with respect to capital movement are reflected in annex III of this directive. This relates to derogation provisions that postpone the implementation of directives already adopted. This can relate on the one hand to directives that should by now already have been implemented and on the other hand to directives that would normally have had to be implemented at an earlier time in the future.

Under article 6, the member states shall take the necessary steps to implement the directive not later than July 1, 1990. As is the case with Greece and Ireland, Spain and Portugal may, notwithstanding the derogation provisions relating to capital movements, included in the Accession Act of 1985 and in annex III, temporarily maintain restrictions on the capital movements mentioned in annex IV, on the conditions and for the periods mentioned in this annex. Such periods extend to not later than December 31, 1992.

Article 6 also provides that, if, before expiry of the period determined for liberalisation of capital movements as mentioned in lists III and IV of annex IV, Portugal or Greece is of the opinion that they are not in a position to proceed with such liberalisation, as a result of difficulties with their balances of payment, or as a result of the fact that their national financial policies have not been adequately adapted, the Commission will examine the economic and financial situation of these member states. Depending on the results of such examination the Commission may propose to the Council to extend the period set for liberalisation, in respect of all or part of the subject movement of capital. The duration of this extension may not exceed three years. This may result in failure to meet the magic date of December 31, 1992.

Article 6, paragraph 3 deals with the dual exchange market of Belgium and Luxembourg. With due observance of the conditions and the periods of annex V, both countries may temporarily maintain the dual exchange market. Annex V is as follows:

'Considering that the system of a dual free and official exchange market as is applied in the Kingdom of Belgium and the Grand Duchy of Luxembourg has not led to a diminishing of the movement of capital but nevertheless forms an improper element within the framework of the European Monetary System and that therefore in the framework of the actual implementation of the directive and in view of a reinforcement of the European Monetary System this has to be put to an end, the above-mentioned member states will commit themselves to abolish this system before December 31, 1992. They will also commit themselves to manage the system until the abolition in such a way that the free capital movement will be guaranteed and that the currency rates on the two markets will not show significant and lasting differences'.

Before December 31, 1988 the Commission will, on the basis of article 6, paragraph 5, present proposals to the Council in order to abolish or to restrict the risks of distortions and tax-evasion or tax-fraud, resulting from differences in the national regulations concerning the taxation of savings and the supervision of its application. Before June 30, 1989 the Council shall hand down its judgement on said proposals, in order to facilitate the implementation of the regulations in the national laws before the entry into force of this directive (on July 1, 1990). Under article 7, paragraph 1, the member states will endeavour, in the regulations that they apply to transfers in respect of capital transactions with non-member countries, to achieve the same degree of liberalisation as in the case of transactions with residents of other member states. However, this will not affect the application in respect of non-member countries of national or Community rules or in particular of any reciprocity conditions, with regard to establishment, financial services and admission of securities to the capital markets.

If, as of July 1, 1990, this directive for the implementation of article 67 of the Treaty has been complied with, the first directive of May 11, 1960 for the implementation of article 67 of the Treaty will be withdrawn. The directives of 1962, 1985 and 1986, that entail an amendment of the first directive of May 11, 1960 will also be withdrawn. In the field of the liberalisation of capital movement only three directives will then remain:

a Council directive of May 31, 1963 on the abolition of all prohibitions or obstacles to payments for services, where the restrictions on the provision of services lie solely in the related payments. (see III).

b Council directive of July 30, 1963 liberalising transfers in respect of invisible transactions not related to the movement of goods, services, capital or persons (see IV).

   This directive has been implemented by nine of the twelve member states. The Commission will examine whether Greece has complied with its implementation obligations. Spain and Portugal benefit from a transitional situation until the end of 1992.

c Council directive of June 24, 1988 for the implementation of article 67 of the Treaty (see current point VII).

   This directive is to be implemented in the national laws of eight of the twelve member states before July 1, 1990. Spain, Portugal, Ireland and Greece may benefit from transitional provisions until not later than the end of 1992.

III. CREDIT INSTITUTIONS AND INVESTMENT FIRMS

3.1 Credit institutions and investment firms in 1993

In preceding sections the path to liberalisation of the capital movements in 1993 has been discussed. This relates to the freedom of banking, securities and insurance capital. However, a free internal banking market in 1993 for credit institutions and investment firms will not be achieved through liberalised banking capital movements alone, but also through freedom of establishment of banks and freedom of provision of banking services. In the following sections, attention is given to EEC regulations concerning this freedom of establishment of banks and their freedom to supply services. Legislation in these areas is based inter alia on articles 52-58 (freedom of establishment) and 59-66 (services) of the EEC Treaty.

The legislation to be discussed relating to establishment and services will be divided into a number of categories. Firstly the category 'establishment and provision of services in the narrow sense' will be discussed. This relates to EEC regulations providing for the removal of restrictions on the freedom of establishment and the freedom to supply services. Subsequently, the coordination legislation will be discussed. This legislation not only removes several restrictions relating to freedom of establishment and freedom to supply services, but also provides coordination of the regulations with which credit institutions and investment firms must comply. Establishment and provision of services in the narrow sense eliminates several restrictions (negative integration), while the remaining legislation provides for coordination of regulations in the prudential area (positive integration).

3.2 Establishment and provision of services by credit institutions in the narrow sense

I GENERAL PROGRAMME TO REMOVE THE RESTRICTIONS ON THE FREEDOM TO SUPPLY SERVICES
(OJEC 32/62 15.1.1962)
GENERAL PROGRAMME TO REMOVE THE RESTRICTIONS ON THE FREEDOM OF ESTABLISHMENT
(OJEC 36/62 15.1.1962)

Under articles 52 and 59 of the EEC Treaty, restrictions on the freedom of establishment and the freedom to provide services are removed gradually (in a number of stages) during the transitional period up till January 1, 1970. Furthermore, articles 54, paragraph 1 and 63, paragraph 1, provide that the Council, in the context of the deadline of January 1, 1970, must draft programmes for the removal of the restrictions that exist within the Community with regard to the freedom of establishment and the freedom to provide services, resulting in the two programmes referred to above.

As regards services it can be remarked that the general programme makes a distinction between services that are defined in article 60 of the EEC Treaty and those that are not. Article 60 determines that the term services refers to those services that are usually normally charged for, *in so far as* the regulations concerning the free movement of goods, capital and persons do not apply to such services. With regard to the liberalisation of services supplied by banks and insurance companies which involve capital movements, this regulation is elaborated in article 61, paragraph 2. The latter article provides that said liberalisation must be realised in accordance with the gradual liberalisation of capital movements. In according with the latter provision, the general programme states with respect to services that services involving capital movements must be liberalised at the same rate as that at which the capital movements themselves are to be liberalised. Services that do not involve capital movements are covered by the timetable for the removal of restrictions by January 1, 1970.

Both general programmes include such a timetable, in which the transitional period until January 1, 1970 is divided into a number of phases. In this context article 54, paragraph 2 and article 63, paragraph 2 of the EEC Treaty provide that the Council may adopt directives in order to implement the general programmes or a phase thereof. The Council has only adopted one directive for the implementation of programmes in the field of banking institutions. This was in 1973, i.e. three years after the expiry of the magic date of January 1, 1970, by which date the restrictions should already have been removed. This directive is discussed below under II.

II COUNCIL DIRECTIVE OF JUNE 28, 1973 CONCERNING THE REMOVAL OF THE RESTRICTIONS ON THE FREEDOM OF ESTABLISHMENT AND THE FREEDOM TO SUPPLY SERVICES FOR SELF-EMPLOYED ACTIVITIES BY BANKS AND OTHER FINANCIAL INSTITUTIONS

(OJEC L 194 16.7.1973, directive 73/183/EEC)

This directive instructs the member states to remove restrictions which in particular:

- prevent beneficiaries from establishing in the host country or providing services there under the same conditions and with the same rights as the subjects of that state;
- arise from administrative procedures the result of which is that, in comparison with the subjects of the host member state, beneficiaries are subject to discriminatory treatment.

As regards banking services involving capital movement, this directive liberalises banking services relating to capital movements covered by the unconditional liberalisation obligation of lists A and B of the first capital directive of May 11, 1960, supplemented and amended by the second directive of December 18, 1962.

Banking services relating to categories of capital movements other than those mentioned in lists A and B, are not liberalised by this directive. The following banking services, included in annex I of the directive and relating to capital movements covered by list A, are liberalised:

Direct investments

- Commercial and financial information (soliciting custom, information on the solvency of client, statistics, forwarding of accountancy data);
- Assistance and representation before the (administrative and judicial) authorities and other competent bodies;
- Advice and assistance to undertakings with a view to their possible merger (seeking foreign partners, expert advice etc);
- Aid in large-scale buying of shares (particularly for take-over bids) in order to obtain a controlling interest in an undertaking (stock exchange formalities, capital appraisals, financial assessment etc.);
- Physical exchange of securities;
- Custody of securities;
- Delivery of securities allotted to the shareholders of a company.

Liquidation of direct investments

- Commercial and financial information (soliciting custom etc.);
- Assistance and representation before the (administrative and judicial) authorities and other competent bodies;
- Advice and assistance to undertakings with a view to facilitating liquidation operations;
- Aid in the large-scale sale of shares;
- Physical exchange of securities;
- Custody of securities.

Investments in real estate and liquidation thereof

- Commercial and financial information;
- Assistance and representation before the (administrative and judicial) authorities and other competent bodies;
- Advice and assistance concerning investments and liquidation thereof;
- Administration of estates (assistance and representation in connection with the upkeep of the property, letting etc.);
- Assistance for the building-up and possible liquidation of sureties and guarantees of all kinds not issued by banks.

Personal capital movements

- Estate management on the occasion of succession (payment of taxes, search of missing persons, etc).

The granting and repayment of short- and medium-term credits in respect of commercial transactions or provision of services in which a resident is participating

- Commercial and financial information (soliciting custom etc.);
- Assistance and representation before the (administrative and judicial) authorities and other competent bodies;
- Advice on the financial management of an undertaking;
- Recovery of claims;
- Collection of bills;
- Domiciling of bills;
- Assistance for the building-up and possible liquidating of sureties and guarantees of all kinds not issued by banks;
- Blocking of cash, bonds or securities belonging to a client and guaranteeing his obligation towards a third party;
- Canvassing on behalf of third parties;
- Services in connection with factoring operations.

Sureties, other guarantees and rights of pledge and transfers connected with them

- Sureties and guarantees issued by banks.

Death duties

- Tax information;
- Tax deposits.

Other capital transactions in list A

- Transfers.

With regard to list B the following banking services, related to capital movements of list B, are liberalised:

Operations in securities dealt in on a stock exchange excluding units of unit trusts

- Receipt of orders to buy and sell;
- Assistance in the issue of bearer certificates representing securities previously issued and dealt in on a stock exchange;
- Servicing of securities (stamping, renewal of coupons, exchange, renewal, regrouping, splitting up, destruction);
- Financial services (payment of coupons, redemption of securities, aid in exercising allotment and subscription rights, etc);
- Financial information (current information, analyses, etc);
- Advice on investments in stocks and shares dealt in on a stock exchange;
- Management of a portfolio of securities dealt in on a stock exchange;
- Acceptance and implementation of powers of attorney for exercising the rights of holders of securities dealt in on a stock exchange (particularly representation at shareholders' meetings and in court);
- Custody of securities;
- Conversion of securities;
- Assistance for entry on the official list of securities assigned to the holders of securities dealt in on a stock exchange;
- Canvassing on behalf of third parties in connection with securities dealt in on a stock exchange;
- Search for another party with a view to buying or selling securities dealt in on a stock exchange;
- Acting as a clearing house.

All the above banking services relating to capital movements, covered by lists A and B, are liberalised unless they are supplied by management and deposit agencies of unit trusts.

A number of services connected with securities and involving the transfer of the provider of the service to the country of the beneficiary are not liberalised. They are:
- receipt of orders to buy and sell;
- participation as intermediary in transfers outside the market and the establishment of these transfers;
- information or advice given pursuant to a public offer;
- payment of coupons;

The directive applies to the banks and other financial institutions mentioned in annex II, excluding the activities of investment firms (category 4 of annex II). The reason for the exclusion of investment firms is that their operations give rise to special problems in drafting regulations on the taking-up and pursuit of their business in the various countries. The liberalisation of their activities will have to be effected in a later directive.

In annex II banks and other financial institutions are divided into the following categories:

Category 1: Banks

Banks
Merchant banks
Discounting banks

Category 2: Savings and loan undertakings

Instalment sales finance undertakings
Retail sales finance undertakings
Commodity sales finance undertakings
Building and loan associations
Real estate credit agencies
Urban mortgage undertakings
Farm mortgage undertakings
Credit undertakings
Short-term credit undertakings
Agricultural loan institutions
Commercial credit undertakings
Industrial credit undertakings
Personal credit undertakings
Development finance undertakings
Savings banks
Savings and loan banks
Discount and loans
Financial institutions
Rediscount undertakings
Finance companies
Financiers for their own account
Holding companies
Investment companies
Finance-raising holding companies. Financial trustees
Pawnbroking

Category 3: Syndicates

Underwriting syndicates
Surety syndicates
Guarantee syndicates

Category 4: Brokers

Stock exchange brokers
Outside brokers
Stock jobbers
Brokers in transferable securities

Category 5: Intermediaries or middlemen

Discount brokers, operating on their own account
Bank brokers
Financial intermediaries or middlemen

Category 6: Miscellaneous

Foreign exchange offices
Precious metals markets
Financial consultancy
Post office giro institutions
Trust companies
Clearing houses

In 1974 the European Court of Justice handed down two important judgements, in the Reyners and Van Binsbergen cases. In these judgements the Court held that the freedom of establishment and the freedom to provide services, entrenched in the EEC Treaty, had become directly enforceable since the end of the transitional period on December 31, 1969. Through these judgements the Treaty provisions concerning the freedom of establishment (articles 52-58) and the freedom to provide services (articles 59-66) became directly applicable.

As a result of these judgements, the directive discussed above for the removal of the restrictions on the freedom of establishment and the freedom to provide services by banks and other financial institutions, became largely redundant. Only banking services connected with capital movements are not directly subject to the Treaty, since they are being liberalised in line with the gradual liberalisation of capital movements. However, the exclusion of investment firms in the directive does not exclude them from the direct application of the Treaty achieved by the judgements.

In spite of the judgements of the Court there still remains a need for directives. Their function is now no longer the elaboration of the Treaty articles concerning establishment and services, but rather to facilitate the exercise of the freedom of establishment and the freedom to provide services, which have been directly applicable since the end of the transitional period.

3.3 Coordination of credit institutions (I)

III FIRST COUNCIL DIRECTIVE OF DECEMBER 12, 1977 ON THE COORDINATION OF LAWS, REGULATIONS AND ADMINISTRATIVE PROVISIONS RELATING TO THE TAKING UP AND PURSUIT OF THE BUSINESS OF CREDIT INSTITUTIONS

(OJEC L 322 17.12.1977, directive 77/780/EEC)

At the end of section II it was stated that there will remain a need for directives in the field of establishment and the provision of services. Their function is no longer to elaborate Treaty articles concerning the freedoms of establishment and provision of services, but rather to facilitate the exercise of these freedoms, which have been directly applicable since the end of the transitional period. The aim of the first coordination directive for *credit institutions*, to be discussed here, is to facilitate the effective possibility of establishment and provision of services across the borders of the member states by coordination of the banking laws. Such coordination relates exclusively to the prudential supervision of banks; the monetary or general economic supervision is outside the scope of the directive.

A draft directive on the coordination of the rules and regulations concerning establishment and the provision of services by *investment firms* is circulating in Brussels and will be discussed later in this chapter.

The first Council directive on the coordination of credit institutions is only a first step towards effective coordination of banking laws in the Community. It is restricted to a number of provisions of a predominantly general character, which are to provide the basis for the preparation of more detailed coordination provisions in subsequent directives. The most important provisions relate to the concept of 'credit institution', the use of a system of authorisations, solvency margins and liquidity ratios and collaboration between the competent national authorities. These four groups will be discussed below.

The concept 'credit institution'

Article 2, paragraph 1 provides that the directive relates to the access to and the pursuit of the business of credit institutions. Article 1 defines a credit institution as an undertaking whose business is to receive deposits or other repayable funds from the public and to grant credits for its own account. In terms of this definition financial institutions such as investment firms, investment funds and insurance companies do not fall within its scope. Furthermore, a branch is defined by article 1 as a place of business which forms a legally dependent part of a credit institution and which carries out directly all or some of the transactions inherent in the business of credit institutions. Any number of places of business set up in the same member state by a credit institution with its head office situated in another member state shall be regarded as a single branch.

A number of institutions with a special character are excluded from the scope of the directive (article 2, paragraph 2): central banks, post office giro services and a number of institutions specified by name for each country.

Authorisation

Authorisation can only be granted by the competent authorities if the following conditions have been complied with (article 3, paragraph 2):

- Separate own funds;
- Adequate minimum own funds.
  The volume of this 'adequate minimum' is not further quantified in the directive;
- Persons who effectively direct the business must be at least two in number.
  In addition these persons must have the necessary reliability and experience to exercise this function.

Member states may establish additional and/or more stringent standards. An important exception is also made in one respect to the freedom granted by the directive, namely that the conditions for authorisation may no longer include the economic need of the market (article 3, paragraph 3a).

Article 2, paragraph 4a, determines that the existing credit institutions that are affiliated with a central body (head office), within the same member state, that controls their operations at the time of the notification of the directive do not need to comply separately with the authorisation requirements, if:

- the obligations of the central body and the obligations of the affiliated institutions are joint and several obligations, or that the obligations of the affiliated institutions are fully guaranteed by the central organ;
- global supervision is exercised on the solvency and the liquidity of all the affiliated institutions and the central body on the basis of consolidated accounts;
- the management of the central body has the power to instruct the management of the affiliated institutions.

Credit institutions that become affiliated with a central body as mentioned above in article 2, paragraph 4a, after notification of the directive, do not need to comply separately with the authorisation requirements if they form a normal expansion of the network under the competence of this central body (article 2, paragraph 4b).

Branches of institutions with their head office in another member state may be subject in the country of establishment to the same authorisation procedures and requirements as those that apply to independently established institutions in that member state (article 4, paragraph 1). Formally this regulation is necessary to determine that these branches may be considered independent entities by the supervisory authorities of the country of establishment in order to supervise them in the same way as they supervise the domestic banks. Thus, the directive falls far short of achieving its objective. As stated in the preamble of the directive the objective of the coordination is to arrive at a system in which credit institutions that have their head office in another member state will be exempt from any national authorisation procedure for the establishment of branches in other member states. In other words, this represents a shifting of the control of branches to the authorities of the country where the head office is established.

The present directive only makes a small step in this direction, namely in that it provides that authorisation of a branch may not be refused solely on the ground that it is established in another member state in a legal form not allowed for credit institutions performing equivalent functions in the host country (article 4, paragraph 2)

Solvency and liquidity ratios

Article 6 requires the member states to keep track of the ratios between asset and liability items, to be further specified, on the balance sheets of credit institutions in order to judge their solvency and liquidity. The intention is to create an instrument that enables the analysis of the solvency and liquidity ratios according to a procedure uniform for the entire Community, without affecting the existing solvency and liquidity regulations and for the time being solely for purposes of observation. The Banking Advisory Committee established on the basis of article 11, (see the sub-paragraph on collaboration between the competent authorities below) is charged with the determination of the relevant balance sheet items and the inspection of the results of the analyses. The above-mentioned observational instrument can be considered as the precursor of harmonised solvency and liquidity regulations.

Collaboration between the competent authorities

Under article 11, a Banking Advisory Committee of the European Community will be established. It will consist of up to three representatives of each member state and of the Commission. These representatives may, occasionally and on condition of prior approval by the Committee, be accompanied by advisors.

The Committee may also invite qualified persons and experts to participate in their meetings. The secretarial activities will be provided by the Commission.

The task of the Committee is threefold. In the first place it must assist the Commission with regard to the proper application of the directive in question as well as the Council directive of June 28, 1973 (discussed under II) concerning the freedom of establishment and provision of services by banks and other financial institutions, in so far as they relate to credit institutions. In addition, the Committee must perform a number of specific tasks defined in the directive, including the tasks discussed above concerning the solvency margin and liquidity ratios of credit institutions. Finally the Committee assists the Commission with the elaboration of new proposals to the Council relating to further coordination in the field of credit institutions. The Banking Advisory Committee is not concerned with the study of specific problems relating to the various credit institutions. The latter involvement remains the preserve of the existing informal contact group of supervisory authorities.

In order to supervise the activities of the credit institutions whose sphere of work covers one or more member states other than the member state of their head office, in particular because they have established branches in such states, the competent authorities of the member states concerned cooperate closely. They provide each other with all information concerning the board of directors, the management and the owners of the credit institutions, thereby facilitating the supervision of these credit institutions and investigation regarding the conditions for granting authorisation. In addition, they provide each other with any information that may facilitate appraisal of the liquidity and solvency of such credit institutions (article 7, paragraph 1).

By virtue of article 14 all member states are to have implemented the directive within 24 months after notification.

IV COUNCIL DIRECTIVE OF JULY 8, 1985 AMENDING DIRECTIVE 77/180/EEC ON THE COORDINATION OF LAWS, REGULATIONS AND ADMINISTRATIVE PROVISIONS RELATING TO THE TAKING UP AND THE PURSUIT OF THE BUSINESS OF CREDIT INSTITUTIONS

(OJEC L 183 16.7.1985, directive 85/345/EEC)

Under this directive Greece may use the criterion of economic need of the market in the authorisation procedure until June 15, 1989. It also provides that the Commission, at the request of Greece, may introduce proposals to the Council before June 15, 1989 in which Greece is authorised to extend the application of the criterion of economic need until December 15, 1992.

V COUNCIL DIRECTIVE OF APRIL 17, 1986 ALLOWING CERTAIN MEMBER STATES TO EXTEND THE DELAY IN APPLICATION OF DIRECTIVE 77/780/EEC CONCERNING CERTAIN CREDIT INSTITUTIONS

(OJEC L 106 23.4.1986, directive 86/137/EEC)

Under this directive Denmark, Greece, Ireland, the Netherlands and the United Kingdom are authorised to postpone the application of directive 77/780/EEC to a number of named credit institutions until December 15, 1988.

VI COUNCIL DIRECTIVE OF OCTOBER 27, 1986 AMENDING DIRECTIVE 77/780/EEC CONCERNING THE LIST OF CREDIT INSTITUTIONS THAT ARE PERMANENTLY EXCLUDED FROM APPLICATION

(OJEC L 309 4.11.1986, directive 86/524/EEC)

This directive updates the list of credit institutions that are permanently excluded from the application of directive 77/780/EEC.

Summarising points III to VI, it can be remarked that the first coordination directive for credit institutions and its later amendments represent a modest start to harmonisation of the economic control on credit institutions.

The first directive forms the basis for more detailed coordination regulations in later directives, which will be discussed below.

3.4 Coordination of consolidated supervision of credit institutions

VII COUNCIL DIRECTIVE OF JUNE 13, 1983 ON THE SUPERVISION OF CREDIT INSTITUTIONS ON A CONSOLIDATED BASIS
(OJEC L 193 18.7.1983, directive 83/350/EEC)

The preamble to the directive mentions as *ultimate* aim the provision of overall consolidated supervision of a credit institution operating in several member states by the competent authorities in the member state where it has its head office. Pending coordination of, inter alia, the annual accounts and the consolidated accounts (see IX), it is not yet possible to introduce an adequate system of consolidated supervision in all member states. This directive is therefore in the nature of a first stage, intended to lay down the principle of supervision on a consolidated basis and to remove the obstacles that until now have prevented the member states from applying this principle on a unilateral basis for transactions throughout the entire territory of the Community. Pending further coordination, the consolidation process will be carried out by the member states according to their national procedures.

Article 1 contains a number of definitions. The definition of a credit institution is the same as that in the first coordination directive of 1977. A financial institution means an undertaking not being a credit institution whose principal activity is to grant credit facilities (including guarantees), to acquire participations or to make investments. Financial institutions do not in principle fall within the scope of the directive, but it is sometimes necessary to include them in the consolidation procedure. This is the case where a credit institution has a participation in a financial institution (see article 4).

Participation is defined as ownership by a credit institution, directly or indirectly, of 25% or more of the capital of another credit or financial institution.

Article 2, paragraph 2 provides that the directive does not apply to credit institutions listed in article 2 of the first coordination directive, that have been permanently excluded from application. The directive applies to all other credit institutions, subject to the provisions of article 3, paragraph 2.

A credit institution that has a participation in another credit or financial institution, is subject to supervision on the basis of consolidation of its financial position with the financial positions of the institutions in which it has such participation (article 3, paragraph 1). The extent and the manner in which this supervision takes place is determined in article 4. The member states or the competent authorities may, however, forgo supervision on a consolidated basis:

- if at least 75% of the activities of the credit institution which has the participation are already consolidated with those of another credit institution which is itself subject to supervision on a consolidated basis by the competent authorities of one of the member states and the credit institution in which it has the participation is included in this supervision on a consolidated basis, or
- if the credit institution or financial institution in which there is a participation is situated in a non-member country where there are legal impediments to the transfer of the necessary information, or
- if the total balance sheet of the credit or financial institution in which there is a participation represents less than the lesser of the following two amounts: 2% of the total balance sheet of the credit institution which has the participation or 10 million ECU, or
- if the nature of the business of the credit institution or the financial institution in which there is a participation is such, that in the opinion of the member state concerned or the competent authorities for the credit institution which has the participation, consolidation of its financial situation would be misplaced or misleading (article 3, paragraph 2).

Article 3, paragraph 3 provides that supervision on a consolidated basis is exercised by the competent authorities of the country in which the parent credit institution which has the participation has its head office. Pending subsequent coordination, and except as otherwise provided in this directive, the supervision will be carried out in accordance with the national procedure applicable in that country.

Article 3, paragraph 4 provides that the supervision referred to in paragraph 3 shall take place at least once a year. Furthermore, it does not affect any supervision on an unconsolidated basis or any supervision carried out by competent authorities of other member states.

Article 4 defines the form and the extent of consolidation. In this context three possibilities are distinguished:

- Where a credit institution has a participation of more than 50% in another credit or financial institution, the relevant member state or the competent authorities for the former credit institution shall, for the purposes of supervision, require either full or proportional consolidation of the financial situation of the institutions concerned.
- Where a credit institution has a participation of 50% or less in another credit or financial institution and, in the opinion of the competent authorities for that credit institution, a situation of effective control exists, it shall be for the relevant member state or competent authorities to determine the method of consolidation.
  Pending further coordination, the competent authorities in the member state in which the parent credit institution has its head office and the competent authorities for the credit or financial institution in which it has the participation may agree that consolidation of such a participation is not required in specified cases.
- Where a credit institution has a participation of 50% or less in another credit institution or in a financial institution and a situation of effective control does not exist, it shall be for the relevant member state or the competent authorities for that credit institution to determine whether and how consolidation is to be effected. Before effecting such a consolidation, these authorities must inform the competent authorities for the credit or financial institution in which there is a participation.

Article 5 lists a number of measures to facilitate the application of supervision on a consolidated basis. On the one hand the member states must see to it that no legal restrictions exist that prevent a credit institution that has a participation from providing the information necessary for supervision on a consolidated basis to be effected in accordance with this directive. On the other hand the member states permit the exchange between their competent authorities of the information necessary for supervision on a consolidated basis in accordance with this directive. In the case of financial institutions the gathering or possession of information shall in no way imply that a supervisory function is being exercised over those financial institutions by the competent authorities. Under article 1, financial institutions do not fall within the scope of the directive.

Article 6 discusses the application of the principle of supervision on a consolidated basis to credit institutions whose parent companies have their head office in non-member countries as well as to credit institutions in non-member countries whose head office is established within the Community. On the basis of reciprocity this supervision is to be regulated in bilateral agreements between the competent authorities of the member states and the non-member countries concerned. Such agreements shall on the one hand seek to ensure that the competent authorities of the member states are able to obtain the necessary information to enable supervision on a consolidated basis of a credit institution situated within the Community with participations in a credit institution or financial institution outside the Community, and on the other hand that the competent authorities of non-member countries can obtain the necessary information to enable parent institutions having head offices within their territory, and which have participations in credit institutions situated in one or more member states, to be supervised.

Article 7 provides that the directive must be implemented before July 1, 1985.

The above-mentioned directive introduces supervision of credit institutions on a consolidated basis. For the time being and in view of the First and Second Concordat of Basle (see below), this consolidation obligation concerns solvency supervision rather than liquidity supervision. Solvency supervision on a consolidated basis is therefore performed by the parent authorities. Supervision of the liquidity of foreign establishments is performed by the host authorities. It proved as yet impossible in 1983 to have the liquidity supervision performed by the parent authority and thus on a consolidated basis. This is connected with the fact that the liquidity of foreign establishments is determined to a large extent by local circumstances, the organisation of the local money market and the possibility of obtaining assets from the local lender of last resort, which is the central bank of the host country. Pending later coordination in this field the supervisors of the host country will continue to be responsible for the supervision of the liquidity of foreign establishments.

Reference has been made above to the First and Second Concordat. The First Concordat of December 1975 and the Second Concordat of July 1983 were achieved within the Committee on Banking Regulations and Supervisory Practices, popularly known as the 'Blunden Committee', after its first chairman, as the 'Cooke Committee' after its second chairman, as the 'Muller Committee' after its third chairman, and as the 'Corrigan Committee' after its fourth and present chairman. Since February 1975 the supervisory authorities of the countries that cooperate within the framework of the Bank for International Settlements (BIS) in Basle, being members of the Group of Ten, and Luxembourg have been collaborating in this Committee. The Group of Ten comprises the original ten countries (Belgium, Germany, Canada, France, Italy, Japan, the Netherlands, Sweden, the United Kingdom and the United States) and Switzerland which joined later. The disastrous year of 1974, with its bank failures (Franklin National Bank in New York, Herstatt Bank in Cologne) emphasised the necessity of intensifying consultation between economic supervisors. It emerged that supervision can only be completely effective through international cooperation.

The First Concordat of December 1975 contained the following principles of cooperation:

1 Supervision on foreign bank establishments is a mutual responsibility for parent and host authorities.
   In this context the foreign establishments of banks may have three forms:
   - Branches.
     These are legally dependent parts of the parent bank.
   - Subsidiaries.
     These are legally independent parts of the parent bank.
   - Joint ventures (consortia).
     These are joint subsidiaries of several shareholders.
2 No foreign bank establishment should escape supervision. For this reason every country must ensure that foreign bank establishments within its territory are subject to supervision. In the case of joint ventures the host authority is practically the only supervisor in a position to exercise supervision.
3 Primary responsibility for the supervision of liquidity should lie with the host authorities, with perhaps a more limited supervisory role with respect to business in foreign currencies or the currency of the parent authorities.

4 Solvency supervision is primarily the prerogative of the parent authority, albeit with stronger emphasis on the role played by the host authority in the case of subsidiaries and especially in the case of joint ventures.

5 Practical cooperation should be promoted on a reciprocal basis in the following three ways:
- by direct exchange of information between parent and host authorities;
- by direct inspection by parent authorities in the territory of the host authority;
- by indirect inspections by host authorities at the request of parent authorities.

The Second Concordat contains three important additions to the First Concordat:

1 One of the most important cornerstones on which the practical division of responsibilities between the supervisors in the different countries should be based, namely supervision on a consolidated basis, is now included in the revised Concordat.

2 Techniques for the avoidance of gaps in the supervision are discussed, on the principle that no international operating bank should escape supervision. Examples are gaps that can arise from inadequate regulation of the supervision in certain countries and from the existence of holding companies and non-banking institutions within a group of affiliated banks (the bankruptcy of Banco Ambrosiano in Luxembourg, which was not a bank but a holding company). The revised Concordat emphasises the importance of close collaboration in this respect between parent and host authority.

3 More detailed treatment is given of the shared responsibility of the parent and host authorities with regard to supervision of the liquidity of foreign bank establishments; the host authority is primarily responsible for supervision of the liquidity of foreign bank establishments in its own country while the parent authority is responsible for supervision of the liquidity of the overall banking group. In view of what is stated in point 1, the latter liquidity supervision of the overall banking group will have to take place on a consolidated basis.

VIII PROPOSAL FOR A COUNCIL DIRECTIVE RELATING TO THE SUPERVISION OF CREDIT INSTITUTIONS ON A CONSOLIDATED BASIS

(OJEC C 315 14.12.1990, proposal (90) 451)

THE PROPOSAL WAS AMENDED IN 1991

(OJEC C 332 21.12.1991, proposal (91) 491)

The proposal widens and reinforces the provisions embodied in the 1983 directive as follows.

- Supervision on a consolidated basis of credit institutions and financial holding companies.

  The consolidated supervision referred to here applies to banking groups of which the parent company is not a credit institution but a financial holding company, i.e. an undertaking whose subsidiaries are exclusively or substantially one or more credit institutions or financial institutions.

  Consolidation inclusive of the financial holding company has the advantage of providing a better understanding of the own funds position of the banking group. In addition, the risks to which the group as a whole is exposed can be more fully gauged. The volume of such exposure can accordingly be compared with the own funds, enabling a more accurate assessment of the group's solvency.

  A further benefit of including the financial holding company in the consolidation is that, from the point of view of supervision, groups with a vertical structure (i.e. those whose parent company is a credit institution holding a succession of subsidiary undertakings and subsidiaries of subsidiary undertakings) can be put on an equal footing with horizontally structured groups (i.e. the parent company of which is a financial holding company whose various subsidiaries are sister companies).

The object of consolidated supervision including the financial holding company is most certainly not to implement regulation of financial conglomerates. Nor is it the intention to give authorities responsible for the supervision of credit institutions a dominant influence in the supervision of groups with diversified activities. The purpose is merely to give these authorities a better insight into the solvency of credit institutions which form part of the group.

- Information to be furnished by mixed-activity holding companies.

  A mixed-activity holding company is a parent undertaking of a banking group which is neither a credit institution nor a financial holding company. The heterogeneity of the group's activities precludes the consolidation of such activities. The proposed directive introduces the obligation on the part of mixed-activity holding companies and their subsidiaries to provide information to the supervisory authorities of the group's credit institutions and in particular as regards indebtedness and transactions between the mixed-activity holding company and its subsidiaries on the one hand and among the credit institutions of the group on the other.

The proposed implementation date of the directive is January 1, 1993. The original 1983 directive will then be repealed.

3.5 Coordination of annual accounts and consolidated annual accounts of credit institutions

IX COUNCIL DIRECTIVE OF DECEMBER 8, 1986 ON THE ANNUAL ACCOUNTS AND CONSOLIDATED ACCOUNTS OF BANKS AND OTHER FINANCIAL INSTITUTIONS
(OJEC L 372 31.12.1986, directive 86/635/EEC)

As indicated under VII, a balanced system of consolidated supervision can only exist if there is coordination of the annual accounts and the consolidated accounts of credit institutions. The directive discussed below provides for this.

The directive combines the scope of two directives adopted earlier (one relates to annual accounts, the other to consolidated accounts) specifically addressing banks and other financial institutions. This relates to the following two directives, adopted earlier:

- Fourth Council directive of July 25, 1978 based on article 54, paragraph 3, subparagraph g of the Treaty, on the annual accounts of certain types of company
  (OJEC L 222 14.8.1978, directive 78/660/EEC)
- Seventh Council directive of June 13, 1983 based on article 54, paragraph 3, subparagraph g of the Treaty, on consolidated accounts
  (OJEC L 193 18.7.1983, directive 83/349/EEC)

Because of their special characteristics, banks and other financial institutions are specifically excluded from the scope of the fourth directive. Article 1, paragraph 2 provides that, 'Pending later coordination, the member states do not need to apply the regulations to banks and other financial institutions, or to insurance companies'. The provisions applicable to banks and other financial institutions (i.e. not to insurance companies) with regard to their annual accounts are incorporated in the directive of December 8, 1986. The seventh directive does apply, in principle, to banks and other financial institutions. Article 42, paragraph 1 of the directive states: 'Credit institutions shall draw up consolidated annual accounts and consolidated annual reports in accordance with directive 83/349/EEC, in so far as this section does not provide otherwise'. Thus the directive of December 8, 1986 follows directive 83/349/EEC with respect to consolidated accounts and only gives changes in relation to directive 83/349/EEC. These changes arise from certain divergent rules concerning the annual accounts of banks and other credit institutions. Since it was not until the directive of December 8, 1986 that the latter rules concerning annual accounts were adopted, the rules, connected with annual accounts, in respect of consolidated accounts could not be included in the seventh directive of 1983. Only when the rules on annual accounts were adopted in the directive of December 8, 1986 was it possible to indicate in the same directive the rules on consolidated accounts, applicable specifically to banks and other financial institutions. The latter were published as deviations from directive 83/349/EEC.

We will now discuss the directive of December 8, 1986.

Article 2, paragraph 1 states that the coordination provisions of this directive apply to:

a Credit institutions as described in article 1 of directive 77/780/EEC (first coordination directive), which are companies as described in article 58, second paragraph of the Treaty.

  Article 1 of the first coordination directive defines a credit institution as an undertaking whose business it is to receive deposits or other repayable funds from the public and to grant credits for its own account.

  Under article 58, second paragraph of the EEC Treaty, companies are defined as firms governed by civil or mercantile law, including cooperative societies or partnerships, and the remaining legal entities governed by public or private law, excluding non-profit companies.

b Financial institutions having one of the legal forms mentioned in article 1, paragraph 1 of directive 78/660/EEC, that on the basis of paragraph 2 of this article, are not subject to that directive.

  Article 1, paragraph 1 of directive 78/660/EEC provides that the coordination rules prescribed by that directive apply to legal and administrative provisions of the member states relating to companies having the following legal forms:

  - in Germany:
    die Aktiengesellschaft, die Kommanditgesellschaft auf Aktien, die Gesellschaft mit beschränkter Haftung;
  - in Belgium:
    de naamloze vennootschap/la société anonyme, de commanditaire vennootschap op aandelen/la société en commandite par actions, de personenvennootschap met beperkte aansprakelijkheid/la société de personnes à responsabilité limitée;
  - in Denmark:
    aktieselskaber, kommanditaktieselskaber, anpartsselskaber;
  - in France:
    la société anonyme, la société en commandite par actions, la société à responsabilité limitée;
  - in Ireland:
    public companies limited by shares or by guarantee, private companies limited by shares or by guarantee;
  - in Italy:
    la società per azioni, la società in accomandita per azioni, la società a responsabilità limitata;
  - in Luxembourg:
    la société anonyme, la société en commandite par actions, la société à responsabilité limitée;
  - in the Netherlands:
    de naamloze vennootschap, de besloten vennootschap met beperkte aansprakelijkheid;
  - in the United Kingdom:
    public companies limited by shares or by guarantee, private companies limited by shares or by guarantee.

Article 1, paragraph 2 of the same directive 78/660/EEC entails that the provisions of this directive do not apply to banks or other financial institutions or to insurance companies. Banks and other financial institutions are therefore covered by the provisions of the subject directive of December 8, 1986.

Finally the subject directive of December 8, 1986 provides that the term 'credit institutions' also includes the financial institutions mentioned under paragraph b, unless the context indicates otherwise. A wider definition of the term credit institution is therefore used here than in the first coordination directive 77/780/EEC.

By virtue of article 2 the rules of this directive do not need to be applied to:

a credit institutions mentioned in article 2, paragraph 2 of directive 77/780/EEC that are permanently excluded from its application;

b institutions in one member state that are connected with a central body in that state, as determined in article 2, paragraph 4 under a) of directive 77/780/EEC. In this case, without prejudice to the application of the subject directive to the central body, the entire body and its affiliated institutions must be included in consolidated accounts with annual report, which must be drawn up, audited and published in accordance with the subject directive.

c the following credit institutions:
- in Greece: the ETEBA-institutions (National investment bank for industrial development) and Trapeza Ependyseon (Investment bank);
- in Ireland: the Industrial and Provident Societies;
- in the United Kingdom: the Friendly Societies and the Industrial and Provident Societies.

The member states prescribe the following format for the compilation of the balance sheets of the credit institutions covered by the subject directive, according to article 4:

LAYOUT OF THE BALANCE SHEET

ASSETS

1 Cash in hand, balances with central banks and post office banks.
2 Treasury bills and other bills eligible for refinancing with the central banks:
   a Treasury bills and similar securities.
   b Other bills eligible for refinancing with central banks (unless national law prescribes that such bills be shown under Asset items 3 and 4).
3 Loans and advances to credit institutions:
   a repayable on demand.
   b other loans and advances.
4 Loans and advances to customers.
5 Debt securities including fixed-income securities:
   a issued by public bodies.
   b issued by other borrowers, showing separately:
   own-debt securities (unless national law requires their deduction from liabilities).
6 Shares and other variable-yield securities.
7 Participating interests, showing separately:
   participating interests in credit institutions (unless national law requires their disclosure in the notes to the accounts).
8 Shares in affiliated undertakings, showing separately:
   shares in credit institutions (unless national law requires their disclosure in the notes to the accounts).
9 Intangible assets as described under Asset headings B and C.I of article 9 of directive 78/660/EEC, showing separately:
   - formation expenses, as defined by national law and in so far as national law permits their being shown as an asset (unless national law requires their disclosure in the notes to the account).

- goodwill to the extent that it was acquired for valuable consideration (unless national law requires its disclosure in the notes to the accounts).

10 Tangible assets as described under Asset heading C.II of article 9 of directive 78/660/EEC, showing separately:
- land and buildings occupied by a credit institution for its own activities (unless national law requires their disclosure in the notes to the accounts).

11 Subscribed capital unpaid, showing separately:
called-up capital (unless national law provides for called-up capital to be included under liabilities, in which case capital called up but not yet paid must be included either in this Asset item or in Asset item 14).

12 Own shares (with an indication of their nominal value or, in the absence of a nominal value, their accounting par value to the extent that national law permits their being shown in the balance sheet).

13 Other assets.

14 Subscribed capital called up but not yet paid (unless national law requires that called-up capital be shown under Asset item 11).

15 Prepayments and accrued income.

16 Loss for the financial year (unless national law provides for its inclusion under Liability item 14).

Total assets.

LIABILITIES

1 Amounts owed to credit institutions:
a repayable on demand.
b with agreed maturity dates or periods of notice.

2 Amounts owed to customers:
a savings, deposits, showing separately:
- those repayable on demand and those with agreed maturity dates or periods of notice where national law provides for such a breakdown (unless national law provides for such information to be given in the notes to the accounts).

b other debts:
ba repayable on demand.
bb with agreed maturity dates or periods of notice.

3 Debts evidenced by certificates:
a debt securities in issue.
b others.

4 Other liabilities.

5 Accruals and deferred income.

6 Provisions for liabilities and charges:
a provisions for pensions and similar obligations.
b provisions for taxation.
c other provisions.

7 Profit for the financial year (unless national law provides for its inclusion under Liability item 14).

8 Subordinated liabilities.

9 Subscribed capital (unless national law provides for called-up capital to be shown under this item. In that case, the amounts of subscribed capital and paid-up capital must be shown separately).

10 Share premium account.

11 Reserves.
12 Revaluation reserves.
13 Profit or loss brought forward.
14 Profit or loss for the financial year (unless national law requires that this item be shown under Asset item 16 or Liability item 7).

Total liabilities

OFF-BALANCE-SHEET ITEMS

1 Contingent liabilities, showing separately:
  - acceptances and endorsements.
  - guarantees and assets pledged as collateral security.
2 Commitments, showing separately:
  commitments arising out of sale and purchase transactions.

LAYOUT OF THE BALANCE SHEET AND THE NOTES THERETO

The layout of the balance sheet is shown above, it may have a horizontal layout only. A number of items are shown as sub-items in the layout. However, they may optionally be shown in the notes. Based on the nomenclature of the directive (abbreviated in some cases), a number of balance sheet items are discussed below.

Assets

Treasury bills and other bills eligible for refinancing with central banks

This item comprises treasury bills, etc. eligible for refinancing (including treasury bills, treasury certificates and similar debt instruments issued by public bodies) as well as other bills (including bills purchased from credit institutions or customers) to the extent that they are eligible for refinancing with central banks. Directive 86/635/EEC calls for a breakdown of this item, to be shown either in the balance sheet or in the notes thereto, into treasury bills, etc. and other bills eligible for refinancing with central banks.

Other bills eligible for refinancing with central banks must, however, be shown under the balance sheet items 'loans and advances to credit institutions' or 'loans and advances to customers' if this is prescribed by national law.

Loans and advances to credit institutions

A breakdown of this item into 'repayable on demand' and 'other loans and advances' is required. 'Other loans and advances' must be further classified into their remaining maturity, for which directive 86/635/EEC prescribes the following schedule:
- not more than three months;
- more than three months but not more than one year;
- more than one year but not more than five years;
- more than five years.

Member states may, however, until January 1, 1988, require or permit the listing by maturity to be based on the originally agreed maturity or period of notice.

Loans and advances to customers

The amounts of loans and advances the term of which is not fixed must be shown and other loans and advances under this heading must be classified according to the same schedule as indicated above for 'Other loans and advances to credit institutions'.

Debt securities and other fixed-income securities

This item comprises negotiable debt securities, including fixed-income securities to the extent that these are not required to be classified under the heading 'Treasury bills and other bills eligible for refinancing with central banks'. Directive 86/636/EEC calls for the following breakdown:
- issued by public bodies and by other borrowers;
- held as financial fixed assets and other;
- listed and unlisted.

Securities held as financial fixed assets are those intended for use on a continuing basis in the normal course of an undertaking's activities.

While financial fixed assets are not the subject of a separate balance sheet item in the directive, the term is nevertheless necessary in connection with the valuation rules. Securities not held as financial fixed assets as defined above, comprise securities forming part of the trading portfolio, or securities which are neither held as financial fixed assets nor included in a trading portfolio. The latter securities will as a rule be of the nature of credits granted. This division into three groups is relevant in the context of the valuation rules.

In addition the following information is called for:
- the criterion used to distinguish between those securities which are and those which are not held as financial fixed assets;
- a statement of movements in securities held as financial fixed assets;
- the balance sheet amount (asset and liability) of the premium and discount related to the securities held as financial fixed assets which are not valued at a purchase price but at the lower or higher amount, as the case may be, repayable a maturity;
- the difference between purchase price and market value, if higher, of securities not held as financial fixed assets;
- the amount of own-debt securities included in the item under review;
- the amount that will become due within one year of the balance sheet date.

Shares and other variable-yield securities

The breakdown and information requirements for this heading are largely in line with those for the previous item, 'debt securities including fixed-income securities'. A breakdown into public bodies and other borrowers, and into differences, not yet written off, between purchase price and higher or lower amount repayable at maturity, are of course not relevant here.

Participating interests/shares in affiliated undertakings

These items must be broken down into listed and unlisted equity participations. If the participating interests and shares are held in credit institutions they should be shown separately. Amounts concerning either participating interests or shares in affiliated undertakings included in the assets and liabilities mentioned below, must likewise be disclosed separately, either as sub-items of the balance sheet items concerned or in the notes. This relates to the following asset and liability items:

ASSETS
- Treasury bills and other bills eligible for refinancing with central banks
- Credit institutions
- Customers
- Debt securities, etc.

LIABILITIES
- Debts evidenced by certificates
- Credit institutions
- Customers
- Subordinated liabilities

Subordinated assets

All subordinated assets must be disclosed either as sub-items of the balance sheet items concerned or in the notes. If these subordinated assets relate to participating interests or shares in affiliated undertakings, this should be stated.

Liabilities

Amounts owed to credit institutions

Directive 86/635/EEC calls for this item to be split into amounts 'repayable on demand' and 'with agreed maturity dates or periods of notice'.
The amounts not repayable on demand must be broken down into remaining maturity in accordance with the following schedule:
- not more than three months;
- more than three months but not more than one year;
- more than one year but not more than five years;
- more than five years.

Member states may, however, until January 1, 1998, require or permit the listing by maturity to be based on the originally agreed maturity or period of notice.

Amounts owed to customers

The same listing by maturity applies to this item, which should be classified into 'savings deposits' and 'other debts'.

Debts evidenced by certificates

This heading, which compromises both debt securities and debts for which negotiable certificates have been issued, must, in terms of directive 86/635/EEC, be split into:
- debt securities in issue.
- other.

The latter sub-item includes, in particular, deposit receipts, *bons de caisse* and liabilities arising out of own acceptances (issued for the credit institution's own refinancing) and promissory notes. The same maturity schedule must be shown for the sub-item 'other' as for 'amounts owed to credit institutions'. The amount of 'debt securities in issue' that will become due within one year of the balance sheet date must be shown.

Subordinated liabilities

As regards this heading, directive 86/635/EEC states that where, in the event of winding-up or bankruptcy, it has been contractually agreed that liabilities, whether or not evidenced by certificates, are to be repaid only after the claims of all other creditors have been met, the liabilities in question are to be shown under this heading.

For every subordinated borrowing which exceeds 10% of the total amount of the subordinated liabilities, directive 86/635/EEC requires details to be shown as to the amount of the borrowing, the currency in which it is denominated, the rate of interest, the maturity date, whether there are circumstances in which early repayment is required and the terms of the subordination. An overall indication of the rules governing other subordinated borrowings should be given.

Reserves

This item must be broken down into legal reserves, reserves for own shares, reserves provided for by the articles of association, and other reserves.

Off-balance-sheet items

Directive 86/635/EEC requires the following to be disclosed as off-balance-sheet items:

1 Contingent liabilities (liabilities arising out of acceptances and the endorsement of rediscounted bills on the one hand, and guarantees and assets pledged as collateral security on the other, to be disclosed separately).
2 Commitments (with commitments arising out of sale and repurchase transactions to be shown separately).

'Contingent liabilities' include in particular those in respect of sureties and irrevocable letters of credit, and liabilities arising out of the endorsement of rediscount bills and own acceptances not being refinancing acceptances. As far as the latter liabilities and acceptances are concerned, directive 86/635/EEC states that they should be shown under this heading only if national law does not require otherwise.

The notes to the accounts must state the nature and amount of any type of contingent liability which is material in relation to an institution's activities.

'Commitments' include every irrevocable commitment which could give rise to a risk. The notes to the accounts must state the nature and amount of any type of commitment which is material in relation to an institution's activities.

In connection with sale and purchase transactions, directive 86/635/EEC states that where the transferee is merely entitled to return the assets at the purchase price or for a different amount agreed in advance on a date specified or to be specified, the transaction in question shall be deemed to be a sale with an option to repurchase and the transferor must enter under off-balance-sheet 'commitments' an amount equal to the price agreed in the event of repurchase. Where the transferee undertakes to return the assets on a date specified or to be specified by the transferor, the transaction in question is deemed to be a genuine sale and repurchase transaction, and the assets transferred must continue to appear in the transferor's balance sheet.

Assets for account of third parties

Assets which a credit institution acquires in the name of and on behalf of third parties, and assets which a credit institution administers in its own name but on behalf of third parties, constitute the core of the trust business.

The assets are of two kinds:

- the credit institution acquires legal title to the assets concerned. Where these assets are in the form of funds, the accounts are in the name of the credit institution;
- regardless of the administrative powers delegated to the credit institution, the third party retains title to the assets. Where these are in the form of funds, the accounts concerned stay in the name of the third party in question.

In the first case, directive 86/635/EEC requires the total amounts of such assets and corresponding liabilities to be shown separately in the balance sheet or in the notes to the accounts of the credit institution, broken down in accordance with the various asset and liability items. However, member states may permit the disclosure of such assets and corresponding liabilities off the balance sheet provided there are special rules whereby such assets can be excluded from the assets available for distribution in the event of the winding-up of a credit institution (or similar proceedings).

In the second case, directive 86/635/EEC requires that these assets not be shown in the balance sheet. Whether or not off-balance-sheet disclosure is required, is not apparent from the directive. Directive 86/635/EEC also requires to be disclosed in the notes the fact that an institution pursues trust activities (described in the directive as management and agency services to third parties) where the scale of business of that kind is material in relation to the institution's activities as a whole. It is not fully clear whether it is of any importance that the assets concerned should be in the name of the credit institution or not.

LAYOUT OF THE PROFIT AND LOSS ACCOUNT

VERTICAL LAYOUT

1 Interest receivable and similar income, showing separately that arising from fixed-income securities.
2 Interest payable and similar charges.
3 Income from securities:
   a Income from shares and other variable-yield securities.
   b Income from participating interests.
   c Income from shares in affiliated undertakings.
4 Commissions receivable.
5 Commissions payable.
6 Net profit or net loss on financial operations.
7 Other operating income.
8 General administrative expenses:
   a Staff costs, showing separately:
      - Wages and salaries.
      - Social security costs, with a separate indication of those relating to pensions.
   b Other administrative expenses.
9 Value adjustments in respect of Asset items 9 and 10.
10 Other operating charges.
11 Value adjustments in respect of loans and advances and provisions for contingent liabilities and for commitments.
12 Value re-adjustments in respect of loans and advances and provisions for contingent liabilities and for commitments.
13 Value adjustments in respect of transferable securities held as financial fixed assets, participating interests and shares in affiliated undertakings.
14 Value re-adjustments in respect of transferable securities held as financial fixed assets, participating interests and shares in affiliated undertakings.

15 Tax on profit or loss on ordinary activities.
16 Profit or loss on ordinary activities after tax.
17 Extraordinary income.
18 Extraordinary charges.
19 Extraordinary profit or loss.
20 Tax on extraordinary profit or loss.
21 Extraordinary profit or loss after tax.
22 Other taxes not shown under the preceding items.
23 Profit or loss for the financial year.

LAYOUT OF THE PROFIT AND LOSS ACCOUNT AND THE NOTES THERETO

The vertical layout of directive 86/635/EEC for the profit and loss account is shown above. The directive also has a horizontal layout, which is not included here. The layouts have some items whose sub-items may be optionally shown in the notes.

Some comments now follow by way of explanation of some of the profit and loss account items. Special attention will be devoted to the substance of these items and the breakdown, if any, of the figures in the notes.

Interest receivable and payable

This heading comprises ordinary interest, the amounts of premium and discount spread on a time basis, fees and commission similar in nature to interest, and the amounts of swap transaction income and charges spread on a time basis.

The following is to be shown separately:
- interest receivable from debt securities and other fixed-income securities;
- interest payable on subordinated liabilities.

Income from securities

This item comprises all dividends and other income from shares and other variable-yield securities, including income from shares in investment companies. The following are to be shown separately:
- income from participating interests;
- income from shares in affiliated undertakings;
- income from other shares.

Also to be shown under this item are income and charges related to participating interests and affiliated undertakings where the equity method of accounting is used. In that case, a legal reserve could be compulsory if and to the extent that the amount of profit is higher than the dividend received.

Net profit or net loss on financial transactions

To be accounted for under this heading are all profits or losses, realised or unrealised, on transactions in securities forming part of a trading portfolio, in foreign currencies (excluding income and charges on swap transactions treated as interest), and on buying and selling operations involving financial instruments and precious metals.

General administrative expenses

In line with the fourth directive, staff costs, broken down into salaries and wages, pension costs and social security costs, must be shown separately.

Value adjustments in respect of loans and advances and provisions for contingent liabilities and for commitments

In those member states which exercise the option provided for in article 37 of directive 86/635/EEC (see below), this item must also include the net profit or loss, whether realised or unrealised, on transactions in securities included in Asset items 5 and 6 of directive 86/635/EEC, which are neither held as financial fixed assets nor included in a trading portfolio. As indicated earlier, the latter securities are of the nature of credits granted. Their inclusion is therefore logical. If material, value adjustments on loans and advances to credit institutions, to customers, to participating interests and to affiliated undertakings must be shown separately in the notes. This breakdown is not required if the member state permits income and charges under this item to be set off.

Value adjustments in respect of transferable securities held as financial fixed assets, participating interests and shares in affiliated undertakings

Member states may permit set-off of the income and charges included in this item. Should this option not be exercised, a breakdown of material value adjustments into financial fixed assets, participating interests and shares in affiliated undertakings must be shown in the notes.

SUNDRY EXPLANATORY NOTES

To complete the picture, a brief summary is given below of further information that has to be disclosed.

° The proportion of its income by geographical markets (in so far as those markets differ substantially from one another and if not prejudicial to the banks' interests) relating to the following items:
  - interest receivable and similar income;
  - income from securities;
  - commission receivable;
  - net profit or loss on financial operations;
  - other operating income.
° The amount of advances and guarantees granted to members of a credit institution's administrative, managerial and supervisory bodies and the commitments entered into on their behalf by way of guarantees of any kind. By way of derogation from the corresponding provision of the fourth directive, the rate of interest, the principal terms and conditions and the amounts repaid, if any, need not be shown.
° The value of leasing transactions, apportioned between the relevant balance sheet items.
° A breakdown of the following items (unless they are immaterial) by amount and according to their nature:
  - other assets;
  - other liabilities;
  - other operating income;
  - other operating charges;
  - extraordinary income;

- extraordinary charges.

° The total amount in national currency of assets and liabilities denominated in foreign currency.

° A statement of the type of unmatured forward transactions outstanding on the balance sheet date indicating whether they are:
  - hedging or
  - trading.

  The resultant income and charges must be included in 'interest payable or receivable' or 'net profit or loss on financial operations', as the case may be.

VALUATION RULES

On the whole, the valuation rules of directive 86/635/EEC are in line with those of the fourth directive. However, while for valuation purposes the latter directive distinguishes, among other things, between fixed and current assets, the balance sheet of 86/635/EEC does not. In particular for valuation purposes, directive 86/635/EEC accordingly requires Assets items 9 and 10 ('intangible assets' [formation expenses, goodwill] and 'tangible assets' [land and buildings] always to be valued as fixed assets. Included under financial fixed assets are participating interests, shares in affiliated undertakings, and securities intended for use on a continuing basis in the normal course of an undertaking's activities (i.e. those held as financial fixed assets and not as part of a trading portfolio or otherwise).

The fourth directive provisions apply to the valuation of tangible fixed assets (land and buildings). Directive 86/635/EEC makes provision for additional valuation rules for:

- debt securities forming part of financial fixed assets;
- securities forming part of a trading portfolio;
- loans and advances to credit institutions and customers, including securities which are neither held as financial fixed assets nor included in a trading portfolio;
- foreign currencies.

Debt securities held as financial fixed assets

The main rule for the valuation of these debt securities, including fixed income securities, is that they must be carried in the balance sheet at purchase price. If (on a continuing basis) their value is lower, the difference must, in pursuance of the provisions of the fourth directive (which have remained intact), be taken to the profit and loss account. Temporary diminutions in value may be taken into account. Where the reason for a diminution in value is no longer relevant, the value re-adjustment must be written back and credited to the profit and loss account.

According to directive 86/635/EEC, the member states may require or permit these debt securities to be carried at the amount repayable at maturity. In that event there are rules in respect of the resultant premiums and discounts.

If the purchase price exceeds the amount repayable at maturity, the difference must either be charged to the profit and loss account, or - provided the member states so require or permit - be released to income in instalments so that it is completely written off by the time the debt securities are repaid. Where the purchase price is less than the amount repayable at maturity, member states may require or permit the difference to be released to income in instalments over the period remaining until repayment.

Securities not held as financial fixed assets (hence forming part of a trading portfolio or of the nature of credits granted)

The main rule for the valuation of these securities is that they must be carried in the balance sheet at the lower of purchase price and market value. If valuation is at purchase price, the difference from market value, if higher, must be stated in the notes. However, the member states may require or permit these securities to be carried in the balance sheet at the higher market value. In that event, the difference between purchase price and higher market value must be stated in the notes.

Loans and advances in the broad sense

The main rule is for loans and advances, and securities not held as financial fixed assets nor forming part of a trading portfolio, to be valued at the lower of purchase price or market value (in line with article 39 of the fourth directive).

However, article 37 of directive 86/635/EEC introduces a very important optional valuation rule for loans and advances to customers and credit institutions and for securities which are neither held as financial fixed assets nor included in a trading portfolio (hereafter referred to as the 'article-37-option'). Member states may, in the context of this option, permit such loans, advances and securities to be carried in the balance sheet at a value lower than that which would result from the application of the main rule, where that is required by the prudence dictated by the particular risks associated with banking.

An invisible difference between the two values would then result which may, however, not be more than 4% of the valuation on the basis of the main rule (the lower of purchase price and market). The credit institution making use of the article-37-option may maintain the resultant lower values until it decides to adjust them. Since member states may permit the set-off of income and charges included under the off-balance-sheet items 'value adjustments in respect of loans and advances and provisions for contingent liabilities and for commitments' and 'value re-adjustments in respect of loans and advances and provisions for contingent liabilities and for commitments', the effect on the profit and loss account of exercising the article-37-option is likewise invisible.

The scope of the article-37-option is restricted to loans and advances to customers and credit institutions and to certain types of securities. This option does not extend to provisions for contingent liabilities and for commitments nor to other risks associated with banking. However, some writers in authoritative professional publications in certain member states hold the view that the scope allowed by directive 86/635/EEC could well be wider than that.

If securities not held as financial fixed assets are valued at purchase price, the difference from a higher market value must be mentioned in the notes. However, this information may be omitted where a member state exercises the article-37-option.

The article-37-option leaves intact the fourth directive requirements concerning the disclosure of the provision for deferred taxes. It is generally assumed that the scope of article 37 is hardly, if at all, affected by these requirements, although a different interpretation of the directive articles seems possible.

In addition to the article-37-option, directive 86/635/EEC introduces a second facility. Those member states which exercise the article-37-option must permit, and those member states which do not exercise this option may permit, the introduction of a fund, whether open or not, called 'fund for general banking risks'. This fund is intended to include those amounts which a credit institution decides to put aside to cover such risks where that is required by the particular risks associated with banking. The net balance of the additions to and withdrawals from this fund must be shown separately in the profit and loss account. Neither the fund's scope nor its amount have been limited in any way. It is shown in the balance sheet as a provision.

Directive 86/635/EEC permits the use of the article-37-option and the fund for general banking risks side by side, so that one bank could have both the lower values, whether invisible or not, in terms of article 37 and the fund. It is also possible that a bank prefers not to have either, but instead opts to take its actual losses from defaulting debtors to its profit and loss account without any adjustments. Depending on circumstances, member states must or may 'permit' both measures, but they cannot 'require' either of them.

Foreign currency

The main rule is that all assets and liabilities denominated in foreign currency, including forward contracts, must be translated at the spot rates of exchange ruling on the balance sheet date. The differences arising from such translation must be shown in the profit and loss account. Further rules apply to the following items:

- *Forward contracts against assets/liabilities above the line (hedging)*

As we saw, the swap income and charges resulting from these contracts are included under the interest receivable or payable, spread over the actual duration of the contract. Translation of these contracts at the spot rate of exchange ruling on the balance sheet date is accordingly wholly in line with the translation of underlying foreign currency. Translation gains or losses will compensate one another.

- *Forward contracts against other forward contracts (trading)*

Member states may require these contracts to be translated at the forward rate ruling on the balance sheet date.

- *Own position*

A credit institution's own position consists of forward transactions, assets or liabilities in foreign currencies not covered or not specifically covered by other forward transactions or by assets or liabilities. Member states may require that positive translation differences arising from a credit institution's own position not be shown in the profit and loss account.

- *Financial fixed assets, tangible and intangible assets (unhedged)*

Member states may require or permit translations at the rate ruling on the date of acquisition.

- *Financial fixed assets, tangible and intangible assets (hedged)*

Member states may require or permit that the profit or loss on translation of these assets and the related hedging transactions be taken in whole or in part to non-distributable reserves.

- *Participating interest at net asset value, etc.*

Where the equity method of accounting is applied, member states may require that translation differences, either in whole or in part, be taken direct to reserves. These positive or negative translation differences are shown separately in the balance sheet or in the notes.

3.6 Coordination of the publication of annual accounting documents of credit institutions

X COUNCIL DIRECTIVE OF FEBRUARY 13, 1989 ON THE OBLIGATION CONCERNING THE PUBLICATION OF ANNUAL ACCOUNTING DOCUMENTS BY BRANCHES ESTABLISHED IN MEMBER STATES BY CREDIT INSTITUTIONS AND FINANCIAL INSTITUTIONS HAVING THEIR HEAD OFFICES OUTSIDE THAT MEMBER STATE
(OJEC L 44 16.2.1989, directive 89/117/EEC)

For the realisation of the European internal market it is required that branches of credit institutions and financial institutions having their head office in another member state should be treated in the same way as branches of such institutions having their head office in the same member state. It is sufficient for the branches of such institutions having their head offices in another member state to publish the annual accounting documents as a whole. It is not permitted to require these institutions to publish separate local annual accounts. This is reflected in article 44, paragraph 3, of the previously discussed Council directive of December 8, 1986 (86/635/EEC) on the annual accounts and consolidated accounts of banks and other financial institutions. Article 44, paragraph 3, stipulates that the annual accounts (including those of branches) and the consolidated accounts (including those of branches and subsidiaries) must be made available to the public in every member state where these credit institutions have branches.

However, in view of the present state of integration, the need for certain information concerning the activities of branches and subsidiaries of credit and financial institutions having their head office outside the involved member state cannot be left out of account. As far as publication by companies and firms, and especially their subsidiaries, is concerned, the required coordination has been brought about by the first Council directive on company law (68/151/EEC, OJEC L 65 14.3.1968). The lack of coordination, concerning disclosure by branches gives rise to disparity in respect of protection of shareholders and third parties between:

- companies which operate in other member states by opening branches, on the one hand, and
- companies which operate in other member states by opening subsidiary companies, on the other.

Such disparities need to be eliminated in order to ensure an equivalent level of protection for those concerned. The Council directive to be discussed below, on the obligations of branches established in a member state of credit and financial institutions having their head office outside that member state, regarding the publication of annual accounting documents, provides for this.

Article 1 stipulates that the coordination measures prescribed by this directive apply to branches established in a member state by credit institutions and financial institutions within the meaning of directive 86/635/EEC, having their head offices outside that member state. Where a credit institution or a financial institution has its head office in a non-member country, this directive applies in so far as the credit institution or financial institution has a legal form which is comparable to the legal forms specified in article 2 of directive 86/635/EEC (see under IX).

Provisions concerning branches of credit and financial institutions having their head office in another member state (article 2):

a Member states must ensure that the branches publish the annual accounting documents of the credit or financial institution in the manner required by the authorities of the host member state. Annual accounting documents, as listed in article 44 of directive 86/635/EEC, are understood to include: annual accounts, consolidated accounts, annual report, consolidated annual report and opinions of the person responsible for auditing the annual accounts and consolidated accounts.
b These documents are to be drawn up and audited in accordance with the provisions of directive 86/635/EEC concerning the annual accounts and the consolidated annual accounts of banks and other financial institutions as enacted by the member state in which the head office of the credit institution or financial institution is established.
c A branch cannot be compelled to publish annual accounts related to its own business operations.
d Member states may, pending further coordination, require branches to publish the following additional information.
  - the income and costs of the branch deriving from items 1, 3, 4, 6 and 7 of article 27 or from items A4, A9, B1 to B4 and B7 of article 28 of directive 86/635/EEC;
  - the average number of staff employed by the branch;
  - the total claims and liabilities attributable to the branch, broken down into those in respect of credit institutions and those in respect of customers, together with the overall amount of such

claims and liabilities expressed in the currency of the member state in which the branch is established;
- the total assets and the amounts corresponding to items 2, 3, 4, 5 and 6 of the assets, 1, 2 and 3 of the liabilities and 1 and 2 of the off-balance-sheet items defined in article 4 and parallel articles of directive 86/635/EEC, and, in the case of items 2, 5 and 6 of the assets a breakdown of securities according to whether they have or have not been regarded as financial fixed assets pursuant to article 35 of directive 86/635/EEC.

Provisions related to branches of credit institutions having their head office in another member state (article 3):

a The member states require branches of credit institutions having their head office in non-member countries to publish the documents specified in article 2 (a), drawn up and audited in the manner required by the law of the country of the head office, in accordance with the provisions set out therein.

b Where such documents are in conformity with, or equivalent to, documents drawn up in accordance with directive 86/635/EEC and the condition of reciprocity, for Community credit institutions and financial institutions ('credit institutions'), is fulfilled in the non-member country in which the head office is situated, article 2 (c) shall apply.

c In cases other than those referred to under b, member states may require branches to publish annual accounts relating to their own activities.

d In the cases specified under b and c member states may require branches to publish the information referred to in article 2 (d) and the amount of endowment capital.

Article 6 defines the final provisions of the directive. Paragraph 1 states that the member states must comply with the directive before January 1, 1991. On the basis of paragraph 2 member states may provide that the provisions of the directive shall apply for the first time to annual accounts for the financial year beginning on January 1, 1993 or during the calendar year 1993.

3.7 Coordination of provisions concerning own funds and solvency of credit institutions

XI COUNCIL DIRECTIVE OF APRIL 17, 1989 ON THE OWN FUNDS OF CREDIT INSTITUTIONS

(OJEC L 124 5.5.1989, directive 89/299/EEC)

XII COUNCIL DIRECTIVE OF DECEMBER 18, 1989 ON A SOLVENCY RATIO FOR CREDIT INSTITUTIONS

(OJEC L 386 30.12.1989, directive 89/647/EEC)

After a general introduction, a survey is given below, classified by subject, of the regulations concerning own funds and solvency adopted within the framework of the Bank of International Settlements (BIS). Developments with respect to each topic within the European Community (EC) are then discussed. In particular an analysis is made of the extent to which the above directives concerning own funds and solvency deviate from the developments within the framework of the BIS. This analysis reveals that there is clear coordination between the two forums.

General introduction

The objective of solvency requirements is to ensure that the own funds of a bank relate to the institution's assets in such a way that possible losses (e.g. a debtor is not able to repay a loan) will be absorbed, without endangering the savings and investments of the suppliers of capital.

There are two possible approaches to the supervision of solvency ratios, namely on the basis of a gearing ratio or on the basis of a risk-asset ratio. While in both cases this is done by reference to assets, in the case of the risk-asset ratio, assets are separately weighted in respect of the exposure they entail in the opinion of the supervisors. A similar risk-weighting can be applied to off-balance-sheet activities, as we shall see below.

In the 1970s and 1980s the solvency ratios of banks deteriorated significantly, one of the causes for this was the occurrence of inflationary tendencies, resulting in a nominal increase of bank assets. Another cause was the 'recycling of petrodollars' through the international banks, which resulted in an increase of granting of credits to national governments and an increase in the granting of credits between banks. Not only did the balance sheet total of the banks increase, but so also did the risks connected with on-balance-sheet and off-balance-sheet (OBS) activities and the risks concerning loans to debt countries. In addition, the process of financial innovation in the 1980s led to a considerable increase in OBS activities, causing a concentration of credit risks in particular for the banking business. In addition to the above developments the profit margins of the banks were seriously affected by increasing competition between banks. The result was the impossibility of increasing own funds adequately in relation to the increased assets and risks.

The current international consensus is that solvency supervision should be strengthened. To maintain fair competition international harmonisation will also be necessary in order to eliminate discrepancies in competition resulting from differences in methods of measuring the solvency ratios (gearing ratio versus risk-asset ratio) and differences in defining own funds in the various countries. To promote such a convergence international talks between supervisors were organised by the Bank for International Settlements (BIS) as well as by the European Community.

Within the context of the BIS the Committee on Banking Regulation and Supervisory Practices was established, until 1989 also named the Cooke Committee, after its chairman, consisting of representatives of the supervisory authorities of the Group of Ten countries plus Luxembourg. The Group of Ten consists of the original ten countries (Belgium, Canada, France, Germany, Italy, Japan, the Netherlands, Sweden, the United Kingdom and the United States) and Switzerland which joined later.

Within the context of the EC the Banking Advisory Committee of the European Community was created, also known as the EC Banking Committee. The twelve EC countries (Belgium, Denmark, France, Germany, Greece, Ireland, Italy, Luxembourg, the Netherlands, Spain, Portugal and the United Kingdom) are represented in this committee. Seven of these countries (Belgium, France, Germany, Italy, Luxembourg, the Netherlands and the United Kingdom) are also represented in the Cooke Committee, thus enabling discussions in the two committees to develop along similar lines over a period of time.

In January 1986 the Federal Reserve Board published a proposal to base solvency supervision on the risk-asset ratio, allowing for off-balance-sheet (OBS) activities, a line followed in the convergence accord of January 1987 between the United States and the United Kingdom. The two countries expressed the hope that their agreement could serve as a guideline for further international consultation. Based on this agreement an accord under the name 'Proposals for international convergence of capital measurement and capital standards' was reached by the twelve countries represented in the BIS. These proposals were ultimately published in their final form in July 1988 in an accord entitled 'International convergence of capital measurement and capital standards'. The EC counterpart to this BIS accord is to be found in the two directives referred to above.

The objectives of the BIS accord are directly related to the above-mentioned deterioration in the solvency position of banks in the 1970s and 1980s. In the first place the soundness and stability of the international banking system will have to be strengthened by establishing uniform effective minimum solvency ratios (the concept of 'effective solvency ratios' will be discussed below). In a number of countries these minimum ratios will force the banks to increase substantially their own funds. Uniformity is necessary to achieve harmonisation of solvency supervision in the international context and, as already indicated, to eliminate disparities in competition. In addition to uniform solvency ratios, a uniform definition of own funds and a uniform method for measuring solvency (the method in which the defined own funds are related to certain asset and OBS items) are required.

A uniform definition of own funds is essential to establish fair competition between banks of different countries.

Banks having their head office in a country with a relatively flexible policy concerning the components of own funds, have less problems in meeting the above uniform solvency ratios than banks with their head office in a country that adopts a narrower definition, implying a competitive advantage for the former banks. Since solvency supervision is exercised on the basis of a consolidated balance sheet for parent company and subsidiaries (see Second Concordat discussed under VII), the location of the head office is significant. A subsidiary from country B established in country A, cannot benefit from the broader definition of own funds of country A, since the balance sheet of this subsidiary is consolidated with the parent company in country B, and the consolidated entity will come under the supervision of country B with a narrower definition of own funds.

To achieve a uniform method for measuring solvency the use of a risk-asset ratio has been proposed, expressing the commonly-defined own funds of each credit institution as a proportion of the commonly-defined risk-weighted value of their assets and off-balance-sheet activities.

In summary, the harmonisation of solvency supervision comes down to the relating of uniformly defined own funds through uniform solvency ratios, to the uniformly defined risk-weighted value of assets and OBS activities. In this process several banks will be forced to strengthen their own funds position. For this reason both the BIS accord and the EC directives make provision for a transitional period until the end of 1992. The various components of harmonisation will be analysed in more detail below.

Definition of own funds

The 'Cooke Committee' breaks the own funds (the capital base) of banks down in two tiers. The first tier is the *core capital (basic equity)*. The second tier is called the *supplementary capital.*
Core capital is made up of:

- Issued and fully paid ordinary shares.
- Common stock and non-cumulative perpetual preferred stock.
- Published reserves, including share premiums, retained profit, general reserves, legal reserves and reserves according to the articles of association.
  Retained profits refers not only to profits retained in previous years but also to allocations during the current year from profit to be retained in the current year.
- (In the case of consolidated accounts) minority interests in the equity of subsidiaries which are less than wholly-owned.

Supplementary capital is made up of the following elements:

- Unpublished or undisclosed reserves provided that:
  - they consist of that part of the accumulated after-tax surplus of retained profits which banks in some countries may be permitted to maintain as an undisclosed reserve;
  - they have the same high quality and character as a disclosed capital reserve, i.e. they are freely and immediately available to cover unexpected future losses. Undisclosed reserves exclude hidden values arising from holdings of securities in the balance sheet at below current market prices. Unrealised, latent capital gains on the securities concerned can be included in a specific way in the revaluation reserve (see below).

° Revaluation reserves.

Revaluation reserves can arise from the revaluation of fixed assets, when the market value of these assets is higher than the purchase value, or they can be a result of long term holdings of equity securities valued in the balance sheet for less than the current market value ('latent' revaluation reserves). For the purpose of arriving at the aggregate of the revaluation reserve, latent revaluation reserves may only be included at 45%. The discount reflects the potential volatility of this form of unrealised capital and the notional tax charge on it.

° General provisions/general loan loss reserves.

To explain the scope of the concept of 'general provision', two concepts can be compared: own funds (including retained profit) and provisions. Provisions can be broken down into specific provisions and general provisions.

The function of a bank's own funds is to absorb unexpected future losses connected with the risks of banking in general. Provisions are held to absorb future losses arising from impairment of the quality of the assets portfolio. A specific provision is ascribed to impairment of particular assets or known liabilities. This means that specific provisions cannot fulfil the general buffer function of own funds. General provisions are held against future, presently unidentified losses. Because of their unspecified nature, general provisions are included in (supplementary) capital. The difference between general (profit) reserves and general provisions is that, although they both have the function of absorbing future deterioration of the assets portfolio, without specifying which assets are involved, the general provisions are held on the basis of indications about the extent of the future impairment (e.g. on the basis of experience), while the purpose of general reserves is to absorb unexpected losses).

° Hybrid (debt/equity) capital instruments.

These combine characteristics of equity capital (own funds - a buffer to absorb unexpected future losses) and of loan capital (the obligation to pay a specific contractual amount to the lenders). The precise specifications differ from country to country. The committee considers that for these hybrid instruments to qualify as core capital they should meet the following requirements:

- they are unsecured, subordinated and fully paid-up;
- they are not redeemable at the initiative of the holder or without the prior consent of the supervisory authority;
- they are available to participate in losses without the bank being obliged to cease trading (unlike conventional subordinated debt, see below);
- they should allow service obligations to be temporarily deferred (as with cumulative preference shares) where the profitability of the bank would not support payment.

In addition to cumulative preference shares, the following are examples of instruments that may be eligible for inclusion:

- long-term preferred shares in Canada;
- 'titres participatifs' and 'titres subordonnés à durée indéterminée' in France;
- 'Genußscheine' in Germany;
- perpetual subordinated debt and preference shares in the United Kingdom;
- mandatory convertible debt instruments in the United States

° Subordinated term debt.

This category includes conventional unsecured subordinated debt instruments with a minimum original fixed term to maturity of over five years and limited redeemable preference shares. Unlike hybrid capital instruments, these instruments are not available to cover losses in the case where a bank continues its activities. For this reason these instruments will be limited to a maximum of 50% of Tier 1 (core-capital). This means that they may be included in the aggregate of supplementary capital (which is used together with core capital for the purpose of solvency evaluation) at the above value. The actual value of these instruments may, of course, be higher.

During the last five years to maturity a cumulative discount factor of 20% per annum will be applied, causing an annual decrease in the contribution of these instruments to supplementary capital.

The 'Cooke Committee' accord also requires that core capital should amount to at least 50% of own funds (capital base) or that supplementary capital may only amount to 100% of core capital. Here, again, this relates to the definition of own funds which is used for solvency evaluation. Actual own funds may differ from this. The above minimum for core capital expresses the aim of the 'Cooke Committee' to make the high quality core capital a substantial part of own funds. In this way a qualitative as well as a quantitative improvement of the own funds position will be achieved.

On April 17, 1989, the Council of Ministers of the EC adopted a directive concerning the own funds of credit institutions. To a large extent this directive is in line with the BIS accord of July 1988.

The EC directive has been drawn up in more detail than the Cooke Committee requirements. This has to do with the fact that an EC directive imposes on member states the obligation to implement its provisions in their national legislation. Compliance may be enforced by the European Court of Justice. Compliance with the BIS accord, however, cannot be enforced by judicial authorities.

The most important articles of the directive are listed below:

Article 2: general principles

1 Subject to the limits imposed in article 6, the unconsolidated own funds of credit institutions shall consist of the following items:

1 capital within the meaning of article 22 of directive 86/635/EEC, in so far as it has been paid up, plus share premium accounts but excluding cumulative preferential shares.
2 reserves within the meaning of article 23 of directive 86/635/EEC and profits or losses in the preceding year brought forward as a result of the application of the final profit or loss. The member states may permit inclusion of interim profits before a formal decision has been taken only if these profits have been verified by persons responsible for the auditing of the accounts and if it is proved to the satisfaction of the competent authorities that the amount thereof has been evaluated in accordance with the principles set out in directive 86/635/EEC and is net of any foreseeable charge or dividend;
3 revaluation reserves within the meaning of article 33 of Council directive 78/660/EEC of July 25, 1978 based on article 54 (3) (g) of the Treaty on the annual accounts of certain types of companies as amended by directive 84/569/EEC;
4 funds for general banking risks within the meaning of article 38 of directive 86/635/EEC;
5 value adjustments within the meaning of article 37, paragraph 2, of directive 86/635/EEC;
6 other items within the meaning of article 3;
7 the commitments of the members of credit institutions set up as cooperative societies and the joint and several commitments of the borrowers of certain institutions organised as funds, as referred to in article 4, paragraph 1;
8 fixed-term cumulative preferential shares and subordinated loan capital as referred to in article 4, paragraph 3.

The following items shall be deducted in accordance with article 6:

9 own shares at book value held by a credit institution;
10 intangible assets within the meaning of article 4, paragraph 9 ('assets') of directive 86/635/EEC;
11 material losses of the current financial year;

12 holdings in other credit and financial institutions amounting to more than 10% of their capital, subordinated claims and the instruments referred to in article 3 which a credit institution holds in respect of credit and financial institutions in which it has holdings exceeding 10% of the capital in each case.

Where shares in another credit or financial institution are held temporarily for the purpose of a financial assistance operation designed to reorganise and save that institution, the supervisory authority may waive this provision;

13 holdings in other credit and financial institutions of up to 10% of their capital, the subordinated claims and the instruments referred to in article 3 which a credit institutions holds in respect of credit and financial institutions other than those referred to in point 12 in respect of the amount of the total of such holdings, subordinated claims and instruments which exceed 10% of that credit institution's own funds calculated before the deduction of items 12 and 13.

Pending subsequent coordination of the provisions on consolidation, member states may provide that, for the calculation of unconsolidated own funds, parent companies subject to supervision on a consolidated basis need not deduct their holdings in other credit institutions or financial institutions which are included in the consolidation. This provision shall apply to all the prudential rules harmonised by Community acts.

2 The concept of own funds as defined in points 1 to 8 of paragraph 1 embodies a maximum number of items and amounts. The use of those items and the fixing of lower ceilings, and the deduction of items other than those listed in items 9 to 13 of paragraph 1 shall be left to the discretion of the member states. Member states shall nevertheless be obliged to consider increased convergence with a view to a common definition of own funds.

To that end the Commission shall, not more than three years after the date referred to in article 9, paragraph 1, submit a report to the European Parliament and to the Council on the application of this directive, accompanied, where appropriate, by such proposals for amendment as it shall deem necessary. Within five years of the date referred to in article 9, paragraph 1, the Council shall, acting by qualified majority on a proposal from the Commission, in cooperation with the European Parliament and after consultation of the Economic and Social Committee, examine the definition of own funds with a view to the uniform application of the common definition.

3 The items listed in points 1 to 5 must be available to a credit institution for unrestricted and immediate use to cover risks or losses as soon as they occur. The amount must be net of any foreseeable tax charge at the moment of its calculation or be suitably adjusted in so far as such tax charges reduce the amount up to which these items may be applied to cover risks or losses.

Article 3: other items referred to in article 2, paragraph 1, point 6

1 The concept of own funds used by a member state may include other items provided that, whatever their legal or accounting designations may be, have the following characteristics:

a they are freely available to the credit institution to cover normal banking risks where revenue or capital losses have not yet been identified;

b their existence is disclosed in internal accounting records;

c their amount is determined by the management of the credit institution, verified by independent auditors, made known to the competent authorities and placed under the supervision of the latter. With regard to verification, internal auditing may be considered as provisionally meeting the aforementioned requirements until such time as the Community provisions making external auditing mandatory have been implemented;

2 Securities of indeterminate term and other instruments that fulfil the following conditions may also be accepted as other items:

a they may not be reimbursed on the bearer's initiative or without the prior agreement of the supervisory authority;
b the debt agreement must provide for the credit institution to have the option of deferring the payment of interest on the debt;
c the lender's claim on the credit institution must be wholly subordinated to those of all non-subordinated creditors;
d the documents governing the issue of the securities must provide for debt and unpaid interest to be such as to absorb losses, while leaving the credit institution in a position to continue trading;
e only fully paid-up amounts shall be taken into account.

To these may be added cumulative preferential shares other than those referred to in article 2, paragraph 1, point 8.

Article 4

1 The commitments of the members of credit institutions set up as cooperative societies referred to in article 2, paragraph 1, point 7, shall comprise those societies' uncalled capital, together with the legal commitments of the members of those cooperative societies to make additional non-refundable payments should the credit institution occur a loss, in which case it must be possible to demand those payments without delay.

The joint and several commitments of borrowers in the case of credit institutions organised as funds shall be treated in the same way as the preceding items.

All such items may be included in own funds in so far as they are counted as the own funds of institutions of this category under national law.

2 Member states shall not include in the own funds of public credit institutions guarantees which they or their local authorities extend to such entities.

However the Kingdom of Belgium shall be exempt from this obligation until December 31, 1994.

3 Member states or the competent authorities may include fixed-term cumulative preferential shares referred to in article 2, paragraph 1, point 8 and subordinated loan capital referred to in that provision in own funds, if binding agreements exist under which, in the event of the bankruptcy or liquidation of the credit institution, they rank after the claims of all other creditors and are not to be repaid until all other debts outstanding at the time have been settled.

Subordinated loan capital must also fulfil the following criteria:
a only fully paid-up funds may be taken into account;
b the loans involved must have an original maturity of at least five years, after which they may be repaid; if the maturity on the debt is not fixed, they shall be repayable only subject to five years' notice unless the loans are no longer considered as own funds or unless the prior consent of the competent authorities is specifically required for early repayment. The competent authorities may grant permission for the early repayment of such loans provided the request is made at the initiative of the issuer and the solvency of the credit institution in question is not affected;
c the extent to which they may rank as own funds must be gradually reduced during at least the last five years before the repayment date;
d the loan agreement must not include any clause providing that in special circumstances, other than the winding up of the credit institution, the debt will become repayable before the agreed repayment date.

Article 5

Until further coordination of the provisions on consolidation, the following rules shall apply:

1 Where the calculation is to be made on a consolidated basis, the consolidated amounts relating to the items listed under article 2, paragraph 1, shall be used in accordance with the rules laid down in directive 83/350/EEC. Moreover, the following may, when they are credit ('negative') items, be regarded as consolidated reserves for the calculation of own funds:
  - any minority interests within the meaning of article 21 of directive 83/349/EEC, where the global integration method is used;
  - the first consolidation difference within the meaning of articles 19, 30 and 31 of directive 83/349/EEC;
  - the translation differences included in consolidated reserves in accordance with article 39, paragraph 6 of directive 86/635/EEC;
  - any difference resulting from the inclusion of certain participating interests in accordance with the method prescribed in article 33 of directive 83/349/EEC.

2 Where the above are debit ('positive') items, they must be deducted in the calculation of consolidated own funds.

Article 6: deduction and limits

1 The items referred to in article 2, paragraph 1, points 3 and 5 to 8, shall be subject to the following limits:
  a the total of items 3 and 5 to 8 may not exceed a maximum of 100% of items 1 plus 2 minus 9,10 and 11;
  b the total of items 7 and 8 may not exceed a maximum of 50% of items 1 plus 2 minus 9,10 and 11;
  c the total of items 12 and 13 shall be deducted from the total of all items.

2 The item referred to in article 2, paragraph 1, point 4 shall constitute a separate category. Provisionally, it shall be included in own funds without limit, but shall not be included when the basis of the limit for the items referred to in points 3 and 5 to 8 is fixed. Within six months of the implementation of this directive the Commission shall, in accordance with the procedure provided for in article 8, propose the final treatment for this item either in original own funds or in additional own funds.

3 The limits referred to in paragraph 1 must be complied with as from the date of the entry into force of the implementing measures for the Council Directive on a solvency ratio for credit institutions and by January 1, 1993 at the latest.

  Credit institutions exceeding those limits must gradually reduce the extent to which the items referred to in article 2, paragraph 1, points 3 and 5 to 8, are taken into account so that they comply with those limits before the aforementioned date.

4 The competent authorities may authorise credit institutions to exceed the limit laid down in paragraph 1 in temporary and exceptional circumstances.

Article 7

Compliance with the conditions laid down in articles 2 to 6 must be proved to the satisfaction of the competent authorities.

Article 8

Without prejudice to the report referred to in article 2, paragraph 2, second subparagraph, the Council will, on proposal of the Commission and by qualifying majority of votes, determine technical adaptations to this directive to:

- clarify the definitions to ensure uniform application of the said directive throughout the Community;
- clarify the definitions to take account, in implementing the said directive, of developments on the financial markets;
- bring the terminology and wording of the definitions into line with that of subsequent acts concerning credit institutions and related areas.

On the basis of article 9 the member states shall bring into force the laws, regulations and administrative provisions necessary for them to comply with this directive no later than the date laid down for the entry into force of the implementing measures of the Council directive on a solvency ratio for credit institutions, and before January 1, 1993.

Method of solvency measurement

In both the BIS accord and the EC directive, solvency is measured by relating the commonly-defined own funds not to the notional principal value of the individual assets and off-balance-sheet exposures but to their credit risk-weighted aggregate. An asset item exposure is made up of the value of the item concerned as disclosed in the balance sheet. The calculation of an OBS exposure is discussed below.

There are five categories of assets, weighted according to broad categories of relative risk, to which the following percentage weights are assigned: 0%, 10%, 20% 50% and 100%. Weights applied to different assets are lower according as the quality of the asset increases. The risk-weighted individual asset and off-balance-sheet exposure must amount to at least 8% of the own funds. In fact this standard solvency ratio implies several effective solvency ratios. For an asset item in the 100% weight of credit risk category for the amount of X, own funds amounting to 0.08x100%xX must be kept, for the 50% category this would be 0.08x50%xX. The effective solvency ratio that applies to the 100% category is 8%, for the 50% category it will be 4%, as shown below:

Weight of credit risk category	Standard solvency ratio	Effective solvency ratio
0%	8%	0.0%
10%	8%	0.8%
20%	8%	1.6%
50%	8%	4.0%
100%	8%	8.0%

The same applies to OBS exposures of X, but since granting of credit guarantees for the amount of Y involves less risks for a bank than the granting of credit for the amount of Y to one single borrower, it is harder to calculate the value of X. It is not certain if a credit guarantee will actually lead to the granting of credit, e.g. a bank grants a credit guarantee a hundred times, but eventually only in fifty cases the credit is actually granted. In this case the credit risk of the bank is not 100xY, but 50%x100xY. This amount (50Y) is the on-balance-sheet credit equivalent of OBS granted credit guarantees for the amount of 100Y. This 50% factor is called the credit conversion factor and represents the number by which the nominal amount of an OBS activity must be multiplied to calculate the OBS credit equivalent. The on-balance-sheet credit equivalent is the OBS exposure for the amount X, or schematically:

OBS activity with the nominal amount of Y	x	credit conversion factor appropriate to this OBS activity	=	on balance sheet credit equivalent X
			=	OBS exposure X

The amount of 50Y is called an on-balance-sheet credit equivalent (OBS exposure), since this amount has the same basis as the actual on-balance-sheet items, where this basis can be defined as the amount subject to credit risk. By applying credit conversion factors for each individual OBS activity, an on-balance-sheet equivalent can be found. This is then placed in one of the five credit risk categories. After multiplication by the relevant credit exposure weighted coefficient the result will be multiplied by 8% (standard solvency ratio).

Schematically:

OBS activity with nominal amount of Y	x	credit conversion factor appropriate to this activity	=	on-balance-sheet credit equivalent for the amount of X
			=	OBS exposure for the amount of X
			x	credit exposure weighted coefficient (0%, 10%, 20%, 50% or 100%)
			=	OBS exposure weighted for credit risk
			x	8% standard solvency ratio
			=	required amount of own funds relating to the OBS activity for the amount Y

OBS activities which are more likely to become on-balance-sheet items will involve a higher credit conversion factor. There are therefore different credit conversion factors for the various OBS activities.

The above shows that both the EC and the BIS place asset exposures and OBS exposures in five credit risk categories having a 0%, 10%, 20%, 50% or 100% weighting. The only difference concerns the allocation of asset items and OBS items to the different credit risk categories.

The credit risk categories according to the BIS accord are listed below:

0% category

- Cash.
- Claims on central governments and central banks denominated in national currency and funded in that currency.
- Other claims on OECD central governments and central banks.
- Claims collateralised by cash or OECD central government securities.
- Claims guaranteed by OECD central governments.

0%, 10%, 20% or 50% category

- Claims on domestic public sector entities, excluding central government, and loans guaranteed by such entities.

The supervisory authorities may themselves set the percentage weights for the above-mentioned claims (0%, 10%, 20% or 50%).

20% category

- Claims on multilateral development banks (IBRD, IADB, AsDB, AfDB, EIB) and claims guaranteed by, or collateralised by securities issued by such banks.
- Claims on banks incorporated in the OECD.
- Loans guaranteed by OECD incorporated banks.
- Claims on banks incorporated in countries outside the OECD with a residual maturity of up to one year and loans with a residual maturity of up to one year and guaranteed by banks incorporated in countries outside the OECD.
- Claims on non-domestic OECD public sector entities, excluding central government, and loans guaranteed by such entities.
- Cash items in process of collection.

50% category

- Loans fully secured by mortgage on residential property that is or will be occupied by the borrower or that is rented.

100% category

- Claims on the private sector.
- Claims on banks incorporated outside the OECD with a residual maturity of over one year.
- Claims on central governments outside the OECD (unless denominated in national currency and funded in that currency, see above 0%).
- Claims on commercial companies owned by the public sector.
- Premises, plant and equipment and other fixed assets.
- Real estate and other investments (including non-consolidated investment participations in other companies).
- Capital instruments used by other banks (unless deducted from capital).
- All other assets.

We examine below the value of the credit conversion factors for off-balance-sheet (OBS) banking transactions agreed by the Cooke Committee. The BIS accord recognises two main groups of off-balance-sheet transactions: credit substitutes and non-credit substitutes. The latter group can in turn be divided into two sub-groups, i.e. contingencies that are and contingencies that are not interest and/or exchange rate related.

A Credit substitutes

While no credit is granted in the case of credit substitutes, the full exposure to credit risk is borne. As regards the aggregation of credit risks, such a credit-replacing OBS activity is a perfect substitute for normal bank lending. This is expressed in a proposed credit conversion factor of 100%.

The products concerned are as follows:

- Standby letters of credit serving as financial guarantees for loans and securities.
  A customer can charge a bank to issue a standby letter of credit which will be used to cover credit granted by other lenders than the bank. The lenders will be ensured that the interest payments and the redemption of the principal sum will be received, since the bank will take over the obligations if the customer defaults. Thus, the credit risk is entirely transferred from the creditor of the customer to the bank.
- Acceptances, including endorsements with the character of acceptances.
  A credit institution, accepting a draft from a customer which is drawn on this credit institution, will be required to make certain future payments to certain persons. The acceptance of a draft is actually equivalent to granting credit for the value of the draft to enable the customer to pay the above-mentioned persons. The amount of the credit risk borne by the credit institution is the same in both cases.
- Sale and repurchase agreements and assets sales with recourse, where the credit risk remains with the credit institution.
- Forward asset purchases, forward forward deposits and the unpaid portion of partly paid shares and securities.
  These represent obligations that are 100% certain to lead to future balance sheet influences.

B Non-credit substitutes that are not interest and/or exchange rate related

Although these activities do expose a credit institution to risk, this risk is less than 100%. In such cases the proposed credit conversion factors are therefore less than 100%, namely 0%, 20% and 50%.

The following OBS activities are concerned:

- Standby letters of credit related to particular transactions forming part of the ordinary business operations of the customer.
  This does not therefore relate to the standby letters of credit discussed under A, which function solely as a financial guarantee for obtaining loans. In this case the credit institution guarantees via the standby letter of credit that the client will always be able to pay the transaction amount. This does not mean, however, that the credit institution will accumulate a 100% credit risk factor, since in return for the payment the customer will acquire goods which will have a certain value. The potential proceeds of sale result in the accumulation by the credit institution of a credit risk lower than the 100% applicable in the case of standby letters of credit used as a financial guarantee. The Cooke Committee proposes a credit conversion factor of 50% for these transactions.
- Other transaction-related contingent items such as performance bonds and bid bonds. A credit conversion factor of 50% will apply.
- Loan commitments.
  A credit institution commits to grant a certain maximum amount of credit during a certain period at a certain interest rate. If it were certain that the customer would use the option of taking up the credit, a credit conversion factor of 100% would be justified, since the loan commitment would become a credit substitute. However, the customer has the option not to make use of the commitment. On these grounds the credit conversion factor is 50% for formal standby facilities and credit lines with an original maturity of over one year, and 0% for similar commitments with an original maturity of up to one year, or which can be unconditionally cancelled at any time.
- Note issuing facilities (NIFs) and revolving underwriting facilities (RUFs).
  Under NIFs and RUFs credit institutions enter into a guarantee or underwriting commitment, which does not appear on the balance sheet. This means that the credit institutions concerned

grant credit guarantees to issuers of short term securities and commit to grant the required capital in case the securities cannot be placed. The credit institutions thus commit to provide funds to the issuer up to the amount of the shortfall in issue proceeds. The credit institutions supply the capital either by adding the securities to their own portfolio and crediting the shortfall in issue proceeds to the issuer, or they grant advances up to the value of the amount of the issue. In the above case, where the credit institutions must provide funds under guarantee commitments, the balance sheet will be influenced by an OBS activity. However this will not always occur. In this connection, the Cooke Committee proposes a credit conversion factor of 50%.

- Short-term self-liquidating trade-related contingencies such as documentary credits collateralised by the underlying shipments. The proposed credit conversion factor is 20%.

C Non-credit substitutes that are interest and/or exchange rate related

These are interest and currency swaps, purchased interest and currency options dealt in on the over-the-counter (OTC) markets and forward-rate-agreements (FRAs).

Solvency guidelines only relate to activities that result in the present in a claim or asset position (either on-balance-sheet or off-balance-sheet) or to commitments that may result in the future in the creation of a claim or asset position. The purchase of an option by a credit institution creates an OBS claim position subject to solvency provisions, since the entitlement to purchase or sell the underlying security, attaching to the purchased option, may become valueless if the counterparty (the writer of the option) defaults. It is strange, however, that written put options are not included in the current proposals. By writing a put option a credit institution commits to purchase a specific quantity of the underlying security at a specific price. If the option is exercised and the credit institution must purchase the underlying security, this results in a claim position. Writing a put option therefore means entering into a commitment which may result in a claim position in the future. This would indicate a need to make this activity subject to solvency provisions.

Options and financial futures traded in on organised exchanges (i.e. not on OTC markets), are not subject to solvency provisions. This applies only in so far as there are daily adjusted margin obligations, which apply to the parties entering into a commitment to purchase or sell a particular underlying security. Any losses connected with compliance with the obligations can be met from the deposited margin amount.

The reason why these off-balance-sheet activities are treated separately from those in category B is that banks are not exposed to any credit risk on the notional principal value of the rights acquired and obligations contracted but only on a fraction of this amount, namely the potential cost of a possible future replacement of the forfeited cash flow, which arises if the counterparty does not fulfil his obligations. These future replacement costs are crucial to the calculation of the on-balance-sheet credit conversion equivalents or credit conversion factors.

Assume for example that a bank purchases dollar/guilder call options on the OTC market, thereby acquiring the right to purchase one million dollars at a dollar/guilder rate of $ 1 = *f* 2. The bank purchases these calls in order to cover an identical *written* position. At a given point in time the purchaser of the options written by the bank exercises his right.

The bank consequently supplies one million dollars at the rate of $ 1 = *f* 2, acquiring these dollars by exercising the options it has bought. If the writer of the latter options is unable to supply these dollars to the bank, the bank will have to purchase the necessary dollars on the spot market. If the spot rate is $ 1 = *f* 2.10, the bank will incur a loss of 1,000,000 x (*f* 2.10 - *f* 2.00) = 100,000 guilders. The bank has borne a credit risk not on the nominal value of the acquired option contract (which amounts to $ 1,000,000 x *f* 2.00 = 2,000,000 guilders), but merely on the replacement cost of *f* 100,000, which corresponds with 100,000/2,000,000 = 5% of this nominal value. A credit conversion factor of 5% would have reflected the correct OBS exposure in this case.

The OBS exposure on an acquired currency call option can be formulated in general terms as:

amount of foreign currency x (spot rate on exercise - exercise price)

The major problem here is that we do not know the spot rate on exercise. This is a future rate that may be either above or below the current spot rate. An estimate of a future spot rate is also necessary for the calculation of the replacement cost in the case of swaps and FRAs.

In this connection a majority of countries represented in the Cooke Committee prefers the current exposure method. A few countries on the other hand prefer the original exposure method. In the Cooke Committee accord it is left to the discretion of the countries themselves which of the two methods is selected.

Both methods are described below.

Current exposure method

This method consists of calculating the *total replacement cost,* being the sum of the present replacement cost market (i.e. the current exposure) and the likely future replacement cost (i.e. the potential future exposure).

Present replacement cost is the cost that would have to be borne to obviate the current exposure arising in the event of a counterparty defaulting on his contractual obligation. In the above option example this would mean that the bank has to supply dollars and must also buy dollars at the current spot rate, since it is not possible for the bank to exercise the purchased options in view of the fact that the writer has defaulted. The current spot market rate is used to calculate current exposure and the technique is accordingly also known as the marking-to-market method. A negative present replacement cost implies a financial gain for the bank in the event of the counterparty defaulting. However, such gains may not be netted with off-balance-sheet items which have a positive replacement cost.

Likely future replacement cost is the extra cost on top of the present replacement cost that could arise as a result of interest or exchange rates ruling at the time the counterparty defaults differing from current rates. Banks, therefore, are not only exposed to credit risk on the present replacement cost, but also on the additional future replacement cost. Accordingly, the potential future replacement cost forms part of the total replacement cost.
This can be shown schematically as follows:

estimated future rate	=	present rate	+	estimated deviation
total replacement cost	=	present replacement cost	+	likely future replacement cost
total exposure	=	current exposure	+	potential exposure

Mathematical and statistical models, in which variables such as maturity and volatility play an important part, are used to calculate the estimated difference from the current spot rate. A longer period to maturity means a longer period during which distortions in interest and/or exchange rates may occur. These result in a higher likely future replacement cost and higher credit-converted amounts. It follows that as the maturity of off-balance-sheet engagements draws nearer, credit conversion factors become lower (for contracts featuring both interest rate and exchange rate risk). Since the Cooke Committee works on the assumption that volatility is higher in exchange rates than in interest rates, exchange rate contracts, assuming equal residual maturity, will have a higher credit conversion factor than interest rate contracts.

This is reflected in the factors agreed by the Cooke Committee :

Residual maturity	*Interest rate contracts*	*Exchange rate contracts*
less than one year	nil	1.0%
one year and over	0.5%	5.0%

By applying these factors to the notional principal amounts of off-balance-sheet contractual rights or obligations, their additional future replacement cost (their add-on) is arrived at. The sum of this add-on and the current replacement cost of an off-balance-sheet item produces its total replacement cost.

The total replacement cost so calculated constitutes the on-balance-sheet equivalent of any off-balance-sheet item which is then allocated to one of the five credit exposure categories, as in the case of a 'genuine' on-balance sheet item. The credit-exposure-weighted off-balance-sheet exposure is obtained by multiplying this equivalent by one of the credit exposure weighting coefficients 0%, 10%, 20%, 50% or 100%). The required level of capital for any off-balance-sheet activity is equal to this weighted exposure times the solvency ratio of 8%.

The total replacement cost of an individual off-balance-sheet item related to the notional principal amount of the contractual right or obligation, produces an effective credit conversion factor. In contrast to that applied in the calculation of the additional future replacement cost, this credit conversion factor changes from day to day. This is because the effective credit conversion factor incorporates not only the additional future replacement cost but also the present replacement cost, the latter being calculated on the basis of daily market rates.

Schematically:

$$\text{effective credit conversion factor for an individual off-balance-sheet activity} = \frac{\text{total replacement cost}}{\text{notional principal amount of acquired OBS rights or obligation}}$$

in which:

total replacement cost	=	present replacement cost	+	additional future replacement cost
		calculated on the basis of daily changing market rates		calculated on the basis of a fixed percentage

Unlike the *fixed effective* credit conversion factors (0%, 10%, 20%, 50% or 100%) which apply for the OBS instruments discussed under A an B, the *variable effective* credit conversion factors as discussed under C, are applied here. This is connected with the fact that, for off-balance-sheet instruments which are neither credit substitutes nor interest and/or exchange rate related, notional and effective credit conversion factors coincide. This is so because the notional principal amount of each OBS right or obligation is multiplied by a *fixed notional* percentage. While off-balance-sheet instruments which are interest and/or exchange rate related also feature such a fixed notional percentage, they have, in addition, a replacement cost component which changes daily. It causes notional and effective factors to differ and effective credit conversion factors to be variable.

Original exposure method

Some of the representatives on the Cooke Committee find the marking-to-market element of the current exposure method --i.e. the fact that interest and exchange rate fluctuations help determine the credit-converted amount-- too complicated. For the rest of the proposals, on the other hand, the Committee favours the use of definite and invariable factors for potential future exposure as well as for classification according to credit risk category.

In their view, an on-balance-sheet credit-equivalent should be calculated using a fixed credit conversion factor valid for the whole of the period to maturity (and so eliminating the unstable element incorporated in the current exposure method) at the time of contracting the off-balance-sheet right or obligation (hence original exposure method).

However, this is not to say that the calculation of fixed credit conversion factors does not take into account the possibility that a bank, owing to interest and exchange rate fluctuations, can be faced with larger exposures. This does occur, but not by continuously marking-to-market, rather by calculating once-only conversion factors comprising a kind of average value for the exposure to interest and exchange rate fluctuations.

Fixed effective and fixed notional credit conversion factors are thus introduced in this method (contrary to the variable effective credit conversion factors in the current exposure method) which have higher values than the fixed notional credit conversion factors of the current exposure method. The sole purpose of these fixed notional factors in the latter method is to provide for the additional future replacement cost. In the current exposure method, on the other hand, the fixed notional factors also provide for the current replacement cost.

The two methods may be compared schematically as follows:

Current exposure method

total replacement cost (RC)	=	present RC	+	additional RC
		calculated on the basis of daily fluctuating market rates		calculated on the basis of fixed notional factors

Original exposure method

total replacement cost (RC)	=	present RC	+	additional RC

sum calculated on the basis of fixed notional factors.

The impact of variables such as maturity and volatility on the current exposure method is equally significant in the case of the original exposure method. The higher the maturity the higher the credit conversion factors. Exchange rate contracts with their higher volatility than for interest rate contracts in the eyes of the Cooke Committee, are also allocated higher conversion factors. The Cooke Committee proposes the following factors. The lower factors (lower because they only provide for the additional, future replacement cost) of the current exposure method are indicated in parentheses except for exchange rate contracts with a maturity of one year and of less than two years.

Maturity	*Interest rate contracts*	*Exchange rate contracts*
less than one year	0.5% (0%)	2.0% (1.0%)
one year and less than two years	1.0% (0.5%)	5.0% (5.0%)
for each additional year	1.0% (0%)	3.0% (0%)

Residual maturity and the (current exposure method) marking-to-market principle that goes with it are not relevant here; relevant to this original exposure method is the original maturity and the related principle of calculating an average value to provide for the exposures to future interest and exchange rate fluctuations in the period to maturity.

In the EC directive on solvency ratios for credit institutions the Cooke Committee accord on credit conversion factors for interest and exchange rate contracts has been followed closely. The proposed rates for the mark-to-market approach correspond exactly with those of the current exposure method. The proposed conversion factors for the original exposure approach also correspond exactly with those of the original exposure method from the BIS agreement of July 1988.

As far as the OBS activities presented under A and B are concerned, the same credit conversion factors are adopted. A credit conversion factor of 100% for items with a full risk, i.e. for items that are complete credit substitutes. A percentage of 50% for items with a medium risk, of 20% for items with a medium/low risk and 0% for low risk items.

The EC directive presents the following classification of off-balance-sheet items:

Full risk (100%)

- Guarantees having the character of credit substitutes.
- Acceptances.
- Endorsements on bills not carrying the name of other credit institutions.
- Transactions with recourse.
- Irrevocable standby letters of credit having the character of credit substitutes.
- Asset sale and repurchase agreements as defined in article 12, paragraphs 1 and 2, of directive 86/635/EEC, if these agreements are treated as off-balance-sheet items pending application of directive 86/635/EEC. This is the directive of December 8, 1986 concerning the annual accounts and consolidated annual accounts of banks and other financial institutions.
- Assets purchased under outright forward purchase agreements.
- The unpaid portion of partly-paid shares and securities.
- Forward forward deposits.
- Other items also carrying full risk.

Medium risk (50%)

- Documentary credits issued and confirmed (see also medium/low risk).
- Warranties and indemnities (including tender, performance, customs and tax bonds) and guarantees not having the character of credit substitutes.
- Asset sale and repurchase agreements as defined in articles 12, paragraphs 3 and 5, of directive 86/635/EEC.
- Irrevocable standby letters of credit not having the character of credit substitutes.
- Undrawn credit facilities (agreements to lend, purchase securities, provide guarantees or acceptance facilities) with an original maturity of more than one year.
- Note issuing facilities (NIFs) and revolving underwriting facilities (RUFs).
- Other items also carrying medium risk.

Medium/low risk (20%)

- Documentary credits in which underlying shipment acts as collateral and other self-liquidating transactions.
- Other items also carrying medium/low risk.

Low risk (0%)

- Undrawn credit facilities (agreements to lend, purchase securities, provide guarantees or acceptance facilities) with an original maturity of up to and including one year or which can be cancelled unconditionally at any time without notice.
- Other items carrying low risk.

The EC directive further distinguishes the credit risk categories listed below. First a number of concepts are defined:

- Zone A: all EC member states and all other countries which are full members of the Organisation for Economic Cooperation and Development (OECD) and those countries which have concluded special lending agreements with the International Monetary Fund (IMF) associated with the Fund's General Agreements to Borrow (GAB).

- Zone B: all other countries not in zone A.

- Non-bank sector: all borrowers other than credit institutions, central banks and central governments, regional governments and local authorities, the European Communities, the European Investment Bank and multilateral development banks.

- Multilateral development banks: the International Bank for Reconstruction and Development, the International Financial Corporation, the Inter-American Development Bank, the Asian Development Bank, the African Development Bank, the Council of Europe Resettlement Fund, the Nordic Investment Bank and the Caribbean Development Bank.

0%-Category

- Cash in hand and equivalent items.
- Asset items constituting claims on Zone A central governments and central banks.
- Asset items constituting claims carrying the explicit guarantees of Zone A central governments and central banks.
- Asset items constituting claims on Zone B central governments and central banks, denominated and funded in the national currencies of the borrowers.
- Asset items constituting claims carrying the explicit guarantees of Zone B central governments and central banks, denominated and funded in the national currency common to the guarantor and the borrower.
- Asset items constituting claims on the European Communities (EC).
- Asset items secured, to the satisfaction of the competent authorities, by collateral in the form of Zone A central government or central bank securities, or securities issued by the European Communities, or by cash deposits placed with the lending institution or by certificates of deposit or similar instruments issued by and lodged with the latter.

20%-Category

- Asset items constituting claims on the European Investment Bank (EIB).
- Asset items constituting claims on multilateral development banks.
- Asset items constituting claims carrying the explicit guarantee of the European Investment Bank (EIB).
- Asset items constituting claims carrying the explicit guarantees of multilateral development banks.
- Asset items constituting claims on Zone A regional governments or local authorities, subject to article 7.
- Asset items constituting claims carrying the explicit guarantees of Zone A regional governments or local authorities, subject to article 7.
- Asset items constituting claims on Zone A credit institutions but not constituting such institutions' own funds as defined in directive 89/299/EEC.
- Asset items constituting claims, with a maturity of one year or less, on Zone B credit institutions, other than securities issued by such institutions which are recognised as components of their own funds.
- Asset items carrying the explicit guarantees of Zone A credit institutions.
- Asset items constituting claims with a maturity of one year or less, carrying the explicit guarantees of Zone B credit institutions.
- Asset items secured, to the satisfaction of the competent authorities, by collateral in the form of securities issued by the EIB or by multilateral development banks.
- Cash items in the process of collection.

50%-Category

- Loans fully and completely secured, to the satisfaction of the competent authorities, by mortgages on residential property which is or will be occupied or let by the borrower.
- Prepayments and accrued income: these assets shall be subject to the weighting corresponding to the counterparty where a credit institution is able to determine it in accordance with directive 86/635/EEC. Otherwise, where it is unable to determine the counterparty, it shall apply a flat-rate weighting of 50%.

100%-Category

- Asset items constituting claims on Zone B central governments and central banks except where denominated and funded in the national currency of the borrower.
- Asset items constituting claims on Zone B regional governments or local authorities.
- Asset items constituting claims with a maturity of more than one year on Zone B credit institutions.
- Asset items constituting claims on the Zone A or Zone B non-bank sectors.
- Tangible assets within the meaning of assets as listed in article 4, paragraph 10, of directive 86/635/EEC.
- Holdings of shares, participations and other components of the own funds of other credit institutions which are not deducted from the own funds of the lending institutions.
- All other assets except where deducted from own funds.

The exceptions of article 7, mentioned in the 20%-category, imply the following. Member states may fix a weighting of 0% rather than 20% for their own regional governments and local authorities if there is no difference in risk between claims on the latter and claims on their central governments because of the revenue-raising powers of the regional governments and local authorities and the existence of specific constitutional arrangements the effect of which is to reduce the chances of default by the latter. A zero weighting fixed in accordance with these criteria shall apply to claims on, and off-balance-sheet items incurred on behalf of, the regional government and local authorities in question and claims on others and off-balance-sheet items incurred on behalf of others and guaranteed by those regional governments and local authorities.

If guarantees have been expressly granted in respect of off-balance-sheet items, they are weighted as if they had been contracted for the guarantor rather than the counterparty.

The following comments can be made on the EC and BIS rules on own funds and solvency:

a As a result of the establishment of various credit conversion factors for off-balance-sheet activities and the introduction of five credit risk categories for both on-balance-sheet activities and on-balance-sheet credit equivalents, differences arise in solvency weighting among the various activities, which impact on the allocation of credits. The latter means that in this way supervisors exert influence on the optimum composition of a bank's portfolio. Or to put it another way, the central bankers are taking the commercial bankers' decisions for them.

Supervisors can claim on the other hand that they are merely creating a new framework within which the banks can determine the composition of their portfolios in complete freedom and in competition with each other. In addition, this new framework is necessary in order to reverse the deterioration in bank solvency, already mentioned. In fact, of course, all regulations are restrictive.

b The implication of classifying individual assets and off-balance-sheet activities into five credit risk categories is to disregard the effects of diversification, as a result of which the total risk within a bank's portfolio could be lower than the sum of all its parts. Only in the improbable case that all the individual assets and OBS activities are in perfect positive correlation, will no diversification effects occur.

c Except for OBS non-credit substitutes which are interest and/or exchange rate related, and for which account is taken of the interest and/or exchange rate risk when estimating the credit risk and credit conversion factors, for other OBS activities and on-balance-sheet activities only the credit risk is taken into account while the interest and/or exchange rate risk is disregarded. However, the risks associated with interest and exchange rate fluctuations can be substantial. Those concerned are aware of this and are currently studying a number of approaches to integrating the interest and exchange rate risks in the risk-asset ratio.

d The rules discussed above represent a tightening of international supervision of solvency. However, a tightening of supervision of liquidity is also of essential importance for the maintenance of stability in the international financial system. In this respect the introduction of a risk-asset ratio is a positive step, since the substitution of high-credit-risk assets and a higher anticipated yield for liquid, low-credit-risk assets, in order to increase banking profits, now becomes less attractive. This is because the higher anticipated yield is accompanied by a higher solvency requirement. The own funds required for this purpose are relatively high-cost, which results in the higher anticipated yield being lower in net terms, thereby militating somewhat against the substitution process.

e Despite the improvement in supervision of solvency represented by the EC and BIS rules, the problem remains that supervision is still exercised on the basis of the book-value balance sheet. The actual exposure of banks to risk, on the other hand, is only expressed in a market-value balance sheet.

A fundamental aspect in this respect is the question to what extent supervisors, in determining solvency, can rely on the book value of assets, if this differs significantly from their market value. This divergence between book value and market value has become all the more topical since the quality of bank assets has decreased, owing to factors such as the international debt crisis and problems in specific sectors of the economy (in the USA: agriculture, energy and real estate). This declining quality has been expressed in the form of a fall in the market value of some assets below their book value.

XIII COUNCIL DIRECTIVE OF DECEMBER 3, 1991 IMPLEMENTING DIRECTIVE 89/299/EEC ON THE OWN FUNDS OF CREDIT INSTITUTIONS
(OJEC L 339 11.12.1991, directive 91/633/EEC)

The 1989 directive on own funds did not definitively recognise the fund for general banking risks as part of either the original own funds (cf. the core capital or basic equity in the BIS accord) or the additional own funds (cf. the supplementary capital in the BIS accord). This 1991 directive on the other hand, allocates the fund for general banking risks to the category of original own funds.

XIV COUNCIL DIRECTIVE OF MARCH 16, 1992 AMENDING DIRECTIVE 89/299/EEC ON THE CREDIT INSTITUTION'S OWN FUNDS
(OJEC L 75 21.3.1992, directive 92/16/EEC)

While, in the case of cooperative societies or funds, the 1989 directive permits the joint and several commitments of borrowers to be treated as own funds, it does not deal with the treatment of such commitments where a cooperative society or fund is a credit institution which is converted into a public limited liability company. Regulating this aspect became relevant when the Danish Government made known its evident interest in converting its mortgage loan institutions, organised as cooperative societies or funds, into public limited liability companies. A temporary derogation, permitting part of their joint and several commitments to be allocated to own funds, is required to make the change-over possible or facilitate it. The 1992 directive provides for such temporary derogation until January 1, 2001.

3.8 Coordination of large exposures of credit institutions

XV COMMISSION RECOMMENDATION OF DECEMBER 22, 1986 ON MONITORING AND CONTROLLING LARGE EXPOSURES OF CREDIT INSTITUTIONS
(OJEC L 33 4.2.1987, recommendation 87/62/EEC)

The preamble of the recommendation states that monitoring and controlling the exposures of a credit institution is an integral part of prudential supervision. Excessive concentration of exposures to a single client or group of connected clients may result in an unacceptable degree of risk concentration, a situation that may be deemed to be prejudicial to the solvency of a credit institution. The recommendation's objective is to establish Community-wide standards for monitoring and controlling large exposures of credit institutions. It was decided to do so by means of a recommendation, since this instrument permits existing systems to be adjusted gradually and new systems to be established without causing dislocation to the banking system of the Community. A directive on monitoring and controlling large exposures of credit institutions can then still be introduced at a later stage.

The recommendation applies to credit institutions as defined in article 1 of the first coordination directive of 1977.

The concept of exposure is defined as any facility granted, whether drawn or undrawn, by a credit institution to a client or a group of connected clients, on- or off-balance-sheet, and includes those commitments and contingent items deemed to be relevant by the respective competent authorities when assessing the identifiable risks of that institution. An indicative list of exposures is given in the appendix to the recommendation. Pending further coordination, the member states have discretion to fix the weighting factor for the elements listed below; however, the Commission recommends that those elements contained in sections A and B(i) of the list given below be weighted at 100%. Since the list is indicative, and therefore cannot be regarded as comprehensive, the Commission would expect member states to include in the term 'exposure' any elements which are broadly of the same character.

The following indicative list is presented:

A On-balance-sheet items
- loans and advances, including overdrafts;
- bill and promissory notes;
- leases;
- shares and other securities;
- loan stocks;
- certificates of deposits.

B Off-balance-sheet items

i Guarantees and similar contingent liabilities:
- acceptances;
- endorsements on bills which do not carry the name of another credit institution;
- guarantees which take the form of credit substitutes;
- documentary credits, issued and confirmed;
- transactions with recourse;
- warranties and indemnities, including tender and performance bonds and customs and tax bonds;
- irrevocable standby letters of credit.

ii Commitments:
- asset sale and repurchase agreements;
- assets purchased under outright forward purchase agreements;
- unpaid portion of partly-paid shares and securities;
- standby facilities, such as irrevocable revolving lines of credit;
- underwriting, including note issuing facilities and revolving underwriting facilities;
- irrevocable undrawn overdraft facilities, commitments to lend, purchase securities or provide guarantees or acceptance facilities.

In the definition of the concept of 'exposure', it emerged that this relates to a concentration of exposures (together forming a large exposure) to one client or a group of connected clients. In this context a group of connected clients is defined as two or more persons, whether natural or legal, jointly representing exposures of the same credit institution and any of its subsidiaries, where such clients are mutually associated in that:
- one of them holds directly or indirectly power of control over the other, or
- their accumulated exposures represent a single risk to the credit institution in as much as they are so interconnected that there is a likelihood that if one of them experiences financial problems the other or all of them are likely to encounter repayment difficulties. Credit institutions should regard the following as examples of interconnection of this type:
  - ° common ownership;
  - ° common directors;
  - ° cross guarantees;
  - ° direct commercial interdependency with no possibility of substitution in the short term.

The recommendation considers an exposure of a credit institution to a client or group of connected clients to be a 'large' exposure when its value has reached or exceeded 15% of own funds.

The above is a description of a large exposure. In addition the recommendation proposes limits to the size of such a large exposure. Credit institutions may not incur an exposure to a client or group of connected clients when its percentage value exceeds 40% of own funds, and the aggregate of these large exposures, entered into in respect of one client or a group of connected clients, may not exceed 800% of own funds.

Depending on the decision of the competent authorities, the above limits need not apply to certain clients of groups of connected clients such as:

a the public authorities of:
 - ° any of the EC member states;
 - ° countries on the IMF list of industrial countries drawn up for statistical purposes;

b the institutions of the EC and international public bodies of which the relevant member state is a member.

In addition, the competent authorities may grant partial or full exemption from the 40% and 800% limits:

a for exposures secured by an explicit irrevocable guarantee or pledge of the organisations mentioned above (public authorities, EC institutions and international public bodies of which the relevant member state is a member);

b for exposures secured by cash deposits or listed securities, provided that the value of the latter is calculated in a prudent manner.

Finally, the competent authorities may grant exemption from the application of this recommendation to interbank exposures having a maturity of six months or less.

The exposures of a credit institution which has a participation, as defined in article 1 of directive 83/350/EEC relating to the supervision of institutions on a consolidated basis (discussed earlier), in another credit institution or financial institution, shall be monitored and controlled on a consolidated basis to the extent and in the manner prescribed by the member state in applying the above directive.

XVI PROPOSAL FOR A COUNCIL DIRECTIVE ON MONITORING AND CONTROLLING LARGE EXPOSURES OF CREDIT INSTITUTIONS
(OJEC C 123 9.5.1991, proposal (91) 68)

If adopted, this proposal will make the provisions of the recommendation binding. The proposal also contains certain amendments to the recommendation, a major one being the percentage of own funds up to which credit institutions may be exposed with respect to a client or group of connected clients (25% instead of 40%). Where that client or group of connected clients is the parent undertaking of the credit institution and/or one or more subsidiaries of that parent undertaking, credit institutions may not have large exposures which in the aggregate exceed 800% of own funds.

The planned date of implementation of the directive is January 1, 1993.

3.9 Coordination of deposit-guarantee schemes of credit institutions

XVII COMMISSION RECOMMENDATION OF DECEMBER 22, 1986 CONCERNING THE INTRODUCTION OF DEPOSIT-GUARANTEE SCHEMES IN THE COMMUNITY
(OJEC L 33 4.2.1987, recommendation 87/63/EEC)

Article 16 of the proposal for a Council directive concerning the reorganisation and the winding-up of credit institutions and deposit-guarantee schemes (to be discussed further under XIV), states the following:

1 Member states shall ensure that the deposit-guarantee schemes that exist in their territory cover the deposits of branches of institutions having their head office in another member state.
2 *As a transitional measure, pending entry into force of a deposit-guarantee scheme in all member states,* the latter shall ensure that the deposit-guarantee-schemes, in which the institutions that have their head office in their territory take part, extend cover to deposits received by branches set up in host countries within the Community which have no deposit-guarantee scheme, under the same conditions as those laid down for guarantee deposits received in the home country.

The Commission produced this recommendation in view of the fact that only six of the twelve EC countries had deposit-guarantee schemes. The thinking behind the recommendation is to achieve more experience with the workings of deposit-guarantee schemes in the Community, before binding regulations are drafted in the form of a proposal for a directive.

The Commission recommends:

1 that member states which already have one or more deposit-guarantee schemes (Belgium, France, Germany, the Netherlands, Spain and the United Kingdom), should check, in the event of the winding-up of a credit institution revealing insufficient assets, that those schemes:
   a guarantee reasonable compensation for depositors who do not posses the means of properly assessing the financial policies of the institution to which they entrust their deposits;
   b cover the depositors of all authorised credit institutions, including the depositors of branches of credit institutions that have their head offices in other member states;
   c distinguish sufficiently clearly between intervention prior to winding-up and compensation after winding-up;
   d clearly set out the criteria for compensation and the formalities in order to receive compensation.
2 that member states which already have plans for introducing deposit-guarantee schemes (Ireland, Italy and Portugal):
   a should check that those plans meet the conditions set out above;
   b should take all appropriate measures to ensure that those deposit-guarantee schemes are adopted by December 31, 1988.
3 that member states which do not have a deposit-guarantee scheme covering all their institutions and which have not yet drawn up plans for such a scheme (Denmark, Greece and Luxembourg):
   a should draw up, in collaboration with the authorities responsible for supervising credit institutions and the professional organisations representing the categories of institutions concerned, a plan for one or more deposit-guarantee schemes meeting the conditions set out above in points 1 (a) to (b);
   b should take all appropriate measures to ensure that those schemes come into force by January 1, 1990.
4 that the member states shall inform the Commission of any amendment in their deposit-guarantee schemes related to points 1, 2 and 3 of this recommendation.

3.10 Coordination of reorganisation, winding-up and deposit-guarantee schemes of credit institutions

XVIII *PROPOSAL FOR A COUNCIL DIRECTIVE ON THE COORDINATION OF LAWS, REGULATIONS AND ADMINISTRATIVE PROVISIONS RELATING TO THE REORGANISATION AND THE WINDING-UP OF CREDIT INSTITUTIONS*

(OJEC C 356 31.12.1985, proposal (85) 788)

AMENDED PROPOSAL FOR A COUNCIL DIRECTIVE CONCERNING THE REORGANISATION AND THE WINDING-UP OF CREDIT INSTITUTIONS AND DEPOSIT-GUARANTEE SCHEMES

(OJEC C 36 8.2.1988, proposal (88) 4)

The purpose of reorganisation measures is to prevent the bankruptcy of a credit institution in difficulties. Where such measures fail, the credit institution will have to be wound up. The proposal for a directive envisages coordination of the main reorganisation and winding-up provisions. In addition, article 16 describes briefly the situation that will exist until the entry into force of a deposit-guarantee scheme in all the member states.

The directive applies to credit institutions and their branches in another member state than the one where their head office is situated, as defined in the first coordination directive of December 1977.

The proposal considers reorganisation measures to be the measures included in appendix I of the proposal where they are intended to safeguard or to restore the financial situation of a credit institution. Examples of such measures are on the spot investigations and expert appraisals, appointment of a special auditor and suspension of all or part of a credit institution's activities.

With respect to the provisions on reorganisation measures, the proposal distinguishes between credit institutions whose head office is inside and those whose head office is outside the Community:

A Credit institutions having their head office within the Community

The competent authorities or courts of the member state where the head office is situated (the home country) are authorised to decide, in accordance with the rules, procedures and practices in force in their territory, on the implementation of one or more reorganisation measures in a credit institution and its branches (article 4, paragraph 1).

The measures decided on by the competent authorities or the competent court of the member state in which the head office is situated are to be fully effective against the governing bodies and creditors of branches situated in other member states, even if the legal system of these other member states does not provide for such measures or their execution is subject to conditions which will not be fulfilled (article 4, paragraph 2). The competent authorities of the member state in which the head office is situated must, prior to deciding on the reorganisation measures, inform the competent authorities of the host member state of their intention and consult them on the effects of such measures in the host country, unless the measure concerned is clearly not likely to have any significant effect on a branch situated in another member state (article 5).

Conversely, a similar duty rests with the authorities of the member state in which the branch is situated if reorganisation measures are being envisaged there (article 6). If, upon receipt of such information, the competent authorities of the home country consider that the difficulties encountered by the branch are not such as to justify the application of article 4, paragraphs 1 and 2, they shall so inform the authorities of the host country, which may decide notwithstanding this to apply one more reorganisation measures in their territory.

B Credit institutions having their head office outside the Community

Pending subsequent coordination of laws, regulations and administrative provisions applying to the branches of credit institutions having their head office outside the Community, the authorities and courts of the host country shall retain the right to implement reorganisation measures in accordance with the rules, procedures and practices in force in their territory, unless provision is made to the contrary in agreements concluded with the home country, in accordance with the Treaty, on the basis of the principle of reciprocity (article 8).

Within the meaning of this directive the procedures listed in appendix 2 to the proposal are regarded as winding-up procedures.

Again, in the discussion of the provisions relating to winding-up procedures the proposal distinguishes between credit institutions having their head office within the Community and outside the Community:

A Credit institutions having their head office within the Community

Article 11, paragraph 2 states that the business of the credit institution shall be wound up in accordance with the law of the home country. On the basis of article 11, paragraph 3, decisions on the winding-up of a credit institution taken by the administrative authorities or courts, shall also be fully effective against the credit institutions' branches situated in other member states. However, the above-mentioned decisions form a restriction to the introduction of other winding-up procedures against these branches. This relates to voluntary winding-up by a credit institution's own statutory bodies.

Article 14 provides that winding-up shall be carried out under the supervision of the competent authorities of the home country in collaboration with the competent authorities of the host country.

B Credit institutions having their head office outside the Community

Article 15 stipulates that where the law of the host country provides for the possibility of winding-up a branch of a credit institution having its head office outside the Community, such winding-up shall be decided on by the competent authorities of the host country.

Deposit-guarantees are defined as all the measures which have the purpose of guaranteeing depositors reasonable compensation, or to prevent depositors from suffering any losses.

Article 16, paragraph 1 states that, in general, member states shall ensure that the deposit-guarantee schemes that exist in their territory also cover the deposits of branches of institutions having their head office in another member state. However, as a transitional measure, pending entry into force of a deposit-guarantee scheme in all member states, the latter shall ensure that the deposit-guarantee schemes, in which the institutions having their head office in their territory take part, extend cover to deposits received by branches set up in host countries within the Community which have no deposit-guarantee scheme, under the same conditions as those laid down for the guaranteeing of deposits received in the home country.

Finally, under article 17 the member states shall adopt the laws, regulations and administrative provisions necessary to comply with this directive not later than January 1, 1990, but may stipulate that these provisions shall not apply until two years after that date.

3.11 Coordination of consumer credit

XIX COUNCIL DIRECTIVE OF DECEMBER 22, 1986 FOR THE APPROXIMATION OF THE LAWS, REGULATIONS AND ADMINISTRATIVE PROVISIONS OF THE MEMBER STATES CONCERNING CONSUMER CREDIT
(OJEC L 42 12.2.1987, directive 87/102/EEC)

There are considerable differences in the laws of member states in the field of consumer credit, limiting the opportunities the consumer has to obtain credit in other member states and affecting adversely the size and nature of the desired credit and the purchase of goods and services. The objective of the directive under review is to end this undesirable situation through harmonisation of the laws concerning consumer credit.

The directive applies to credit agreements in which a consumer is the borrower. A consumer is defined as a natural person who, in transactions covered by the directive, is acting for purposes which can be regarded as outside his trade or profession. A creditor is a natural or legal person who grants credit in the course of his trade, business or profession, or a group of such persons. In terms of such agreements a creditor grants or promises to grant to a consumer a credit in the form of a deferred payment, a loan or other similar financial accommodation. Agreements for the provision on a continuing basis of a service or a utility under which the consumer has the right to pay for them, for the duration of their provision, by means of instalments, are not deemed to be credit agreements for the purpose of this directive (article 1).

By virtue of article 2, the directive does not apply to:
a credit agreements or agreements promising to grant credit
  - intended primarily for the purpose of acquiring or retaining property rights in land or in an existing or projected building;
  - intended for the purpose of renovating or improving a building;

b hiring agreements under which the title does not ultimately pass to the hirer;
c credits granted or made available without payment of interest or any other charge;
d credit agreements under which no interest is charged provided the consumer agrees to repay the credit in a single payment;
e credit in the form of advances on current account, other than on credit card accounts;
f credits for amounts less than ECU 200 or more than ECU 20,000;
g credit agreements under which the consumer is granted a period not exceeding three months within which to repay the credit or is required to repay the credit by a maximum number of four payments within a period not exceeding 12 months.

Article 3 stipulates that any advertisement must indicate the annual percentage rate of charge calculated as the total cost of the credit to the consumer expressed as an annual percentage of the amount of credit granted.

Under article 4, credit agreements are to be made in writing. Such written agreements are to include:
a a statement of the annual percentage rate of charge;
b a statement of the conditions under which the annual percentage rate of charge may be amended;
c other essential terms of the agreement.

The annex to the directive contains a list of such 'other essential terms' which member states may require to be included in the written agreement. The following conditions are concerned:
1 Credit agreements relating to the supply of certain goods or the provision of certain services:
  i a description of the goods or services to which the agreement relates;

ii the cash price and the price stipulated in the credit agreement;
iii if relevant, the amount of the down payment, the number and the amount of the instalments and the dates when they are due, or the method to determine this information if unknown at the time of conclusion of the contract;
iv a statement implying a reduction in case of accelerated payment by the consumer;
v a statement mentioning the owner of the goods (in case the property rights are not immediately transferred to the consumer) and the conditions under which the consumer becomes the owner of the goods;
vi a description of possibly required securities;
vii the time for consideration;
viii an indication of required insurance, if appropriate, and mentioning of the insurance cost in case the consumer cannot choose the insurer himself.

2 Credit agreements involving credit cards:
i the credit limit, if any;
ii the repayment conditions or the manner to determine these repayments;
iii the time for consideration.

3 Credit agreements implying continuous credit and which are not covered by the directive in any other way:
i the credit limit, if any or the method by which it is determined;
ii the conditions regarding use and repayment;
iii the time for consideration;

4 Other credit agreements covered by the directive:
i the credit limit, if any;
ii mentioning of possibly required securities;
iii the conditions of repayment;
iv the time for consideration;
v a statement mentioning the consumer's right to a reduction in case of accelerated discharge of his obligation as provided for in article 8.

Under article 5, member states shall make it mandatory to disclose at least the total cost of the loan to the consumer as long as no decision has been taken on the implementation of a Community method or methods for computing the annual percentage rate of charge.

Notwithstanding the exclusion provided for in article 2, paragraph 1e, where there is an agreement between a credit institution or financial institution and a consumer for the granting of credit in the form of an advance on a current account, other than on credit card accounts, the consumer shall be informed at the time or before the agreement is concluded:

- of the credit limit, if any;
- of the annual rate of interest and the charges applicable from the time the agreement is concluded and the conditions under which these may be amended;
- of the procedure for terminating the agreement.

Under article 12, member states shall:

a ensure that persons offering credit or offering to arrange credit agreements shall obtain official authorisation to do so, either specifically or as suppliers of goods and services; or
b ensure that persons granting credit or arranging for credit to be granted shall be subject to inspection or monitoring of their activities by an institution or official body; or
c promote the establishment of appropriate bodies to receive complaints concerning credit agreements or credit conditions and to provide relevant information or advice to consumers regarding them.

Member states may provide that the authorisation referred to under (a) above, shall not be required where persons offering to conclude or arrange credit agreements satisfy the definition of credit institutions in the first directive of 1977 and are authorised in accordance with the provisions of that directive.

Article 14, paragraph 1, provides that member states shall ensure that credit agreements shall not derogate, to the detriment of the consumer, from the provisions of national law implementing or corresponding to this directive. Under paragraph 2 of this article member states shall ensure that the provisions which they adopt in implementation of this directive are not circumvented as a result of the way in which agreements are formulated, in particular by the device of distributing the amount of credit over several agreements.

Member states shall bring into force the measures necessary to comply with this directive not later than January 1, 1990.

XX COUNCIL DIRECTIVE OF FEBRUARY 22, 1990 AMENDING DIRECTIVE 87/102/EEC FOR THE APPROXIMATION OF THE LAWS, REGULATIONS AND ADMINISTRATIVE PROVISIONS OF THE MEMBER STATES CONCERNING CONSUMER CREDIT

(OJEC L 61 10.3.1990, directive 90/88/EEC)

Article 5 of directive 87/102/EEC discussed above holds out the prospect of a Community method or methods for the computation of the annual percentage rate of charge for consumer loans. As a first step towards the introduction of such a method, the directive under review puts forward a mathematical formula. The Council believes that it would be appropriate to establish common rules for such a formula, even though the expense items to be taken into account in computing the annual percentage rate of charge have not yet been determined. The annual percentage rate of charge in this formula is the discount rate which ensures equality between the amount of the credit and the present value of the interest and repayments during the term of the loan.

3.12 Coordination of mortgage credit

XXI PROPOSAL FOR A COUNCIL DIRECTIVE ON THE FREEDOM OF ESTABLISHMENT AND THE FREE SUPPLY OF SERVICES IN THE FIELD OF MORTGAGE CREDIT

(OJEC C 42 14.2.1985, proposal (84) 730)

THE PROPOSAL WAS AMENDED IN 1987

(OJEC C 161 19.6.1987, proposal (87) 255)

On the basis of the EEC Treaty and the Reyners and Van Binsbergen judgements of the European Court in 1974, all undertakings have been entitled to establish and provide services anywhere within the territory of the Community since the end of the transitional period (January 1, 1970). To facilitate the effective exercise of this freedom, the Council adopted the first coordination directive on credit institutions in December 1977.

Notwithstanding the above, there are still obstacles to the freedom of establishment and provision of services in the field of mortgage credit. These are the result of the prohibition to grant mortgage credit secured on real property situated in another member state on the one hand, and of the difference in conditions under which credit institutions are allowed to undertake mortgage business in the various countries on the other hand. The objective of the proposal in question is to change this undesirable situation.

The proposal applies to all credit institutions covered by the first Council directive of 1977, the activities of which consist wholly or partially of receiving funds from the public collected in the form of deposits or the proceeds from mortgage bonds or other debentures or securities and of reimbursable deposits, and in granting loans to the public secured by mortgage on real property for the purpose of acquiring or retaining property rights in building land or in existing or projected buildings or for renovating or improving buildings. Such credit institutions will be referred to as designated credit institutions.

Home member states shall authorise designated credit institutions to undertake mortgage credit activities in any other member state in respect of real property situated anywhere in the Community (by means of establishment in another member state or by means of cross-border provision of services). Furthermore, they shall not restrict the use in another member state of any financial technique permitted for mortgage credit activities in the home member state (article 3).

Under article 4, paragraph 1, the host member states, subject to the exception contained in paragraph 3, shall repeal all legal or administrative provisions preventing or obstructing a designated credit institution having its head office in another member state, from undertaking mortgage credit activities in their territory in accordance with the financial techniques permitted under the law of its home member state, or shall amend such provisions as to make the operation of such techniques possible.

Where the introduction of new financial techniques alters the conditions of competition in a member state, that member state shall authorise all designated credit institutions established in its territory who are adversely affected by the change to adopt similar techniques or take equivalent measures (article 4, paragraph 2). The proposals in paragraphs 1 and 2 regarding permitted financial techniques represent the practical implementation of the principle of mutual recognition. Mutual recognition therefore takes precedence over harmonisation of financial techniques. However, pending coordination relating to bonds secured by mortgage, the host member state may require that issues of such bonds on its territory conform with the relevant provisions in force in that member state (article 4, paragraph 3).

Article 6 introduces a transitional period of not more than seven years after the adoption of this directive. After this period all capital movements related to mortgage credit must have been liberalised by the directives on liberalisation of the movement of capital, discussed earlier. During this transitional period, a host member state may require both funding and lending transactions to be in its own currency, or where other currencies are permitted, it may require matching between assets and liabilities in each currency. In all cases, however, the designated credit institution in question may use the ECU as an alternative. The home member state is also entitled to require the above-mentioned congruence of assets and liabilities in a particular currency.

Finally, supervision of designated credit institutions is dealt with. Until other appropriate provisions for control are made by a later directive, supervision of any form of *establishment* in another member state of a designated credit institution shall be exercised by the supervisory authority of that host member state in close cooperation with the supervisory authority of the home member state and in accordance with the legal provisions in the host member state which are not inconsistent with this directive. In accordance with the principle of home country control, the supervision of such credit institution related to *cross-border supply of services* will be exercised by the supervisory authority of the home member state.

3.13 Coordination of credit institutions (II)

XXII SECOND COUNCIL DIRECTIVE OF DECEMBER 15, 1989 ON THE COORDINATION OF LAWS, REGULATIONS AND ADMINISTRATIVE PROVISIONS RELATING TO THE TAKING UP AND PURSUIT OF THE BUSINESS OF CREDIT INSTITUTIONS AND AMENDING DIRECTIVE 77/780/EEC

(OJEC L 386 30.12.1989, directive 89/646/EEC)

The most important objectives of the directive

1 The second coordination directive for credit institutions forms the cornerstone of all directives for the business of credit institutions in the context of the achievement of the internal market in 1992. In amplification of the body of legislation already enacted in the field of liberalisation of capital movement and other instruments of the banking business (concerning own funds, large exposures, harmonised solvency ratios, deposit-guarantee schemes), the directive aims to:
- remove the remaining obstacles to the freedom of establishment in the field of credit institutions;
- ensure full freedom to provide services.

2 The approach of the directive is expressly based on the principle of achieving only the essential harmonisation necessary and sufficient to secure mutual recognition and supervision by the home member state as mentioned in the White Paper. The aim is to enable the granting to a credit institution of a single authorisation (licence) recognised throughout the Community for both the freedom of establishment and the freedom to provide services, by the end of 1992.

Freedom of establishment

The most important conditions for the freedom of establishment were laid down in the first coordination directive of 1977. However three obstacles to the freedom of establishment have remained. In the first place, a bank wishing to open a branch in another member state is required to have the host country's authorisation. Furthermore the bank concerned is subject to the control of the host country and the activities of the bank can be restricted by the laws of that country. In the third and last place, branches in most member states are required to maintain a certain minimum capital as if this represented the establishment of a new bank. These three obstacles will be removed by this new directive.

Freedom to provide services

At the moment there are no Community procedures to facilitate the freedom to supply services in the field of banking. Such a freedom is essentially achieved only in member states with fully liberalised capital movement. The recently adopted directive on the liberalisation of capital movements (June 24, 1988) will, to a great extent, ensure the freedom to provide services, but not all the services of credit institutions are covered. Banks are still required to obtain authorisation by most host member states in order to market their services. In addition their services are limited to services provided by domestic banks and the banks are subject to the supervision of the host member state.

A single licence and the agreed list of activities of credit institutions

At the heart of the directive is the requirement of a single licence along with an agreed list of banking activities which this licence will cover. The list is an annex to the directive and has been

drawn up with a view to a liberal model of the banking business. The most important and far-reaching aspect of the list is the inclusion of all forms of transactions in securities, particularly:
- transactions of credit institution for their own account or for the account of customers in all types of security (short term and long term);
- participation in share issues and the provision of services related to such issues;
- portfolio management and advice.

Harmonisation of essential supervisory requirements

Supervision by the home country is only possible after harmonisation of the essential supervisory requirements. The requirements that will be harmonised by this directive concern:
- the initial capital necessary for authorisation and the execution of activities (articles 4 and 10);
- the supervision of qualifying holdings and holdings of banks in sectors outside the banking business (articles 11 and 12);
- sound administrative and accounting procedures (article 13).

However, these regulations are not sufficient to ensure the solvency of the institution and the protection of the depositors. The above regulations concerning mutual recognition and supervision by the home member states (articles 18-24) will consequently only be brought into force (article 24) after implementation of the regulations concerning own funds and solvency ratios, but by January 1, 1993 at the latest.

On April 17, 1989 the directive on the own funds of credit institutions was adopted by the Council. On December 18, 1989 the directive on solvency ratios for credit institutions was adopted. In the light of essential supervision requirements, reference can also be made to the Commission's recommendations on large exposures and deposit-guarantee schemes. Both may possibly be transformed into directives in the future.

Coordination of the supervision of credit institutions

The competent supervisory authorities of the home member states will be responsible for the application and control of the above-mentioned harmonised subjects.

However, the directive states that, pending further coordination, the competent authorities of the host member states shall retain responsibility in the first instance for the supervision of the liquidity of credit institutions and for monetary policy.

The directive also provides for extensive collaboration between the supervisory authorities of the host member states and of the home member states.

EXPLANATORY NOTES

1 Definitions and scope

Articles 1 and 2

Article 1 provides a list of definitions, based on directives adopted earlier. Article 2 determines the scope of the directive and determines that it will apply, in principle, to all credit institutions. Some exceptions, already defined in the first coordination directive of 1977 (77/780/EEC), are also indicated.

Article 3
This article prohibits persons or undertakings that are not credit institutions from carrying on the business of taking deposits or other repayable funds from the public. This prohibition does not apply to the taking of deposits or other repayable funds by a member state or a member state's regional or local authorities or by public international bodies of which one or more member states are members, provided that those activities are subject to regulations and controls intended to protect depositors and investors applicable to those cases.

2 *Harmonisation of authorisation conditions*

In directive 77/780/EEC a system of mandatory authorisation was introduced. However, it was considered desirable to harmonise further the authorisation conditions in that directive, in particular with a view to the application of the concept of mutual recognition of supervision requirements.

a Adequate initial capital

Article 4
The first coordination directive stipulated that a credit institution on starting its operations has to have an adequate minimum of own funds. Although this requirement has been incorporated in the national legislation of all member states, the value of initial capital differs substantially from member state to member state. The second Council directive requires credit institutions to have an initial capital of ECU 5 million to qualify for authorisation. This provision ensures that banks in the Community that are active in another member state have adequate initial capital. However, member states may establish stricter standards for their own credit institutions. In addition, and in view of the fact that in some member states the field of operations or permitted activities of certain categories of credit institution are subject to restrictions imposed by legal regulations, this article provides that member states may deviate from the above-mentioned general rule by requiring a lower initial capital of at least 1 million ECU for such institutions.

b Identities of major share holders and qualifying holdings

The ownership of a credit institution its control by interest groups not belonging to the banking business are important points of attention for the supervisory authorities of the Community, especially in a period when highly complex corporate structures are commonplace. The risks connected with cross-financing and conflicts of interests are particularly evident in an environment characterised by substantial changes in the structure of financial systems. The directive therefore stipulates that prior to authorisation, the competent authorities must have been informed of the identity of the (direct or indirect) shareholders or members holding a qualifying holding in the institution, and the amount of such holding.

This applies to direct and indirect shareholders or members, regardless of whether they are natural persons or legal entities. This procedure enables the competent authorities to consider the suitability of the shareholders and members and to reject undesirable corporate structures at the moment of the establishment of the institution. Article 11 of the directive is very closely related to this and provides for a disclosure procedure concerning the proposed acquisition of an existing credit institution.

c A single licence for the banking business and abolition of the initial capital

Article 6
This article contains two fundamental starting-points that are a logical result of the mutual recognition approach.

In the first place the *introduction of a single licence for the banking business* (article 6, paragraph 1). As of January 1, 1993 host member states may no longer require authorisation for the establishment of branches of credit institutions authorised in other member states. This is in accordance with the fundamental principle of supervision by the home member states, which is advocated in the entire Community banking regulations and stipulates that the supervision of a credit institution and its activities performed by a branch or because of its provision of services will be subject to the competent authorities of the home member state. The present directive provides for a procedure between the authorities of the home member state and those in the host member state in the case of the establishment of branches (articles 19 and 21).

The second principle is the *abolition of the initial capital*, still required in a great number of member states for the authorisation of branches of credit institutions already authorised in other member states. The directive also provides for a transitional period: until the entry into force on January 1, 1993, host member states may not, as a condition of the authorisation of branches of credit institutions authorised in other member states, require initial endowment capital exceeding 50% of the initial capital required by national rules for the authorisation of credit institutions of the same nature (article 6, paragraph 3). This provision is effective from January 1, 1990.

Credit institutions are entitled to the free use of the funds no longer required pursuant to the above regulations (article 6, paragraph 3).

d Consultation procedures

Article 7
This article provides for consultation between the competent authorities where a credit institution authorised in another member state wishes to establish a subsidiary. A similar procedure applies in the case of a subsidiary of a parent undertaking of a credit institution recognised in another member state and in the case of authorisation of an undertaking which is controlled by the same natural persons or legal entities as control a credit institution authorised in another member state.

3 Relations with non-member countries

Articles 8 and 9
In the present state of Community law, *subsidiaries* within the Community belonging to banks from non-member countries are considered as Community undertakings from the moment of their establishment (article 58 of the EEC Treaty) and accordingly have the right of establishment and the freedom to provide services. However, *branches* of credit institutions from non-member countries are not entitled to these benefits. In this context the first coordination directive provides for certain procedures for the authorisation of branches from non-member countries.

Since the Community will be one of the most open financial markets in the world, the Council holds the view that in this mutually dependent financial world, EC banks and other financial institutions should be granted reasonable access to, and equal treatment in other world markets. Although the Council is concerned with the liberalisation of financial markets within the framework of the internal market, it in no way intends to lose sight of the progress of attempts to liberalise financial markets on a global scale, such as those being undertaken during the present GATT-negotiations concerning the provision of services.

In the Council's opinion, a directive shaping the legal and supervisory framework for the banking business, must comprise a common approach to the policies of the member states concerning the first establishment of a credit institution from a non-member country. An authorisation may, in fact, affect not only the member state of first establishment but also all other member states. This warrants the application of a procedure of reciprocity in appropriate cases.

Article 8 provides for a procedure of mandatory prior exchange of information between the competent authorities and the Commission with regard to a request for authorisation for a subsidiary whose parent undertaking is governed by the laws of a non-member country or for the acquisition by such parent undertaking of a holding in a Community institution such that the latter would become its subsidiary. The principle of reciprocity is described further in article 9. Whenever it appears to the Commission that a non-member country is not granting Community credit institutions *effective market access* comparable to that granted by the Community to credit institutions from that non-member country, the Commission may submit proposals to the Council for the granting of a suitable mandate to undertake negotiations in order to obtain comparable competitive opportunities for Community credit institutions. The Council decides by qualified majority.

Should it appear to the Commission, however, that Community credit institutions in a non-member country are not accorded *national treatment*, affording them the same competitive opportunities as are available to domestic credit institutions, and that the conditions for effective market access have not been fulfilled, it may open negotiations to have this wrong redressed. In addition to opening negotiations it may, in accordance with the procedures laid down in article 22, paragraph 2, be resolved that the competent authorities of the member state restrict or suspend their decisions concerning future applications for authorisation or applications for authorisation filed prior to the time of the resolution, and concerning the acquisition of undertakings by direct or indirect parent companies governed by the laws of the non-Community state in question. These measures are valid for three months. Before this term expires, however, the Council can, depending on the results of the negotiations, at the motion of the Commission decide by qualified majority of the votes whether the measures are to remain in force.

The above restriction or suspension therefore applies only where national treatment is at stake. This implies a limited interpretation of the reciprocity principle. Community credit institutions for example, will not be entitled to a universal licence in the United States of America if US banks are likewise unable to obtain such licence in the USA (segregation of commercial and investment banking), notwithstanding the fact that US banks will qualify for a universal banking licence in the European internal market.

The above-mentioned sanctions do not apply to the setting up of subsidiaries by credit institutions or their subsidiaries duly authorised in the Community, or to the acquisition of holdings in Community credit institutions by such institutions or subsidiaries. This also represents a further limitation of the reciprocity principle.

4 Harmonisation of the conditions relating to the pursuit of the business of credit institutions

Article 10

This article contains a fundamental principle of supervision: a credit institution's own funds may not fall below the amount of initial capital required pursuant to article 4 at the time of its authorisation. However, the member states may decide that credit institutions already in existence when the directive is implemented, and the own funds of which do not attain the levels prescribed for initial capital in article 4, may continue to carry on their activities, provided that their own funds may not fall below the highest level reached after the date of the notification of this directive.

a Supervision of qualifying holdings

Article 11
Article 11 contains a double information duty. Natural persons or legal entities considering the (direct or indirect) acquisition of a qualifying holding in a credit institution must notify the competent authorities of this intention beforehand. The same applies whenever a natural person or a legal entity intends to enlarge the size of such holding in a way that would make the voting rights or shares held equal to or greater than 20%, 33% or 50%, or that would make the credit institution into a subsidiary. The duty to notify the competent authorities beforehand also applies in the reverse situation where the qualifying holding is disposed of either in full or in part. This provision enables the supervisory authorities to be informed promptly about changes in holdings. This enables them to review the structures of undertakings and where appropriate to reject them on account of the adverse impact on sound and prudent management of banking activities.

In addition to the above information duty, credit institutions shall each year furnish the competent authorities with the names of the shareholders and members of a credit institution and the size of their qualifying holdings, in accordance with the names registered at the annual general meeting of shareholders and members, or in accordance with regulations relating to companies listed on stock exchanges. If the authorities find that sound and prudent management of banking activities is at issue as a result of the influence of the shareholders or members, they may take measures to put an end to this situation. Such measures may consist for example of injunctions, sanctions against directors and managers or the suspension of the exercise of the voting rights attaching to the shares held by the shareholders or members in question.

b Participation by credit institutions in sectors other than the credit or financial sector

Article 12
The 1983 directive concerning consolidated supervision applies to holdings of credit institutions in other credit institutions or financial institutions and states that no new provisions in this area will be needed for the time being. However, the Council holds the opinion that holdings of credit institutions in sectors other than the credit or financial sector, need to be regulated separately in the interests of the financial stability of credit institutions. This is motivated by two reasons. Firstly, the risk of snowballing (in the event of such a subsidiary getting into financial difficulties) and secondly that in the investment process itself credit institutions immobilise their assets. A majority of the member states therefore already have regulations in this area. In view of differing national practices and the prospect of a single internal market for banking, the Council consequently holds the opinion that harmonisation is necessary in this area.

The second coordination directive therefore contains regulations that require banks to meet certain objective criteria if they intend to acquire or keep holdings in institutions other than those in the credit or financial sector. The directive introduces two limits in this connection: i) a credit institution may not hold a qualifying holding of an amount greater than 15% of its own funds in an undertaking which is neither a credit institution nor a financial institution, and ii) the total amount of the qualifying holdings in undertakings other than credit institutions and financial institutions may not exceed 60% of the own funds of the credit institution. The member states need not apply the limits to holdings in insurance companies. The limits do not apply to shares held temporarily during a financial reconstruction or rescue operation or during the normal course of underwriting a share issue or in an institution's own name but on behalf of others. If, however, in exceptional circumstances, the limits are exceeded, the competent authorities may require a credit institution either to increase its own funds or to take other equivalent measures. A more far-reaching alternative solution is that member states provide that 100% of the amounts by which a credit institution's qualifying holdings exceed those limits must be covered by own funds and that the latter shall not be included in the calculation of the solvency ratio.

Article 13
The presence of sound administrative and accounting procedures and adequate internal control mechanisms constitute fundamental safeguards for the sound management of credit institutions. The competent authorities of the home member state must therefore require that every credit institution complies with this.

c *Responsibilities of the home member state*

Article 14
As indicated above in the opening remarks, the main principle of the directive is supervision by the home member state; i.e. supervision of a credit institution by the competent authorities of the home member state, even where cross-border activities are at issue.

In view of the insufficient degree of harmonisation of solvency requirements and monetary cooperation within the Community, the host member states retain the first responsibility for the supervision of the liquidity of the branches of credit institutions and retain primary responsibility for the application of monetary policy.

Given the present developments and the lack of soundness in securities markets, in addition to the absence of adequate measures in this context in the most member states, the directive stipulates that, pending further coordination, the competent authorities of the host member states may apply their national regulations in order to ensure the supervision of the market exposure borne by credit institutions operating on their securities markets. To this end they will collaborate with the competent authorities of the home member states. This has become necessary in view of the events of October 1987, since in particular the directive on solvency ratios only deals with the credit risk (i.e. the risk attributable to a certain counterparty on receipt of a bank loan or a guarantee). Clearly, however, securities transactions (and particularly market-making) involve market or position exposure (i.e. the risk of a general fall in the market, to which everyone who has taken an open position is exposed).

d *On-the-spot verification*

Article 15
The subject directive provides a possibility that the competent authorities of the home member state, after having informed the competent authorities of the host member state, carry out on-the-spot verification activities in branches of credit institutions established in other member states. The competent authorities of the home member state may also request the competent authorities of the host member states to carry out such verification. However, the above shall not affect the right of the competent authorities of the host member state to carry out, in the discharge of their responsibilities under this directive, on-the-spot verifications of branches established within their territory.

e *Obligation of professional secrecy*

Article 16
Although the obligation of professional secrecy for supervisory authorities is included in article 12 of the first coordination directive, it is considerably extended by the second coordination directive. The new obligations concern in particular:

- All persons working or who have worked for the competent authorities, as well as auditors or experts acting on behalf of the competent authorities. No confidential information which they may receive in the course of their duties may be divulged to any person or authority whatsoever, except in cases covered by criminal law;
- Exchanges of information between competent authorities about matters concerning supervision. This information is covered by professional secrecy;
- Member states may conclude cooperation agreements, providing for exchanges of information, with the competent authorities of non-member countries only if the information disclosed is subject to guarantees of professional secrecy at least equivalent to those referred to in this article.

f Sanctions

Article 17

On the basis of this article the member states determine that their competent authorities may adopt or impose penalties or measures aimed specifically at ending observed breaches or the causes of such breaches, against credit institutions or those who effectively control the business of credit institutions which breach laws, regulations or administrative provisions concerning the supervision or pursuit of their activities.

5 Provisions relating to the freedom of establishment and the freedom to provide services

Article 18

This article is essential for the application of the system of mutual recognition in banking. According to the system advocated by the directive, credit institutions that fulfil the following two conditions can enjoy mutual recognition:
- they should be authorised and controlled by the competent authorities in their home country, in accordance with Community banking directives;
- by establishing a branch or through the free provision of services they should pursue business activities mentioned on the approved list in the annex to the directive.

This means that the following cases are not eligible for mutual recognition:
- institutions that are not authorised as credit institutions and are not supervised as such, even if they perform activities listed in the annex;
- activities not listed in the annex, even if they are legally regulated in their own member state.

The approved list in the annex to the directive contains all the activities presently forming the core of the business of banks. In order to keep up with the development of new banking activities, the list may be amended in accordance with the procedures laid down in the directive.

The list contains the following business integral to banking and covered by mutual recognition:
1 Acceptance of deposits and other repayable funds from the public;
2 Lending, including in particular, consumer credit, mortgage credit, factoring with or without recourse, financing of commercial transactions (including forfaiting);
3 Financial leasing;
4 Money transmission services;
5 Issuing and administering means of payment (e.g. credit cards, traveller's cheques and bankers' drafts);
6 Guarantees and commitments;
7 Trading for own account or for account of customers in;
a money market instruments (cheques, bills, CDs, etc);

b foreign exchange;
c financial futures and options;
d swaps and similar finance instruments;
e transferable securities;
8 Participation in share issues and the provision of services related to such issues;
9 Advice to undertakings on capital structure, industrial strategy and related questions and advice and services relating to mergers and the purchase of undertakings;
10 Agency services on the interbank markets;
11 Portfolio management and advice;
12 Custody and management of securities;
13 Credit reference services;
13 Safe custody services.

The annex thus includes the list of core activities of banks referred to in article 18. By virtue of the principle of reciprocity, every authorised credit institution may pursue these activities in another member state, in accordance with the provisions of articles 19, 20 and 21, provided that it is authorised to do so in its own member state. The member states allow these activities to be pursued by the credit institutions using the financial techniques of the home country as long as the latter are in accordance with the legal regulations concerning the general interest in the host member state. On the other hand, a credit institution that has not obtained a licence in accordance with the present directive is not eligible for mutual recognition, even if the activity performed is included in the list and is possible in its own member state without prior authorisation. However, an unauthorised credit institution can still operate in other member states by virtue of the Treaty provisions on the freedom of establishment and the freedom to provide services. This means that, if a licence is required in another member state for certain activities, a branch of an interested institution must also apply for a licence. Should the host country not require such a licence, the unauthorised credit institution will in practice be able to pursue such activities and would accordingly be in the same position as institutions benefitting from mutual recognition.

Article 19

This article prescribes a number of detailed procedures regarding the collaboration between the competent authorities of the member states in the context of the freedom of establishment.

The procedures require that a credit institution planning to establish a branch in the territory of another member state notify the competent authorities of its home member state and supply the required information (as to the member state in which it plans to establish a branch, the proposed activities and the names and addresses of those responsible for controlling the activities of the branch).

After studying the application, the competent authority, if it has reason to doubt the soundness of the administrative structure or the financial position of the credit institution, may refuse to pass the information on to the authorities of the member states concerned. The reasons for any such refusal must be given within three months. The competent authorities of the host member state have two months after receipt of the information on the application in which to prepare for supervision of the branch.

Article 20

As far as the freedom to supply services is concerned, notification to the competent authorities of the home member state by the credit institution of its plan to supply services in another member state is deemed sufficient. The competent authorities of the home member state inform the competent authorities of the host member state of the application within one month after receipt of notification.

Article 21
According to this article host member states may, for statistical purposes, require all credit institutions which operate a branch in their territory periodically to report to their competent authorities on the business pursued in their territory. Branches established in another member state may be required to abide by the same reporting regulations as national credit institutions in order that liquidity requirements can be supervised and monetary policy can be implemented.

A procedure to enforce fulfilment is provided for cases in which a credit institution with a branch or in the context of provision of services does not act in accordance with the legal regulations of the host member state, adopted in implementation of the provisions of this directive relating to the powers of the host country authorities. If the institution concerned does not take the necessary action, the competent authorities of the host member state shall inform the competent authorities of the home member state accordingly. The latter shall take all appropriate measures as quickly as possible to ensure that the subject institution puts an end to the irregular situation in which it finds itself. The nature of those measures shall be communicated to the competent authorities of the host member state.

If, however, the subject institution persists in violating the legal rules of the host member state, the latter state may, after informing the competent authorities of the home member state, take appropriate measures to prevent further irregularities and, in particular, to prevent that institution from initiating further transactions within its territory.

6 *Final provisions*

a Executional power of the Commission

Article 22
In accordance with the procedure to be discussed below, it is possible that the following technical adaptations to this directive will be made:
- expansion or adaptation of the terminology used in the list of activities covered by mutual recognition, to take account of developments on financial markets;
- alteration of the amount of initial capital to take account of economic and monetary developments;
- the areas in which the competent authorities must exchange information;
- clarification of the definitions to ensure uniform application of this directive throughout the Community;
- clarification of the definitions in order to take account in the implementation of this directive of developments on financial markets;
- adaptation of the terminology and wording of definitions in accordance with subsequent directives on banking and related matters.

The essence of the procedure referred to above is that, in the context of technical adaptation, the Commission will be assisted by a committee composed of the representatives of the member states and chaired by a representative of the Commission. The Commission representative may submit to the committee a draft of the measures to be taken. The committee will deliver its opinion on the draft. The opinion will be delivered by the majority laid down in article 148, paragraph 2, of the Treaty. The chairman of the committee does not vote. The Commission will adopt the measures envisaged if they are in accordance with the opinion of the committee. If they are not in accordance with the opinion of the committee, or if no opinion is delivered, the Commission will submit to the Council a proposal concerning the measures to be taken. The Council will act by a qualified majority. If the Council does not act within three months of the referral to it, the

Commission will adopt the measures proposed, unless the Council has decided against those measures by a simple majority.

b Provisions concerning 'grandfathering'

Article 23
Under this article rights in the area of freedom of establishment and freedom to supply services, previously acquired by authorised credit institutions and branches of institutions will not be adversely affected by the directive.

c Application of the directive

Article 24
Except for article 6, paragraph 2, this second coordination directive has to have been implemented by the member states by January 1, 1993. The date for article 6, paragraph 2, is January 1, 1990.

3.14 Coordination of investment firms

XXIII PROPOSAL FOR A COUNCIL DIRECTIVE ON INVESTMENT SERVICES IN THE SECURITIES FIELD
(OJEC C 43 22.2.1989, proposal (88) 778)

THE PROPOSAL WAS AMENDED IN 1990
(OJEC C 42 22.2.1990, proposal (89) 629)

The council directive of June 28, 1973 on the abolition of restrictions on the freedom of establishment and the freedom to provide services in respect of self-employed activities of banks and other financial institutions has been discussed earlier. However, it emerged that this directive did not apply to investment firms. In 1974, the European Court of Justice handed down the Reyners and Van Binsbergen judgements in which it held that the right of establishment and the right to supply services entrenched in the EEC Treaty had been directly applicable since the end of the transitional period on December 31, 1969. As a result of these judgements, the Treaty provisions on the freedom of establishment (articles 52-58) and the freedom to supply services (articles 59-66) acquired direct effect, including with regard to investment firms. No Community legislation in the field of establishment and supply of services by investment firms has subsequently been enacted. A draft directive dealing with the establishment and the supply of services by investment firms is currently circulating in Brussels. This proposed directive can be seen as the counterpart to the second Council directive for credit institutions. The aim of the proposed directive is the introduction of a European passport for the provision of a number of services in the field of investment, based on mutual recognition of the licence granted by the home member state. A further aim is to liberalise membership of securities and financial futures and options exchanges in the host member state.

It is the aim of the Commission that both directives should come into force by January 1, 1993. This will prevent distortions in competition among the securities departments of credit institutions (coming within the scope of the second Council directive) and investment firms (coming within the scope of the directive for investment firms). The proposed directive for investment firms will be discussed below.

A large number of articles of the proposed directive for investment firms are similar to those of the second Council directive for credit institutions. Article 1 contains a number of definitions. A credit institution is an undertaking whose business it is to receive deposits or other repayable funds from the public and to grant credits for its own account. An investment firm, on the other hand, is any natural or legal person whose business it is to provide investment services. An investment service is any service related to any of the instruments listed in the annex to the directive. In section A, this annex gives a list of the activities coming within the scope of the directive. Section B then lists the instruments to which these activities can relate.

Section A lists the following activities:
1 Brokerage, i.e. the acceptance of investors' orders relating to any or all of the instruments referred to in section B and/or the execution of such orders on an exchange or market on an agency basis against payment of commission;
2 Dealing as principal, i.e. the purchase and sale of any or all of the instruments referred to in section B for own account and at own risk with a view to profiting from the margin between bid and offer prices;
3 Market making, i.e. maintenance of a market in any or all of the instruments referred to in section B by dealing in such instruments. This means that the dealer concerned must quote bid and offer prices on an ongoing basis (and not just when it is convenient to him), so that it is possible at all times for investors to perform transactions in a particular instrument;
4 Portfolio management, i.e. the management against payment of portfolios composed of any or all of the instruments referred to in section B undertaken for investors otherwise than on a collective basis, i.e. geared to the wishes of a particular client. Collective portfolio management does not come within the scope of the subject draft directive, but is regulated by the legislation on undertakings for collective investment in securities (UCITS), to be discussed in chapter 4;
5 Arranging or offering underwriting services in respect of issues of instruments referred to in the first item of section B and distribution of such issues to the public;
6 Professional investment advice given to investors on an individual basis or on the basis of private subscription in connection with one or more of the instruments referred to in section B;
7 Safekeeping and administration of any of the instruments referred to in section B otherwise than in connection with the management of a clearing system.

Section B lists the following instruments:
1 Transferable securities including units in undertakings for collective investment in transferable securities (UCITS);
2 Money market instruments, including certificates of deposit and Eurocommercial paper;
3 Financial futures and options;
4 Exchange rate and interest rate instruments.

Apart from definitions of a credit institution, an investment service and an investment firm, the proposal for a directive on investment services in the securities field includes definitions of a home member state, host member state, branch, qualifying holding, parent undertaking, subsidiary and members of a stock exchange or organised securities market.

If the investment firm is a natural person, the home member state is the member state in which this natural person has his principal place of business. If the investment firm is a legal person, the home member state is the member state in which the registered office of the legal person is situated or, if it has no registered office, the member state in which its head office is situated. The host member state is the member state where an investment firm has a branch or into which it supplies services. A branch of an investment firm is a legally dependent part of an investment firm and which provides an investment service for which the investment firm has been authorised.

A qualifying holding is a direct or indirect holding in an investment firm which represents 10% or more of the capital or the voting rights or which makes it possible to exercise a significant influence over the management of the investment firm in which the holding subsists. The definition of parent undertaking is based on articles 1 and 2 of directive 83/349/EEC (seventh Council directive on company law concerning consolidated accounts). The same applies to the definition of subsidiary. Any subsidiary of a subsidiary shall also be regarded as a subsidiary of the parent undertaking which is at the head of those undertakings.

Under Article 2, the proposed directive applies to all investment firms. Investment firms that are authorised as credit institutions and which under the terms of their banking licence are allowed to effect investment transactions are only subject to article 9,paragraph 2, and articles 11 and 13. For the rest, the latter credit institutions are governed by the regulations of the second Council directive on the coordination of credit institutions.

Articles 3, 4, 5 and 6 deal with the harmonisation of authorisation conditions.

On the basis of article 3 investment firms shall obtain authorisation in their home country before commencing to provide one or more of the investment services listed in section A of the annex. The competent authorities of the home country shall not grant authorisation unless:

- the investment has sufficient initial capital in relation to the nature of its activities. (A future directive will deal in more depth with the quantitative interpretation of the term 'sufficient');
- the persons who effectively direct the business of the investment firm are of sufficiently sound repute and experience.

Member states shall also require applications for authorisation to be accompanied by a programme of operations setting out inter alia the types of business envisaged and the structural organisation of the investment firm. The applicant will be informed within three months of submission of a complete application for authorisation whether or not authorisation is granted. Reasons shall be given whenever an authorisation is refused.

The competent authorities may withdraw the authorisation issued to an investment firm only if the investment firm:

- does not make use of the authorisation within twelve months, expressly renounces the authorisation or has ceased to engage in investment business for more than six months, if the member state concerned has made no provision for the authorisation to lapse in such cases;
- has obtained the authorisation through false statements or any other irregular means;
- no longer fulfils the conditions under which authorisation was granted;
- no longer possesses sufficient financial resources or can no longer be relied upon to fulfil its obligations towards its creditors, and in particular no longer provides security for the assets entrusted to it;
- falls within one of the other cases where national law provides for withdrawal of authorisation.

Article 4 is the counterpart of article 5 of the second coordination directive on credit institutions. Under article 4, the competent authorities shall not grant authorisation for the taking up of the business of investment firms before they have been informed of the identities of the shareholders or members, whether direct or indirect, natural or legal persons, that have qualifying holdings, and of the amounts of those holdings. The competent authorities shall refuse authorisation if, taking into account the need to ensure the sound and prudent management of an investment firm, they are not satisfied as to the suitability of the above-mentioned shareholders or members.

Article 5 lays down that member states shall not apply to branches of investment firms having their registered office outside the Community, when commencing or carrying on their business, provisions that result in more favourable treatment than that accorded to branches of investment firms having their registered office in a member state.

Article 6 reflects article 7 of the second coordination directive on credit institutions. There must be prior consultation with the competent authorities of the other member state involved on the authorisation of an investment firm which is:
- a subsidiary of an investment firm authorised in another member state, or
- a subsidiary of the parent undertaking of an investment firm authorised in another member state, or
- controlled by the same persons, whether natural or legal, as control an investment firm authorised in another member state.

Article 7 deals with relations with non-member countries and as such is the counterpart of articles 8 and 9 of the second coordination directive on credit institutions. The contents of article 7 regarding investment firms is equivalent to articles 8 and 9 regarding credit institutions. Here too, the terms *effective market access* and *national treatment* play a crucial part. Whenever it appears to the Commission that community investment firms in a non-member country are not receiving national treatment offering the same competitive opportunities as are available to domestic investment firms and that the conditions of effective market access are not being fulfilled, it may initiate negotiations in order to remedy the situation. In addition to initiating negotiations, it can also be decided that, in accordance with the procedure laid down in article 23, that the competent authorities of the member state must limit or suspend their decisions regarding requests pending at the moment of the decision or future requests for authorisation and the acquisition of holdings by direct or indirect parent undertakings governed by the non-member country in question. The duration of the measures referred to may not exceed six months (this six months period will probably be changed into three months, to give the same period as that mentioned in the second coordination directive). Before the end of this period of six months, and in the light of the result of the negotiations, the Council may, acting on a proposal from the Commission, decide by a qualified majority whether the measures shall be continued. The limitations or suspension referred to above may not apply to the setting up of subsidiaries by investment firms duly authorised in the Community or by their subsidiaries, or to the acquisition of holdings in Community investment firms by such firms or subsidiaries.

Articles 8-11 deal with the harmonisation of the conditions governing the pursuit of the business of investment firms.

Article 8 corresponds with article 10 of the second coordination directive. The article stipulates that the own funds of an investment firm may not fall below the amount of initial capital required pursuant to article 3 at the time of its authorisation. The member states may, however, decide that investment firms already in existence when the directive is implemented, the own funds of which do not attain the levels for initial capital referred to in article 3, may continue to carry on their activities. In that event, their own funds may not fall below the highest level reached after the date of the notification of this directive.

Article 9 is new. Paragraph 1 instructs the competent authorities of the home member state to require continuing compliance by an investment firm authorised by them with the conditions referred to in article 3. Paragraph 2 applies not only to investment firms, but also to investment firms that are credit institutions and are authorised on the basis of their banking licence to pursue transactions in securities. According to paragraph 2 the competent authorities of the home member state shall require that investment firms authorised by them make sufficient provision against market risk attaching to securities positions, in accordance with the rules to be prescribed in a future directive. Paragraph 3 of article 9 applies only to investment firms and prescribes that the supervision of compliance with the conditions referred to in articles 3 and 4 shall be within the exclusive regulatory competence of the home member state's competent authorities irrespective of whether or not the investment firm establishes a branch or provides services in another member state.

Article 10 is identical to article 11 of the second coordination directive and also prescribes the double information duty. Firstly for every natural or legal person considering the acquisition, directly or indirectly, of a qualifying holding in an investment firm. They shall first inform the competent authorities of the intended holding. The same duty applies in cases where a natural or legal person intends to increase his qualifying holding so that the proportion of the voting rights or of the capital held by him would reach or exceed 20%, 33% or 50% or so that the investment firm would become his subsidiary. The duty also applies in the reverse case of disposal of a part of or of the entire qualifying holding.

In addition to the above, investment firms shall also, at least once a year, inform the competent authorities of the names of shareholders and members possessing qualifying holdings and the sizes of such holdings as shown, for example, by the information adopted at the annual general meetings of shareholders and members or by information received as a result of compliance with the regulations relating to companies listed on stock exchanges.

If the competent authorities are of the opinion that sound and prudent management of the investment firm is at issue as a result of the influence of the shareholders or members, the member states may take measures to put an end to this situation. Such measures may consist in particular of injunctions, sanctions against directors and managers or the suspension of the exercise of the voting rights attaching to the shares held by the shareholders or members in question.

Article 11 is partly the counterpart of article 13 of the second coordination directive and also applies to investment firms authorised as credit institutions. Under this article the member states are required to draw up prudential rules to be observed on a continuing basis by the investment firms that have been authorised by their competent authorities. Supervision of compliance with such prudential rules falls within the exclusive competence of the home member state regardless of whether the investment firm has established a branch or provides services in another member state. These prudential rules require that the investment firm:

- has sound administrative and accounting procedures and internal control mechanisms;
- arranges for securities belonging to investors to be kept separately from its own securities;
- except in the case of investment firms that are credit institutions, arranges for money belonging to investors to be placed in an account or in accounts which are separate and distinct from the firm's own account;
- is either a member of a general compensation scheme designed to protect investors who are prevented from having claims because of the bankruptcy or default of the investment firm or makes individual arrangements which provide investors with equivalent protection. Pending further harmonisation of compensation schemes, branches of investment firms are subject to the compensation scheme in force in the host member state provided that payment or contribution to such a compensation scheme shall be calculated by reference to their income in respect of investment activity carried out in that state;
- provides the competent authorities of the home member state with such information on request and at such intervals as they may determine (but not less frequently than quarterly) in order that they may assess its financial soundness, including the adequacy of its provision in respect of market risk;
- arranges for adequate records to be kept related to executed transactions which shall be at least sufficient to enable the home member state's authorities to monitor compliance with prudential rules which they are responsible for applying, including rules related to market risk. Such records shall be retained for periods to be laid down by the competent authorities;
- is organised in such a way that conflicts of interest between the firm and its clients or between one of its clients and another do not result in clients' interests being prejudiced.

Member states may provide that the rules set out in the second, third and fourth indents of the above paragraph do not apply where the service is provided to business or professional investors or where the investment service does not involve the investment firm in handling any money or securities on behalf of clients.

Articles 12-16 contain provisions concerning the freedom of establishment and the freedom to provide services.

Article 12 is the equivalent of article 18 of the second coordination directive and is crucial for the application of the system of mutual recognition for investment firms. Host member states shall ensure that any investment services and any activities which are ancillary thereto may be provided in their territories, in accordance with the provisions of articles 14, 15 and 16, either by the establishment of a branch or by way of the provision of services, by any investment firm authorised to provide the relevant service under this directive by the competent authorities of its home member state. Host member states may not make the establishment of a branch or the provision of services subject to an authorisation requirement to provide endowment capital or any measure having equivalent effect.

Article 13 has no counterpart in the second coordination directive on credit institutions. The article applies not only to investment firms, but also to investment firms that are credit institutions and are authorised by virtue of their banking licence to provide investment services. The article concerns the position in the host member state of investment firms which have been authorised to provide broking, dealing or market-making services by the competent authorities of their home member state. These firms are to be given access, either directly or indirectly, to membership of stock exchanges and organised securities markets of host member states where similar activities are provided and also to membership of clearing and settlement systems which are available to members of such exchanges and markets. Direct membership of the stock exchanges or organised securities markets of the host member state implies the establishment there. Indirect membership is effected by incorporating a subsidiary in the host member state or by taking over an existing undertaking which is a member. In both cases membership remains subject to compliance with the rules governing the structure and organisation of the stock exchange or organised securities market in question and the clearing and settlement system of the host country. Where the host member state's stock exchange or organised securities market does not require the physical presence of the investment firms concerned, they can, on the same basis but without establishing a branch in the host member state, become members of such exchanges and markets. Article 13 ends with a provision stating that host member states shall likewise ensure that investment firms which are authorised to deal in financial futures and options by the competent authorities of their home member state can have access to membership of financial futures and options exchanges and membership of clearing houses in the host member state under the same conditions as set out above.

Article 14 corresponds with article 19 of the second directive. The article prescribes a number of detailed procedures concerning collaboration between the member states in the context of the *freedom of establishment*. An investment firm wishing to establish a branch in another member state shall notify the competent authorities of its home member state. In addition the investment firm is required to provide the necessary information (the member state in whose territory it plans to establish a branch, the types of business envisaged and the names and addresses of the managers of the branch).

After examining the application the competent authorities can, if they have reason to doubt the adequacy of the administrative structure or the financial situation of the investment firm, refuse to communicate the information to the competent authorities of the host member state concerned. They shall give reason for their refusal within three months after receipt of all the information. The competent authorities of the host member state have two months after receipt of the information on the application in which to prepare for supervision of the branch.

Article 15, corresponding with article 20 of the second directive, deals with the collaboration between the competent authorities in the context of the *freedom to provide services*. As far as the freedom to provide services is concerned, it is deemed sufficient for the investment firm to notify the competent authorities of the home member state of its intention to provide services in another member state. The competent authorities of the home member state shall within one month after receipt of the notification, send that notification to the competent authorities of the host member state.

Article 16 has its counterpart in article 21 of the second directive. In accordance with this article the host member states may, for statistical purposes, require that all investment firms having branches within their territories shall report periodically on their activities in those host member states to the competent authorities of those host member states. A procedure to enforce fulfilment is provided in the event that an investment firm having a branch or providing services is not complying with the legal provisions adopted in that state pursuant to the provisions of this directive involving powers of the host member state competent authorities.

If the investment firm concerned fails to take the necessary steps, the competent authorities of the host member state shall inform the competent authorities of the home member state accordingly. The latter authorities shall, at the earliest opportunity, take all appropriate measures to ensure that the investment firm concerned puts an end to that irregular situation. The nature of those measures shall be communicated to the competent authorities of the host member state. If the investment firm persists in violating the legal rules of the host member state, the latter state may, after informing the competent authorities of the home member state, take appropriate measures to prevent or punish further irregularities and, in particular, to prevent that investment firm from initiating further transactions within its territory.

Articles 17-22 deal with authorisation and the authorities responsible for authorisation and supervision. In part these articles correspond with articles in the second directive. It is striking, however, that these articles are incorporated in the second directive under the title 'harmonisation of the conditions governing pursuit of the business' and are incorporated here under a separate title. (The section concerning investment firms has been discussed above). On the basis of article 17 the member states shall designate the authorities which are to carry out the duties provided for in this directive. Said authorities must be public authorities or bodies officially recognised by national law or by public authorities to be part of the supervisory system prevailing in the relevant member state. The authorities concerned must be granted all powers necessary to carry out their task.

Article 18 describes the supervisory authorities. Where there are several competent authorities in the same member state they shall collaborate closely in order to supervise the activities of investment firms operating there. The member states shall also permit such collaboration to take place between such competent authorities and public authorities responsible for the supervision of credit and other financial institutions and insurance companies as regards the respective entities supervised by them.

Where investment services are provided on a service basis across frontiers or by the establishment of branches in one or more member states other than the home member state the competent authorities of the member states concerned shall collaborate closely in order to supervise the activities of the investment firm concerned. They shall supply one another on request with all the information concerning the management and ownership of such investment firms that is likely to facilitate their supervision and the examination of the conditions for their authorisation and all information likely to facilitate the monitoring of such firms.

Article 19 provides for on-the-spot verification. It provides for the possibility for the competent authorities of the home member state, after having first informed the competent authorities of the host member state, to have on-the-spot verification carried out in branches of investment firms established in other member states. The competent authorities of the home member state may also ask the competent authorities of the host member state to carry out this verification. This article shall not affect the right of the competent authorities of the host member state to carry out on-the-spot verifications of branches established within their territory, in discharge of their responsibilities under this directive.

Article 20, being the equivalent of article 16 of the second directive, contains a duty of professional secrecy for the supervisory authorities. The duty applies to:
- Persons working or who have worked for the competent authorities, as well as auditors or experts acting on behalf of the competent authorities. No confidential information which they may receive in the course of their duties may be divulged to any person or authority whatsoever, without prejudice to cases covered by criminal law.
- Exchange of information between competent authorities about subjects concerning supervision. The information shall be subject to professional secrecy.
- Exchange of information between the competent authorities of a member state and the competent authorities of a non-member country as a result of a cooperation agreement.
  Such cooperation agreements may only be concluded if the information disclosed is subject to guarantees of professional secrecy at least equivalent to those referred to in this article.

Article 21 concerns court appeals. The member states must ensure that decisions taken in respect of an investment firm in pursuance of laws, regulations and administrative provisions adopted in accordance with this directive may be subject to the right to apply to the court. The same shall apply where an application for authorisation is deemed to be refused in accordance with article 3.

Article 22 corresponds with article 17 of the second directive and introduces sanction possibilities. Member states shall provide that their respective authorities may, as against investment firms, or those who effectively control the business of such firms which infringe laws, regulations or administrative provisions concerning the supervision or pursuit of their activities, adopt or impose in respect of them penalties or measures aimed specifically at ending observed breaches or the cause of such breaches.

Articles 23-25 contain the final provisions of the directive. Article 23 is equivalent with article 22 of the second coordination directive on credit institutions. In accordance with the procedure discussed below, the following technical adaptations may be made to this (proposed) directive:
- expansion of the content of the list in the annex or adaptation of the terminology used in that list to take account of developments on financial markets;
- alteration of the amount of initial capital referred to in article 3 to take account of developments in the economic and monetary field;
- the areas in which the competent authorities must exchange information;
- clarification of the definitions in order to ensure uniform application of this directive throughout the Community;
- clarification of the definitions in order to take account in the implementation of this directive of developments on financial markets;
- adaptation of the terminology and wording of definitions in accordance with later measures concerning investment firms and related matters.

The procedure referred to above is as follows: the Commission shall be assisted by a committee composed of representatives of the member states and chaired by a representative of the Commission. The representative of the Commission may submit to the committee a draft of the measures to be taken. The committee shall deliver its opinion on the draft. The opinion shall be delivered by the majority laid down in article 148, paragraph 2, of the EEC Treaty. The votes of the representatives of the member states within the committee shall be weighed in the manner set out in that article. The chairman shall not vote. The Commission shall adopt the measures envisaged if they are in accordance with the opinion of the committee.

If the measures envisaged are not in accordance with the opinion of the committee, or if no opinion is delivered, the Commission shall submit to the Council a proposal relating to the measures to be taken. The Council shall act by qualified majority. If, on the expiry of three months from the date of referral to the Council, the Council has not acted, the proposed measures shall be adopted by the Commission.

Article 24 corresponds with article 23 of the second directive, and provides that rights already acquired by investment firms in the area of freedom of establishment and the freedom to provide services shall not be affected by this directive.

Article 25 (the counterpart of article 24 of the second directive) provides that the subject proposal for a Council directive on investment firms, if adopted by the Council, shall be implemented by the member states by January 1, 1993. This corresponds with the date of implementation of the second coordination directive on credit institutions.

XXIV PROPOSAL FOR A COUNCIL DIRECTIVE ON CAPITAL ADEQUACY OF INVESTMENT FIRMS AND CREDIT INSTITUTIONS

(OJEC C 152 21.6.1990, proposal (90) 141)

THE PROPOSAL WAS AMENDED IN 1992

(OJEC C 50 25.2.1992, proposal (92) 13)

The proposal for a Council directive envisages the creation of a common framework for the supervision and monitoring of market risks of investment firms and credit institutions. A further aim is to establish rules on the definition of own funds (based on Council directive 89/299/EEC whose scope now extends to investment firms) and to establish the amounts of minimum initial capital of investment firms (for credit institutions these amounts were already fixed in the second banking coordination directive 89/646/EEC).

As far as controlling solvency is concerned, both credit institutions and investment firms are to apply the credit risk capital requirements as laid down in the directive on solvency ratios (directive 89/647/EEC) to all of their non-trading book business. Additional market risk capital requirements are to be met on the risks connected with the trading book business of credit institutions and investment firms (position risk, settlement and counterparty risk, and large exposures arising on the trading book). In addition, there is a foreign exchange risk capital requirement on the overall business (both trading and non-trading book business) if the overall net foreign exchange position exceeds an agreed level. While no capital requirements have been set in respect of interest rate risk, the proposal contains a provision that the competent authorities shall require firms to set up systems to monitor and control the interest rate risk on all of their business, and that those systems will be subject to approval by the competent authorities.

If the proposal is adopted as directive, it is expected to be implemented on January 1, 1993.

IV. SECURITIES MARKETS AND UNDERTAKINGS FOR COLLECTIVE INVESTMENT IN TRANSFERABLE SECURITIES (UCITS)

4.1 Securities markets and undertakings for collective investment in transferable securities in 1993

This chapter concerns Community rules relating to securities markets and undertakings for collective investment in transferable securities. These rules will be important for the achievement of the internal market in the field of securities by December 31, 1992.

Firstly the coordinating provisions concerning the securities markets will be discussed. They are broken down into the following categories: Coordination of the conditions for the admission of securities, coordination of prospectus for public issues and the European code of conduct relating to transactions in transferable securities. Finally, coordination rules relating to undertakings for collective investment in transferable securities will be discussed.

4.2 Coordination of the admission of securities

I COUNCIL DIRECTIVE OF MARCH 5, 1979 COORDINATING THE CONDITIONS FOR THE ADMISSION OF SECURITIES TO THE OFFICIAL STOCK EXCHANGE LISTING (OJEC L 66 16.3.1979, directive 79/279/EEC)

The objective of the coordination of the conditions for the admission of securities to the official listing on stock exchanges situated or operating in the member states is to provide equal protection for investors at Community level and to facilitate the listing of any given security on a number of stock exchanges in the Community. Accordingly a greater interpenetration of national securities markets will result, contributing to the efforts to establish a European capital market. This coordination must apply to securities, regardless of the legal status of their issuers, and must therefore also apply to securities issued by non-member states or their regional or local authorities or international public bodies.

The above-mentioned coordination should in the first stage be sufficiently flexible to enable account to be taken of present differences in the structures of the securities markets in the member states. For this reason, coordination is for the time being limited to the establishment of minimum conditions for the admission of securities to official listing on stock exchanges situated or operating in the member states, without however giving issuers any right to listing. This partial coordination of the conditions for admission to official listing constitutes a first step towards subsequent closer alignment of the rules of member states in this field.

Article 1 of the directive indicates that the directive concerns securities which are admitted to official listing or are the subject of an application for admission to official listing on a stock exchange situated or operating within a member state. Member states may decide not to apply this directive to:

- units issued by collective investment undertakings other than the closed-end type;
- securities issued by a member state or its regional or local authorities.

Article 2 defines two terms used in article 1:

a Collective investment undertakings other than the closed-end type shall mean unit trusts and investment companies:
  - the object of which is the collective investment of capital provided by the public, and which operate on the principle of risk spreading, and
  - the units of which are, at the request of holder, repurchased or redeemed, directly or indirectly, out of the assets of these undertakings (investment undertakings of the closed-end type do not have this option). Actions take by such undertakings to ensure that the stock exchange value of its units does not significantly vary from their net asset value shall be regarded as equivalent to such repurchase or redemption.

b Units shall mean securities issued by collective investment undertakings as representing the rights of participants in the assets of such undertakings.

Under article 4, paragraph 1, the *admission of securities to official listing* shall be subject to the conditions set out in schedules A and B, relating to shares and debt securities respectively. Paragraph 2 provides that the *issuers of securities admitted to the official listing* must fulfil the obligations set out in schedules C and D, relating to shares and debt securities respectively. By way of illustration the contents of schedule A will be discussed below.

Schedule A, concerning the conditions for the admission of shares to official listing on a stock exchange is divided into two sections:

- Conditions relating to *companies* for the shares of which admission to official listing is sought.
  These conditions concern the legal position of the company, the minimum size of the company and the company's minimum period of existence.
  The legal position of the company must be in conformity with the laws and regulations to which it is subject, as regards both its formation and its operation under its articles of association. As far as the minimum size is concerned, the foreseeable market capitalisation of the shares for which admission to official listing is sought or, if this cannot be assessed, the company's capital and reserves, including profit or loss, from the last financial year, must be at least one million European units of account. With respect to the minimum period of existence, a company must have published or filed its annual accounts in accordance with national law for the three financial years preceding the application for official listing.
- Conditions relating to the *shares* for which admission to official listing is sought.
  These conditions concern the legal position of the shares, the negotiability of the shares, the public issue preceding admission to official listing, the distribution of the shares, the listing of shares of the same class, the physical form of the shares and the shares issued by companies of a non-member state.
  The legal position of the shares must be in conformity with the laws and regulations to which they are subject. The shares must also be freely negotiable. In the case of a public issue that precedes admission to official listing, the first listing may be made only after the end of the period during which subscription applications may be submitted. As far as the distribution of the shares is concerned, it is required that a sufficient number of the shares must be distributed to the public in one or more member states not later than the time of admission. A sufficient number of shares is deemed to have been distributed if the shares in respect of which application for admission has been made are in the hands of the public to the extent of at least 25% of the subscribed capital represented by the class of shares concerned or if, in view of the large number of shares of the same class and the extent of the distribution to the public, the market will operate properly with a lower percentage. The condition concerning the listing of shares of the same class means that the application for admission to official listing must cover all the shares of the same class already issued. For the admission to official listing of shares issued by companies which are nationals of another member state it is sufficient and necessary that their

physical form comply with the standards laid down in that other member state. The physical form of shares issued by companies which are nationals of a non-member state must afford sufficient safeguard for the protection of the investors. Closely related to this is the condition concerning shares issued by companies from a non-member state. If the shares issued by a company which is a national of a non-member state are not listed in either the country of origin or in the country in which the major proportion of the shares is held, they may not be admitted to official listing unless the competent authorities are satisfied that the absence of a listing in the country of origin or in the country in which the major proportion of shares is held is not due to the need to protect investors.

Subject to the prohibitions provided for in article 6 and in schedule A and B, the member states may make the admission of securities to official listing subject to more stringent conditions than those set out in schedules A and B or to additional conditions, provided that these more stringent and additional conditions apply generally for all issuers or for individual classes of issuer and that they have been published before application for admission of such securities is made (article 5, paragraph 1). By virtue of paragraph 2 member states may impose on the issuers of securities admitted to official listing more stringent obligations than those set out in schedules C and D or additional obligations, provided that these more stringent or additional obligations apply generally for all issuers or for individual classes of issuer. Article 5, paragraph 3 provides for a derogation clause. It states that member states may, under the same conditions as those laid down in article 7, authorise derogations from the additional or more stringent conditions and obligations referred to in paragraphs 1 and 2. Article 7 prescribes that any derogations from the conditions for the admission of securities to official listing which may be authorised in accordance with schedules A and B must apply generally for all issuers where circumstances justifying them are similar. The prohibition in Article 6 means that member states may not make the admission to official listing of securities issued by companies or other legal persons who are nationals of another member state subject to the condition that the securities must already have been admitted to official listing on a stock exchange situated or operating in one of the member states.

Article 8 deals with the admission to official listing of debt securities issued by companies and other legal persons covered by the laws of a member state and which are set up, governed by or managed pursuant to a special law. Member states may decide not to apply the conditions set out in schedule B and the obligations set out in items A (4) (a) and (b) of schedule D where repayments and interest payments in respect of those securities are guaranteed by a member state or one of its federal states.

Article 9 deals with the national authorities competent to admit securities to official listing on a stock exchange situated or operating within their territories. These national authorities shall be designated by the member states themselves. By way of derogation from article 5, member states may, solely in the interest of protecting the investors, give the competent authorities power to make the admission of a security to official listing subject to any special condition which the competent authorities consider appropriate and of which they have explicitly informed the applicant (article 10) The general applicability of the more stringent or additional conditions as referred to in article 5, is restricted here.

By virtue of article 14 the competent authorities may decide to suspend the listing of a security where the smooth operation of the market is, or may be, temporarily jeopardised or where the protection of investors so requires. The competent authorities may even decide that the listing of a security be discontinued if they are satisfied that, owing to special circumstances, normal regular dealings in a security are no longer possible.

The competent authorities shall cooperate wherever necessary for the purpose of carrying out their duties and shall exchange any information required for that purpose (article 18, paragraph 1).

Member states shall take the measures necessary to implement this directive in national legislation within two years of its notification. An extension of this period by one year is possible for member states simultaneously introducing this directive and the proposed Council directive (to be discussed under II) on the particulars to be published when securities are admitted to official stock exchange listing (article 22, paragraph 2). The directive to be discussed under IV, extended the period in question until June 30, 1983.

II COUNCIL DIRECTIVE OF MARCH 17, 1980 COORDINATING THE REQUIREMENTS FOR THE DRAWING UP, SCRUTINY AND DISTRIBUTION OF THE LISTING PARTICULARS TO BE PUBLISHED FOR THE ADMISSION OF SECURITIES TO OFFICIAL STOCK EXCHANGE LISTING

(OJEC L 100 17.4.1980, directive 80/390/EEC)

For the protection of actual or potential investors, safeguards are required in most member states from undertakings seeking to procure savings from the public, either at the time of the issue of securities or at the time of their admission to official stock exchange listing. Such safeguards require the provision of information which is sufficient and as objective as possible as regards the financial position of the issuer and the particulars of the securities for which admission to official listing is requested. The form in which this information is required is usually the publication of listing particulars. However the problem is that the safeguards required differ from member state to member state. These differences not only make it more difficult for undertakings to obtain admission of securities to official listing on stock exchanges but also hinder the acquisition by investors residing in one member state of securities listed on stock exchanges of other member states. The aim of this directive is to achieve a degree of equivalence in the safeguards required in each member state, sufficient to ensure the provision of information which is appropriate and as objective as possible to actual or potential security holders. However, taking into account the limited degree of liberalisation of capital movements in the Community in 1980 and the fact that a control mechanism at the time the securities are offered does not yet exist in all member states, this directive confines itself to restricting coordination to the admission of securities to official stock exchange listing.

From article 1 it can be concluded that the directive in question applies to the same securities as those discussed under I. This is not surprising since both directives are closely related. The directive discussed earlier deals with the conditions for admission to official stock exchange listing. Once these conditions have been fulfilled, actual listing can be initiated on the basis of listing particulars. This directive ensures coordination of the safeguards required for the provision of appropriate and as objective as possible information to actual or potential investors in the securities concerned.

Article 4 provides that the listing particulars shall contain the information which, according to the particular nature of the issuer and of the securities for the admission of which application is being made, is necessary to enable investors and their investment advisers to make an informed assessment of the assets and liabilities, financial position, profits and losses, and prospects of the issuer and of the rights attaching to such securities.

Without prejudice to the obligation referred to in article 4, member states shall ensure that, subject to the possibilities for exemption provided for in articles 6 and 7, listing particulars contain at least the items of information provided for in schedules A, B or C for shares, or debt securities or certificates representing shares (article 5, paragraph 1). The following information is concerned:

- Information concerning those responsible for listing particulars and the auditing of accounts;
- Information concerning the admission to official listing and the shares or loan in question;
- General information about the issuer and its capital;
- Information concerning the issuer's activities;
- Information concerning the issuer's assets and liabilities, financial position and profits and losses;
- Information concerning administration, management and supervision;
- Information concerning the recent development and prospects of the issuer.

Articles 6 and 7 contain derogation provisions entailing complete or partial exemption from the obligation to publish listing particulars:

Article 6

Member states may empower the authorities responsible for checking the listing particulars within the meaning of this directive (hereafter referred to as 'the competent authorities') to grant partial or complete exemption from the obligation to publish listing particulars in the following cases:

1 The securities for which admission to official listing is applied for are:
   a securities which have been the subject of a public issue;
   b securities issued in connection with a takeover offer;
   c securities issued in connection with a merger involving the acquisition of another company or the formation of a new company, the division of a company, the transfer of all or part of an undertaking's assets and liabilities or as consideration for the transfer of assets other than cash and where, not more than twelve months before the admission of the securities to official listing, a document, regarded by the competent authorities as containing information equivalent to that of the listing particulars provided for by this directive, has been published in the same member state. Particulars shall also be published of any material changes which have occurred since such document was prepared. The document must be made available to the public at the registered office of the issuer and at the offices of the financial organisations retained to act as the latter's paying agents, and any particulars of material changes shall be published in accordance with article 20, paragraph 1 and article 21, paragraph 1.

2 The securities for which admission to official listing is applied for are:
   a shares allotted free of charge to holders of shares already listed on the same stock exchange; or
   b shares resulting from the conversion of convertible debt securities or shares created after an exchange for exchangeable debt securities, if shares of the company whose shares are offered by way of conversion or exchange are already listed on the same stock exchange; or
   c shares resulting from the exercise of the rights conferred by warrants, if shares of the company whose shares are offered to holders of the warrants are already listed on the same stock exchange; or
   d shares issued in substitution for shares already listed on the same stock exchange if the issuing of such new shares does not involve any increase in the company's issued share capital, and, where appropriate, the information provided for in chapter 2 of schedule A is published in accordance with articles 20, paragraph 1 and 21, paragraph 1.

3 The securities for which admission to official listing is applied for are:
   a shares of which the number or the estimated market value or the nominal value or, in the absence of a nominal value, the accounting par value, amounts to less than 10% of the number or of the corresponding value of shares of the same class already listed on the same stock exchange; or
   b debt securities issued by companies and other legal persons which are nationals of a member state and which:
   - in carrying on their business, benefit from state monopolies, and

- are set up or governed by a special law or pursuant to such a law or whose borrowings are unconditionally and irrevocably guaranteed by a member state or one of a member state's federal states; or

c debt securities issued by legal persons, other than companies, which are nationals of a member state, and
- were set up by a special law, and
- whose activities are governed by that law and consist solely in:
  i raising funds under state control through the issue of debt securities, and
  ii financing production by means of the resources which they have raised and resources provided by a member state, and
- the debt securities of which are, for the purposes of admission to official listing, considered by national law as debt securities issued or guaranteed by the state; or

d shares allotted to employees, if shares of the same class have already been admitted to official listing on the same stock exchange; shares which differ from each other solely as to the date of first entitlement to dividends shall not be considered as being of different classes; or

e securities already admitted to official listing on another stock exchange in the same member state; or

f shares issued in consideration for the partial or total renunciation by the management of a limited partnership with a share capital of its statutory rights over the profits, if shares of the same class have already been admitted to official listing on the same stock exchange; shares which differ solely as to the date of first entitlement to dividends shall not be considered as being of different classes; or

g supplementary certificates representing shares issued in exchange for the original securities, where the issuing of such new certificates has not brought about any increase in the company's issued capital, and provided that certificates representing such shares are already listed on the same stock exchange, and where:
- in the case of a, the issuer has complied with the stock exchange publicity requirements imposed by the national authorities and has produced annual accounts and annual and interim reports which these authorities have considered adequate,
- in the case of c, listing particulars complying with this directive have already been published, and
- in all the cases referred to in points a to g information concerning the number and type of securities to be admitted to official listing and the circumstances in which such securities have been issued has been published in accordance with articles 21, paragraph 1 and 21, paragraph 1.

Article 7

The competent authorities may authorise omission from the listing particulars of certain information provided for by this directive if they consider that:

a such information is of minor importance only and is not such as will influence assessment of the assets and liabilities, financial position, profits and losses and prospects of the issuer; or

b disclosure of such information would be contrary to the public interest or seriously detrimental to the issuer, provided that, in the latter case, such omission would not be likely to mislead the public with regard to facts and circumstances, knowledge of which is essential for the assessment of the securities in question.

Subject to the possibilities for exemption referred to in articles 6 and 7, the listing particulars in the special cases referred to in articles 8 - 17 are drawn up in accordance with the directions given in those articles.

The regulations governing the drawing up of the listing particulars have been discussed above. However, this directive also gives rules for the scrutiny and publication of listing particulars.

In this context, article 18 states that no listing particulars may be published until they have been approved by the competent authorities. The competent authorities approve the publication of the listing particulars only if they are of the opinion that they satisfy all the requirements set out in this directive.

Article 20 deals with the distribution of the listing particulars. They must be published either:

- by insertion in one or more newspapers circulated throughout the member state in which the admission to official listing of securities is sought, or widely circulated therein, or
- in the form of a brochure to be made available, free of charge, to the public at the offices of the stock exchange or stock exchanges on which the securities are being admitted to official listing, at the registered office of the issuer and at the offices of the financial organisations retained to act as the latter's paying agents in the member state in which the admission of securities to official listing is sought.

In addition, either the complete listing particulars or a notice stating where the listing particulars have been published and where they may obtained by the public must be inserted in a publication designated by the member state in which the admission of securities to official listing is sought.

In accordance with article 21 listing particulars must be published within a reasonable period, to be laid down in national legislation or by the competent authorities, before the date on which official listing becomes effective.

Under article 27 member states shall take the measures necessary to comply with this directive within 30 months of its notification. The directive to be discussed below under IV extended this period until June 30, 1983.

III COUNCIL DIRECTIVE OF FEBRUARY 15, 1982 ON INFORMATION TO BE PUBLISHED ON A REGULAR BASIS BY COMPANIES THE SHARES OF WHICH HAVE BEEN ADMITTED TO OFFICIAL STOCK EXCHANGE LISTING

(OJEC L 48 20.2.1982, directive 82/121/EEC)

The protection of investors in securities admitted to official stock exchange listing requires that the investors be supplied with appropriate regular information throughout the entire period during which the securities are listed. Coordination of requirements for this regular information has similar objectives to those envisaged for the listing particulars that have to be published prior to official listing, namely to improve the protection of investors and to make it more equivalent, to facilitate the listing of these securities on more than one stock exchange in the Community, and in doing so to contribute towards the establishment of a genuine Community capital market.

The fourth directive on annual accounts coordinates the laws, regulations and administrative provisions of the member states concerning the annual accounts. For this reason the directive under review will not bring about further coordination in the area of annual accounts, but it does bring about coordination concerning the contents and distribution of a single report covering the first six months of the financial year (the half-yearly report). For the following reasons this regular information needs to be coordinated only for companies whose *shares* are admitted to official stock exchange listing:

- because of the rights they confer on their holders, the protection of investors by means of the publication of a half-yearly report is not essential in the case of ordinary debentures;
- convertible or exchangeable debentures and debentures with warrants may be admitted to official listing pursuant to the directive discussed in I, only if the related shares are already listed on the same stock exchange or on another regulated, regularly operating, recognised open market or

are so admitted simultaneously. The above includes the earlier mentioned condition that the shares must have been admitted to official listing on a stock exchange.

Consequently article 1 states that the directive applies to companies the shares of which are admitted to official listing on a stock exchange situated or operating in a member state, whether the admission is of the shares themselves or of certificates representing them and whether such admission precedes or follows the date on which this directive enters into force. The directive does not apply to investment companies other than those of the closed-end type.

The member states shall ensure that the companies publish half-yearly reports on their activities and profits and losses during the first six months of each financial year. They may subject companies to obligations more stringent than those provided by this directive or to additional obligations, provided that they apply generally to all companies or to all companies of a given class.

The half-yearly report shall consist of figures and an explanatory statement relating to the company's activities and profits and losses during the relevant six-month period. The figures shall indicate at least the net turnover and the profit or loss before or after deduction of tax.

Where a company publishes consolidated accounts it may publish its half-yearly report in either consolidated or unconsolidated form. However, the member states may allow the competent authorities, where the latter consider that the form not adopted would have contained additional material information, to require the company to publish such information.

The powers of the competent authorities concerning non-member countries are then dealt with. If a company governed by the law of a non-member country publishes a half-yearly report, the competent authorities may authorise it to publish that report instead of the half-yearly report provided for in this directive, provided that the information given is equivalent to that which would result from the application of this directive.

Finally, article 12 provides that the member states shall bring into force the measures necessary to comply with this directive not later than June 30, 1983. However, member states may postpone application of these measures until 36 months from the date on which they bring said measures into force.

IV COUNCIL DIRECTIVE OF MARCH 3, 1982 AMENDING DIRECTIVE 79/279/EEC COORDINATING THE CONDITIONS FOR THE ADMISSION OF SECURITIES TO OFFICIAL STOCK EXCHANGE LISTING (DISCUSSED UNDER I) AND DIRECTIVE 80/390/EEC COORDINATING THE REQUIREMENTS FOR THE DRAWING UP, SCRUTINY AND DISTRIBUTION OF THE LISTING PARTICULARS TO BE PUBLISHED FOR THE ADMISSION OF SECURITIES TO OFFICIAL STOCK EXCHANGE LISTING (DISCUSSED UNDER II)

(OJEC L 62 5.3.1982, directive 82/148/EEC)

This directive provides that, if the member states wish to implement the directives discussed under I, II and III *simultaneously*, the final date on which the member states must bring into force the measures necessary to comply with these three directives is set for June 30, 1983. Originally this date applied only to directive III; for directives I and II this date represents an extension. Furthermore, for directives I and II the member states may postpone application of the measures referred to above until 36 months after the date on which they bring these measures into force. In specific terms this means a final deadline of June 30, 1986.

The option of implementing the three directives simultaneously is an expression of the fact that there is a close relationship between the three directives. This relationship concerns the following:

- The objective of each of the directives is the coordination of certain regulations concerning securities admitted to official stock exchange listing or for which admission is requested;
- The three directives aim to establish, at the Community level, a coordinated information policy on the securities concerned.

V COUNCIL DIRECTIVE OF JUNE 22, 1987 AMENDING DIRECTIVE 80/390/EEC COORDINATING THE REQUIREMENTS FOR THE DRAWING UP, SCRUTINY AND DISTRIBUTION OF THE LISTING PARTICULARS TO BE PUBLISHED FOR THE ADMISSION OF SECURITIES TO OFFICIAL STOCK EXCHANGE LISTING

(OJEC L 185 4.7.1987, directive 87/345/EEC)

Article 24 of directive 80/390/EEC provides that where the application for admission of the same securities to official listing on stock exchanges situated or operating in several member states, the competent authorities shall collaborate and use their best endeavours to agree to a single text to be used by all the member states concerned. However, this provision does not entail full mutual recognition of the listing particulars. The directive under review achieves this mutual recognition and contributes to the completion of the securities market in the year 1993.

The directive provides the following. Where, for the same securities, applications to official listing on stock exchanges situated or operating in two or more member states, including the member state in which the issuer's registered office is situated, are made simultaneously or within a short interval, listing particulars shall be drawn up in accordance with the rules laid down in this directive in the *member state in which the issuer has its registered office* and approved by the competent authorities of that state. If the issuer's registered office is not situated in one of those member states, the issuer must choose one of those states under the legislation of which the listing particulars will be drawn up and approved.

Once approved in accordance with the above, listing particulars must be recognised by the other member states in which admission to official listing has been applied for, without it being necessary to obtain the approval of the competent authorities of these states and without their being able to require that additional information be included in the listing particulars. The competent authorities may, however, require that listing particulars include information specific to the market of the country of admission, concerning matters such as the income tax system, the financial organisation retained to act as paying agents for the issuer in that country, and the way in which notices to investors are published.

The provisions concerning reciprocity with non-member countries are an extension of the above. The Community may, by means of agreements concluded with one or more non-member countries pursuant to the Treaty, recognise listing particulars drawn up and scrutinised in accordance with the rules of the non-member country or countries, as meeting the requirements in this directive, subject to reciprocity, and provided that the rules concerned give investors protection equivalent to that afforded by this directive, even if those rules differ from the provisions of this directive.

Member states shall take the measures necessary to comply with this directive by January 1, 1990. For Spain this date shall be replaced by January 1, 1991 and for Portugal by January 1, 1992.

VI COUNCIL DIRECTIVE OF APRIL 23, 1990 AMENDING DIRECTIVE 80/390/EEC CONCERNING THE MUTUAL RECOGNITION OF THE LISTING PARTICULARS TO BE PUBLISHED FOR THE ADMISSION TO OFFICIAL STOCK EXCHANGE LISTING

(OJEC L 112 3.5.1990, directive 90/211/EEC)

This directive is closely connected with the directive coordinating the requirements for the drawing up, scrutiny and distribution of the prospectus to be published where transferable securities are offered to the public, to be discussed below under VII. This directive was adopted by the Council on April 17, 1989. Article 21 stipulates that, when transferable securities are offered to the public simultaneously or within a short interval of one another in two or more member states, a prospectus drawn up and approved in accordance with articles 7, 8 or 12 of the directive must be recognised as a public offer prospectus in the other member states involved, on the basis of mutual recognition. The Council considers it desirable that the said public offer prospectus should also be recognised as listing particulars in the other member states, in cases where, shortly after the public offer (up to three months thereafter) an application is submitted for admission to official stock exchange listing. The subject directive achieves this effect.

4.3 Coordination of public offer prospectuses

VII COUNCIL DIRECTIVE OF APRIL 17, 1989 COORDINATING THE REQUIREMENTS FOR THE DRAWING UP, SCRUTINY AND DISTRIBUTION OF THE PROSPECTUS TO BE PUBLISHED WHEN TRANSFERABLE SECURITIES ARE OFFERED TO THE PUBLIC

(OJEC L 124 5.5.1989, directive 89/298/EEC)

The council directive of March 17, 1980 coordinating the requirements for the drawing up, scrutiny and distribution of the listing particulars to be published for the admission of securities to the official stock exchange listing, discussed under II, represents an important stage in the progress towards a Community information policy. However, such a policy also requires that when transferable securities are offered to the public for the first time in a member state, *whether or not they are subsequently listed* (in case of a later listing a prospectus in accordance with the requirements mentioned in directive II must be published), a prospectus containing information of this nature must be made available to investors. The directive in question stipulates the requirements with which this prospectus must comply.

As was the case with directive II, it is necessary to coordinate the contents of the public offer prospectus in order to achieve equivalence of the minimum safeguards afforded to investors in the various member states and to promote the interpenetration of national securities markets. This coordination is especially necessary where this prospectus may also be accepted as listing particulars for admission to the official stock exchange listing (as discussed under II), if it contains equivalent information as required by that directive.

The provisions of the directive are listed below:

General provisions

Article 1

1 This directive applies to transferable securities which are offered to the public for the first time in a member state provided that these securities are not already listed on a stock exchange situated or operating in that member state.
2 Where an offer to the public is for part only of the transferable securities from a single issue, the member states need not require that another prospectus be published if the other part is subsequently offered to the public.

Article 2

This directive does not apply:

1 to the following types of offer:

- a where transferable securities are offered to persons in the context of their trades, professions or occupations, and/or
- b where transferable securities are offered to a restricted circle of persons, and/or
- c where the selling price of all the transferable securities does not exceed ECU 40,000, and/or
- d where the transferable securities offered can be acquired only for a consideration of at least ECU 40,000 per investor;

2 to transferable securities of the following types:

- a to transferable securities offered in individual denominations of at least ECU 40,000;
- b to units issued by collective investment undertakings other than of the closed-end type;
- c to transferable securities issued by a member state or by one of a member state's regional or local authorities or by public international bodies of which one or more member states are members;
- d to transferable securities offered in connection with a take-over bid;
- e to transferable securities offered in connection with a merger.
- f to shares allotted free of charge to the holders of shares;
- g to shares or transferable securities equivalent to shares offered in exchange for shares in the same company if the offer of such new securities does not involve any overall increase in the company's issued capital;
- h to transferable securities offered by their employer or by an affiliated undertaking to or for the benefit of serving or former employees;
- i to transferable securities resulting from the conversion of convertible debt securities or from the exercise of the rights conferred by warrants or to shares offered in exchange for exchangeable debt securities, provided that a public offer prospectus or listing particulars relating to those convertible or exchangeable debt securities or those warrants were published in the same member state;
- j to transferable securities issued, with a view to their obtaining the means necessary to achieve their disinterested objectives, by associations with legal status or non-profit making bodies, recognised by the state;
- k to shares or transferable securities equivalent to shares, ownership of which entitles the holder to avail himself of the services rendered by bodies such as 'building societies', 'crédits populaires', 'Genossenschaftsbanken', or 'industrial and provident societies', or to become a member of such a body;
- l to Euro-securities which are not the subject of a generalised campaign of advertising or canvassing.

Article 3

For the purposes of this directive:

a 'collective investment undertakings other than of the closed-end type' shall mean unit trust and investment companies:

- the object of which is the collective investment of capital provided by the public, and which operate on the principle of risk spreading, and
- the units of which are, at the holder's request, repurchased or redeemed, directly or indirectly, out of the assets of those undertakings. Actions taken by such undertakings to ensure that the stock exchange value of their units does not significantly vary from their net asset value shall be regarded as equivalent to such repurchase or redemption;

b 'units of a collective investment undertaking' shall mean transferable securities issued by a collective investment undertaking representing the rights of the participants in such an undertaking over its assets;

c 'issuers' shall mean companies and other legal persons and any undertakings the transferable securities of which are offered to the public;

d 'transferable securities' shall mean shares in companies and other transferable securities equivalent to shares in companies, debt securities having a maturity of at least one year and other transferable securities equivalent to debt securities, and any other transferable security giving the right to acquire any such transferable securities by subscription or exchange;

e 'Euro-securities' shall mean transferable securities which:
- are to be underwritten and distributed by a syndicate at least two of the members of which have their offices in different states, and
- are offered on a significant scale in one or more states other than that of the issuer's registered office, and
- may be subscribed for or initially acquired only through a credit institution or other financial institution.

Article 4

Member states shall ensure that any offer of transferable securities to the public within their territories is subject to the publication of a prospectus by the person making the offer.

Article 5

Member states may provide for partial or complete exemption from the obligation to publish a prospectus where the transferable securities being offered to the public are:

a debt securities or other transferable securities equivalent to debt securities issued in a continuous or repeated manner by credit institutions or other financial institutions equivalent to credit institutions which regularly publish their annual accounts and which within the Community, are set up or governed by a special law or pursuant to such a law, or are subject to public supervision to protect savings;

b debt securities or other transferable securities equivalent to debt securities issued by companies and other legal persons which are nationals of a member state and which:
- in carrying on their business, benefit from state monopolies, and
- are set up or governed by a special law or pursuant to such a law or whose borrowings are unconditionally and irrevocably guaranteed by a member state or one of a member state's regional or local authorities;

c debt securities issued by legal persons, other than companies, which are nationals of a member state, and
- were set up by a special law, and
- whose activities are governed by that law and consist solely in:
  i raising funds under state control through the issue of debt securities, and
  ii financing production by means of the resources which they have raised and resources provided by a member state and/or acquiring a holding in such production, and
- the debt securities of which are, for the purposes of the admission to official listing, considered by national law as debt securities issued or guaranteed by the state.

Article 6

If a full prospectus has been published in a member state within the previous twelve months, the following prospectus drawn up by the same issuer in the same state, but relating to different transferable securities, may indicate only those changes likely to influence the value of the securities which have occurred since publication of the full prospectus. However, that prospectus may be made available only accompanied by the full prospectus to which it relates or by a reference thereto.

Contents and arrangements for the scrutiny and distribution of the prospectus for transferable securities for which admission to official stock exchange listing is sought

Article 7

Where a public offer relates to transferable securities which at the time of the offer are the subject of an application for admission to official listing on a stock exchange situated or operating within the same member state, the contents of the prospectus and the procedures for scrutinising and distributing it shall, subject to adaptations appropriate to the circumstances of a public offer, be determined in accordance with directive 80/390/EEC.

Article 8

1 Where a public offer is made in one member state and admission is sought to official listing on a stock exchange situated in another member state, the person making the public offer shall have the possibility in the member state in which the public offer is to be made of drawing up a prospectus the contents and procedures for scrutiny and distribution of which shall, subject to adaptations appropriate to the circumstances of a public offer, be determined in accordance with directive 80/390/EEC.

2 Paragraph 1 shall apply only in those member states which in general provide for the prior scrutiny of public offer prospectuses.

Article 9

A prospectus must be published or made available to the public not later than the time when an offer is made to the public.

Article 10

1 Where a prospectus in accordance with article 7 or 8 is to be published, the advertisements, notices, posters and documents announcing the public offer must be communicated in advance to the competent authorities. The aforementioned documents must mention that there is a prospectus and state where the prospectus is published.

2 If the member states authorise the distribution of the documents referred to above before the prospectus is available, those documents must state that a prospectus will be published and indicate where the members of the public will be able to obtain it.

3 The prospectus must be published either:
   - by insertion in one or more newspapers circulated throughout the member state in which the public offer is made, or
   - in the form of a brochure to be made available, free of charge, to the public in the member state in which the public offer is made and at the registered office of the person making the public offer and at the offices of the financial organisations retained to act as paying agents of the latter in the state where the offer is made.

4 In addition, either the complete prospectus or a notice stating where the prospectus has been published and where it may be obtained by the public must be inserted in a publication designated by the member state in which the public offer is made.

Contents and arrangements for the distribution of the prospectus for transferable securities for which admission to official stock exchange listing is not sought

Article 11

1 Where a public offer relates to transferable securities other than those referred to in articles 7 and 8, the prospectus must contain the information which, according to the particular nature of the issuer and of the transferable securities offered to the public, is necessary to enable investors

to make an informed assessment of the assets and liabilities, financial position, profits and losses and prospects of the issuer and of the rights attaching to the transferable securities.

2 In order to fulfil the obligation referred to in paragraph 1, the prospectus shall, subject to the possibilities for exemption provided for in articles 5 and 13, contain in as easily analysable and comprehensible a form as possible, at least the information listed below:

a those responsible for the prospectus (names, functions and declarations by them that to the best of their knowledge the information contained in the prospectus is in accordance with the facts and that the prospectus makes no omission likely to affect its import);

b the offer to the public and the transferable securities being offered (nature of the securities being offered, the amount and purpose of the issue, the number of securities and the rights attaching to them; the income tax withheld at source; the period during which the offer is open; the date on which entitlement to dividends or interest arises; the persons underwriting or guaranteeing the offer; any restrictions on the free transferability of the securities being offered and the markets on which they may be traded; the establishments serving as paying agents; if known, the price at which the securities are offered, or else, if national rules so provide, the procedure and timetable for fixing the price if it is not known when the prospectus is drawn up; methods of payment; the procedure for the exercise of any right of pre-emption and the methods of and time-limits for delivery of the securities);

c the issuer (name, registered office; its date of incorporation, the legislation applicable to the issuer and the issuer's legal form, its objects, indication of the register and of the entry number therein) and its capital (amount of the subscribed capital, the number and main particulars of the securities of which the capital consists and any part of the capital still to be paid up; the amount of any convertible debt securities, exchangeable debt securities or debt securities with warrants and the procedure for conversion, exchange or subscription; where appropriate, the group of undertakings to which the issuer belongs; in the case of shares, the following additional information must be supplied: any shares not representing capital, the amount of the authorised capital and the duration of the authorisation; in so far as they are known, indication of the shareholders who directly or indirectly exercise or could exercise a determining role in the management of the issuer);

d the issuer's principal activities (description of its principal activities, and, where appropriate, any exceptional factors which have influenced its activities; any dependence on patents, licences or contracts if these are of fundamental importance; information regarding investments in progress where they are significant; any legal proceedings having an important effect on the issuer's financial position);

e the issuer's assets and liabilities, financial position and profits and losses (own accounts and where appropriate, consolidated accounts; if the issuer prepares consolidated annual accounts only, it shall include those accounts in the prospectus; if the issuer prepares both own and consolidated accounts, it shall include both types of accounts in the prospectus; however, the issuer may include only one of the two, provided that the accounts which are not included do not provide any significant additional information); interim accounts if any have been published since the end of the previous financial year; the name of the person responsible for auditing the accounts; if that person has qualified them or refused an audit report, the fact must be stated and the reasons given;

f the issuer's administration, management and supervision (names, addresses, functions; in the case of an offer to the public of shares in a limited-liability company, remuneration of the members of the issuer's administrative, management and supervisory bodies);

g to the extent that such information would have a significant impact on any assessment that might be made of the issuer, recent developments in its business and prospects (the most significant recent trends concerning the development of the issuer's business since the end of the preceding financial year, information on the issuer's prospects for at least the current financial year).

3 Where a public offer relates to debt securities guaranteed by one or more legal persons, the information specified in paragraph 2 (c) to (g) must also be given with respect to the guarantor or guarantors.
4 Where a public offer relates to convertible debt securities, exchangeable debt securities or debt securities with warrants or to the warrants themselves, information must also be given with regard to the nature of the shares or debt securities to which they confer entitlement and the conditions of and procedures for conversion, exchange or subscription. Where the issuer of the shares is not the issuer of the debt securities or warrants the information specified in paragraph 2 (c) to (g) must also be given with respect to the issuer of the shares or debt securities.
5 If the period of existence of the issuer is less than any period mentioned in paragraph 2, the information need be provided only for the period of the issuer's existence.
6 Where certain information specified in paragraph 2 is found to be inappropriate to the issuer's sphere of activity or its legal form or to the transferable securities being offered, a prospectus giving equivalent information must be drawn up.
7 Where shares are offered on a pre-emptive basis to shareholders of the issuer on the occasion of their admission to dealing on a stock exchange market, the member states or bodies designated by them may allow some of the information specified in paragraph 2, (d), (e) and (f) to be omitted, provided that investors already possess up-to-date information about the issuer equivalent to that required by this article as a result of stock exchange disclosure requirements.
8 Where a class of shares has been admitted to dealing on a stock exchange, the member states or bodies designated by them may allow a partial or complete exemption from the obligation to publish a prospectus if the number or estimated market value or the nominal value, or in the absence of a nominal value, the accounting par value of the shares offered amounts to less than 10% of the number or of the corresponding value of shares of the same class already admitted to dealing, provided that investors already possess up-to-date information about the issuer equivalent to that required by this article as a result of stock exchange disclosure requirements.

Article 12

1 However, the member states may provide that the person making a public offer shall have the possibility of drawing up a prospectus the contents of which shall, subject to adaptations appropriate to the circumstances of a public offer, be determined in accordance with directive 80/390/EEC.
2 The prior scrutiny of the prospectus referred to in paragraph 1 must be carried out by the bodies designated by the member states even in the absence of a request for admission to official stock exchange listing.

Article 13

1 The member states or the bodies designated by them may authorise the omission from the prospectus referred in article 11 of certain information prescribed in this directive:
   a if that information is of minor importance only and is not likely to influence assessment of the issuer's assets and liabilities, financial position, profits and losses and prospects; or
   b if disclosure of that information would be contrary to the public interest or seriously detrimental to the issuer, provided that, in the latter case, omission would not be likely to mislead the public with regard to facts and circumstances essential for assessment of the transferable securities.
2 Where the initiator of an offer is neither the issuer nor a third party acting on the issuer's behalf, the member states or the bodies designated by them may authorise omission from the prospectus of certain information which would not normally be in the initiator's possession.
3 The member states or the bodies designated by them may provide for partial or complete exemption from the obligation to publish a prospectus where the information which those making the offer are required to supply by law, regulation or rules made by bodies enabled to

do so by national laws is available to investors not later than the time when the prospectus must be or should have been published or made available to the public, in accordance with this directive, in the form of documents giving this information at least equivalent to that required by article 11.

Article 14
A prospectus must be communicated, before its publication, to the bodies designated for that purpose in each member state in which the transferable securities are offered to the public for the first time.

Article 15
A prospectus must be published or made available to the public in the member state in which an offer to the public is made in accordance with the procedures laid down by that member state.

Article 16
A prospectus must be published or made available to the public not later than the time when an offer is made to the public.

Article 17
1 When a prospectus complying with article 11 or 12 is or must be published, the advertisements, notices, posters and documents announcing the public offer distributed or made available to members of the public by the person making the public offer, must be communicated in advance to the bodies designated in accordance with article 14, if such bodies carry out prior scrutiny of public offer prospectuses. In such a case, the latter shall determine whether the documents concerned should be checked before publication. Such documents must state that a prospectus exists and indicate where it is published.
2 If member states authorise the dissemination of the documents referred to in paragraph 1 before the prospectus is available, those documents must state that a prospectus will be published and indicate where members of the public will be able to obtain it.

Article 18
Any significant new factor or significant inaccuracy in a prospectus capable of affecting assessment of the transferable securities which arises or is noted between the publication of the prospectus and the definitive disclosure of a public offer must be mentioned or rectified in a supplement to the prospectus, to be published or made available to the public in accordance with at least the same arrangements as were applied when the original prospectus was disseminated or in accordance with the manner laid down by the member states or by the bodies designated by them.

Cooperation between member states

Article 19
The member states shall designate the bodies, which may be the same as those referred to in article 12, which shall cooperate with each other for the purposes of the proper application of this directive and shall use their best endeavours, within the framework of their responsibilities, to exchange all the information necessary to that end. Member states shall inform the Commission of the bodies thus designated. The Commission shall communicate that information to the other member states.

Member states shall ensure that the bodies designated have the powers required for the accomplishment of their task.

Article 20

1 Where, for the same transferable securities, public offers are made simultaneously or within a short interval of one another in two or more member states and where a public offer prospectus is drawn up in accordance with article 7, 8 or 12, the authority competent for the approval of the prospectus shall be that of the member state in which the issuer has its registered office if the public offer or any application for admission to official listing on a stock exchange is made in that member state.

2 However, if the member state referred to in paragraph 1 does not provide in general for the prior scrutiny of public offer prospectuses and if only the public offer or an application for admission to listing is made in that member state, as well as in all other cases, the person making the public offer must choose the supervisory authority from those in the member states in which the public offer is made and which provide in general for the prior scrutiny of public offer prospectuses.

Mutual recognition

Article 21

1 If approved in accordance with article 20, a prospectus must, subject to translation if required, be recognised as complying or be deemed to comply with the laws of the other member states in which the same transferable securities are offered to the public simultaneously or within a short interval of one another, without being subject to any form of approval there and without those states being able to require that additional information be included in the prospectus. Those member states may, however, require that the prospectus include information specific to the market of the country in which the public offer is made concerning in particular the income tax system, the financial organisations retained to act as paying agents for the issuer in that country, and the way in which notices to investors are published.

2 A prospectus approved by the competent authorities within the meaning of article 24a of directive 80/390/EEC must be recognised as complying or be deemed to comply with the laws of another member state in which the public offer will be made, even if partial exemption or partial derogation has been granted pursuant to this directive, provided, however, that:

a the partial exemption or partial derogation in question is of a type that is recognised in the rules of the other member state concerned; and

b the circumstances that justify the partial exemption or partial derogation also exist in the other member state concerned.

Even if the conditions laid down in (a) and (b) of the first subparagraph are not fulfilled, the member state concerned may deem a prospectus approved by the competent authorities within the meaning of article 20 to comply with its laws.

3 The person making the public offer shall communicate to the bodies designated by the other member states in which the public offer is to be made the prospectus that he intends to use in that state. That prospectus must be the same as the prospectus approved by the authority referred to in article 20.

4 The member states may restrict the application of this article to prospectuses concerning transferable securities of issuers who have their registered office in a member state.

Cooperation

Article 22

1 The competent authorities shall cooperate wherever necessary for the purpose of carrying out their duties and shall exchange any information required for that purpose.

2 Where a public offer concerning transferable securities giving a right to participate in company capital, either immediately or at the end of a maturity period, is made in one or more of the

member states other than that in which the registered office of the issuer of the shares to which those securities give entitlement is situated, while that issuer's shares have already been admitted to official listing in that member state, the competent authorities of the member state of the offer may act only after having consulted the competent authorities of the member state in which the registered office of the issuer of the shares in question is situated in cases where the public offer prospectus is scrutinised.

Article 23

1 Member states shall provide that all persons then or previously employed by the authorities referred to in article 20 shall be bound by the obligation of professional secrecy. This shall mean that they may not divulge any confidential information received in the course of their duties to any person or authority whatsoever, except by virtue of provisions laid down by law.
2 Paragraph 1 shall not prevent the various member state authorities referred to in article 20 from forwarding information as provided for in this directive. The information thus exchanged shall be covered by the obligation of professional secrecy applying to the persons employed then or previously by the authority receiving such information.
3 Without prejudice to cases covered by criminal law, the authorities referred to in article 20 receiving information pursuant to article 21 may use it only to carry out their functions or in the context of an administrative appeal or in court proceedings relating to the carrying out of those functions.

Negotiations with non-member countries

Article 24

The Community may, by means of agreements with one or more non-member countries concluded pursuant to the Treaty, recognise public offer prospectuses drawn up and scrutinised in accordance with the rules of the non-member country or countries concerned as meeting the requirements of this directive, subject to reciprocity, provided that the rules concerned give investors protection equivalent to that afforded by this directive, even if those rules differ from the provisions of this directive.

The final provision stipulates that the member states shall take the measures necessary for them to comply with this directive by April 17, 1991.

4.4 Coordination of information

VIII COUNCIL DIRECTIVE OF DECEMBER 12, 1988 ON THE INFORMATION TO BE PUBLISHED WHEN A MAJOR HOLDING IN A LISTED COMPANY IS ACQUIRED OR DISPOSED OF

(OJEC L 348 17.12.1988, directive 88/627/EEC)

A policy of adequate information of investors in the field of transferable securities is likely to improve investor protection, to increase investors' confidence in securities markets and thus to ensure that securities markets function correctly. In this context it is important to inform investors of major holdings and of changes in those holdings in Community companies, the shares of which are admitted to official listing on stock exchanges situated or operating within the Community. With a view to these objectives the following provision was made in schedule C, point 5, (c), of the Council directive of March 5, 1979 coordinating the conditions for the admission of securities to official exchange listing: A company the shares of which have been admitted to official listing on a stock exchange within the community must inform the public of any changes in the structure (shareholders and break-down of holdings) of the major holdings in its capital as compared with the information previously published on that subject as soon as such changes come to its notice.

The problem is that said companies can inform the public of changes in major holdings only if they themselves have been informed of such changes. Most member states do not require investors to inform companies when they acquire or dispose of major holdings in their capital. Moreover, where such a requirement does exist there are significant differences in the procedures for applying it. The directive in question sets out to establish coordinated rules in this respect throughout the Community.

Under article 1 this directive applies to natural persons and legal entities in public or private law who, directly or through intermediaries, acquire or dispose of holdings meeting the criteria laid down in article 4 which involve changes in the holdings of voting rights in companies incorporated under their law the shares of which are officially listed on a stock exchange or exchanges situated or operating within one or more member states. Where the acquisition or disposal of a major holding is effected by means of certificates representing shares this directive shall apply to the bearers of those certificates, and not to the issuer.

The directive does not apply to the acquisition or disposal of major holdings in collective investment undertakings. Acquiring a holding means, for the purposes of this directive, not only purchasing a holding, but also acquisition by any other means whatsoever, including acquisition in one of the situations referred to in article 7 (article 2). Member states may subject the natural persons, legal entities and companies referred to in article 1 to requirements stricter than those provided for in this directive or to additional requirements, provided that such requirements apply generally to all those acquiring or disposing of holdings and all companies or to all those falling within a particular category acquiring or disposing of holdings or of companies (article 3).

Article 4 defines a number of thresholds. Where a natural person or legal entity referred to in article 1 acquires or disposes of a holding in a company referred to in article 1 and where, following that acquisition or disposal, the proportion of voting rights held by that person or legal entity reaches, exceeds or falls below one of the thresholds of 10%, 20%, 1/3, 50% and 2/3, he shall notify the company and at the same time the competent authority or authorities referred to in article 13 within seven calendar days of the proportion of voting rights held by that person or legal entity following the acquisition or disposal. Member states need not apply:

- the threshold of 20% and 1/3 where they apply a single threshold of 25%,
- the threshold of 2/3 where they apply the threshold of 75%.

Pursuant to article 5 the member states shall provide that at the first annual general meeting of a company referred to in article 1 to take place more than three months after this directive has been transposed into national law, any natural person or legal entity as referred to in article 1 must notify the company concerned and at the same time the competent authorities concerned where he holds 10% or more of its voting rights, specifying the proportion of voting rights actually held unless that person or entity has already made a declaration in accordance with article 4. Within one month of that general meeting, the public shall be informed of all the holdings of 10% or more in accordance with article 10.

Article 6 deals with the case of a group of undertakings required to draw up consolidated annual accounts. If the person or entity acquiring or disposing of a major holding as defined in article 4 is a member of a group of undertakings required under directive 83/349/EEC to draw up consolidated annual accounts, that person or entity shall be exempt from the obligation to make the declaration provided for in articles 4 and 5 if it is made by the parent undertaking or, where the parent undertaking is itself a subsidiary undertaking, by its own parent undertaking.

Article 7 concerns the determination of the percentage of the voting rights. For the purpose of determining whether a natural person or legal entity is required to make a declaration, the following shall be regarded as voting rights held by that person or entity:

- voting rights held by other persons or entities in their own names but on behalf of that person or entity;
- voting rights held by an undertaking controlled by that person or entity;
- voting rights held by a third party with whom that person or entity has concluded a written agreement which obliges them to adopt, by concerted exercise of the voting rights they hold, a lasting common policy towards the management of the company in question;
- voting rights held by a third party under a written agreement concluded with that person or entity or with an undertaking controlled by that person or entity providing for the temporary transfer for consideration of the voting rights in question;
- voting rights attaching to shares owned by that person or entity which are lodged as security, except where the person or entity holding the security controls the voting rights and declares his intention of exercising them, in which case they shall be regarded as the latter's voting rights;
- voting rights attaching to shares of which that person or entity has the life interests;
- voting rights which that person or entity or one of the other persons or entities mentioned in the above indents is entitled to acquire, on his own initiative alone, under a formal agreement; in such cases, the notification prescribed in article 4 shall be effected on the date of the agreement.
- voting rights attaching to shares deposited with that person or entity which that person or entity can exercise at its discretion in the absence of specific instructions of the holders.

In accordance with article 8, 'controlled undertaking' means, for the purpose of this directive, any undertaking in which a natural person or a entity:

a has a majority of the shareholders' or members' voting rights; or

b has the right to appoint or remove a majority of the members of the administrative, management or supervisory body and is at the same time a shareholder in, or member of, the undertaking in question; or

c is a shareholder or member and alone controls a majority of the shareholders' or members' voting rights pursuant to an agreement entered into with other shareholders or members of the undertaking.

For the purpose of the above a parent undertaking's right as regards voting, appointment and removal includes the rights of any other controlled undertaking and those of any person or entity acting in his own name but on behalf of the parent undertaking or of any other controlled undertaking.

Article 9 states that the competent authorities may exempt from the declaration provided for in article 4 the acquisition or disposal of a major holding by a professional dealer in securities, in so far as that acquisition or disposal is effected in his capacity as a professional dealer in securities and in so far as the acquisition is not used by the dealer to intervene in the management of the company concerned.

The competent authorities shall require the professional dealers in securities to be members of a stock exchange situated or operating within a member state or to be approved or supervised by a competent authority such as referred to in article 12.

A company which has received a declaration as referred to in article 4 must in turn disclose it to the public in each of the member states in which its shares are officially listed on a stock exchange as soon as possible but not more than nine calender days after the receipt of that declaration (article 10).

A member state may provide for said disclosure to the public to be made not by the company concerned, but by the competent authority, possibly in cooperation with that company.

These disclosures must be made by publication in one or more newspapers distributed throughout or widely in the member state or states concerned or be made available to the public either in writing in places indicated by announcements to be published in one or more newspapers distributed throughout or widely in the member state or states concerned or by other equivalent means approved by the competent authorities.

The competent authorities may, exceptionally, exempt the companies referred to in article 1 from the obligation to notify the public set out in article 10 where those authorities consider that the disclosure of such information would be contrary to the public interest or seriously detrimental to the companies concerned, provided that, in the latter case such omission would not be likely to mislead the public with regard to the facts and circumstances knowledge of which is essential for the assessment of the transferable securities in question (article 11).

Member states shall designate the competent authority or authorities for the purposes of this directive and shall inform the Commission accordingly, specifying, where appropriate, the division of duties between those authorities.

Member states shall ensure that the competent authorities have such powers as may be necessary for the performance of their duties.

The competent authorities in the member states shall cooperate wherever necessary for the purpose of performing their duties and shall exchange any information useful for that purpose (article 12).

For the purpose of this directive, the competent authorities shall be those of the member state the law of which governs the companies referred to in article 1 (article 13).

Article 14 entails a duty of professional secrecy for the competent authorities. Under article 15 member states provide for appropriate sanctions in cases where the natural persons or legal entities or companies referred to in article 1 do not comply with the provisions of this directive.

Member states shall take the measures necessary for them to comply with this directive before January 1, 1991.

IX COUNCIL DIRECTIVE OF NOVEMBER 13, 1989 COORDINATING REGULATIONS ON INSIDER DEALING

(OJEC L 334 18.11.1989, directive 89/592/EEC)

The secondary market in transferable securities, on which securities already issued are traded, plays an important role in the financing of business, since a buyer of newly issued securities can sell such securities on this market at a later date. The smooth operation of the secondary market depends to a large extent on the confidence it inspires in investors. The factors on which such confidence depends include the guarantees afforded to investors that they are all on an equal footing and that they will be protected against the improper use of insider information. By benefiting certain investors as compared with others, insider dealing is likely to undermine the confidence of the latter investors and may therefore prejudice the smooth operation of the secondary market in transferable securities. In most member states there are, however, no rules or regulations prohibiting insider dealing and the rules or regulations that do exist in other member states differ considerably from one member state to another. The objective of this directive is to adopt coordinated rules at the Community level in this field.

Insider dealing only exists when inside information is misused. The activities of market-makers, bodies authorised to act as counterparty, or stockbrokers with inside information do not in themselves represent misuse of inside information, provided that the first two of these categories confine themselves to buying and selling securities in the context of their normal business and that stockbrokers confine themselves to executing orders.

Estimates drawn up on the basis of publicly available data cannot be regarded as inside information and therefore any transaction carried out on the basis of such estimates does not constitute insider dealing within the meaning of this directive.

In article 1 of the directive two definitions are presented.

1 'inside information' shall mean information which has not been made public of a precise nature relating to one or several issuers of transferable securities or to one or several transferable securities, which, if it were made public, would be likely to have a significant effect on the price of the transferable security or securities in question.

2 'transferable securities' mean:

   a shares and debt securities as well as securities equivalent to shares and debt securities;
   b contracts or rights to subscribe for, acquire or dispose of securities referred to in a;
   c futures contracts, options and financial futures in respect of securities referred to in a;
   d index contracts in respect of securities referred to in a,

   when a to d are admitted to trading on a market which is regulated and supervised by authorities recognised by public bodies, and which operates regularly and is accessible directly or indirectly to the public.

Under article 2 each member state shall prohibit any person who:

- by virtue of his membership of the administrative, management or supervisory bodies of the issuer, or
- by virtue of his holding in the capital of the issuer, or
- because he has access to such information by virtue of the exercise of his employment, profession or duties, possesses inside information, from taking advantage of that information with full knowledge of the facts by acquiring or disposing of, for his own account or for the account of a third party, either directly or indirectly, transferable securities of the issuer or issuers to which that information relates.

  If said person is a company or other type of legal person, the above prohibition shall apply to the natural persons who take part in the decision to carry out the transaction for the account of the legal person concerned. The above prohibition applies to any acquisition or disposal of transferable securities effected through a professional intermediary. Each member state may provide that this prohibition shall not apply to acquisitions or disposals of transferable securities effected without the involvement of a professional intermediary outside a market as defined in article 1, paragraph 2.

This directive does not apply to transactions carried out in pursuit of monetary, exchange-rate or public debt-management policies by a sovereign state, by its central bank or any other body designated to that effect by the state, or by any person acting on their behalf.

Under article 3 member states shall prohibit any person subject to the prohibition laid down in article 2 who possess inside information from:

- disclosing that inside information to any third party unless such disclosure is made in the normal course of the exercise of his employment, profession or duties;
- recommending a third party, on the basis of that inside information, to acquire or dispose of, or arrange for the acquisition or disposal by a third party of, transferable securities admitted to trading on its securities markets as referred to in article 1, paragraph 2.

Article 4 extends the prohibition referred to in article 2 to any person other than those provided for in article 2 who, with full knowledge of the facts, possess inside information, the direct or indirect source of which could not be other than a person referred to in article 2.

Article 5 deals with the geographical scope of the prohibition. Each member state shall apply the prohibitions provided for in articles 2, 3 and 4 at least to action undertaken within its territory to the extent that the transferable securities concerned are admitted to trading on a market of a member state. In any event, each member state shall regard a transaction carried out within its territory, if it is carried out on a market as defined in article 1, paragraph 2, situated or operating within that territory.

In accordance with article 6 each member state may adopt provisions more stringent than those laid down by this directive or additional provisions, provided that such provisions are applied generally. In particular it may extend the scope of the prohibition laid down in article 2 and impose on persons referred to in article 4 the prohibitions laid down in article 3.

Finally, the directive provides that each member state shall determine the penalties to be applied for infringement of the measures taken pursuant to this directive. These penalties shall be sufficiently severe to promote compliance with those measures.

The date of implementation of this directive is June 1, 1992.

4.5 European code of conduct relating to transactions in transferable securities

X COMMISSION RECOMMENDATION OF JULY 25, 1977 CONCERNING A EUROPEAN CODE OF CONDUCT RELATING TO TRANSACTIONS IN TRANSFERABLE SECURITIES

(OJEC L 212 20.8.1977, recommendation 77/534/EEC)

THE RECOMMENDATION WAS RECTIFIED IN 1977

(OJEC L 294 18.11.1977)

The European code of conduct for transactions in transferable securities formulates a number of principles, already very widely recognised in all European countries, concerning the handling of securities transactions. This constitutes an attempt by the Commission to create a common set of professional ethics capable of considerably facilitating the process of harmonisation through directives.

The European code of conduct comprises the following principles:

Objectives

This code of conduct is to be seen in the general context of the development and integration of securities markets within the European Community, and seeks to establish certain general principles, supported by supplementary guidelines.

The objective of the code is to establish standards of ethical behaviour on a Community wide basis, so as to promote the effective functioning of securities markets (i.e. by creating the best possible conditions for matching the supply of and demand for capital), and to safeguard the public interest.

Definitions

In the code, the following expressions shall have the meaning ascribed to them below:
- *transferable securities*: all securities which are or may be the subject of dealings on an organised market.
- *financial intermediaries*: all persons professionally concerned in transactions in transferable securities.
- *principals*: all persons who issue orders to buy or sell securities, namely those occupying a strategic position with regard to a security and the market in it (e.g. company directors or managers, holders or buyers of major shareholdings) and all those who are in a position to influence public opinion (e.g. financial analysts and journalists).
- *securities markets*: the official stock exchange and all the markets organised by or under the supervision of the competent authorities and also all transactions in transferable securities as defined above including privately negotiated dealings between individuals in transferable securities - the word market (in the singular) being used only for the official stock exchange and the organised markets.
- *competent authorities* are those who have the task of ensuring the proper working of the market and the proper flow of information for the market at national level, principally the stock exchange authorities and supervisory agents.

General principles

1 The objective of this code and the general principle should be observed even in cases not expressly covered by supplementary principles. Every transaction carried out on the securities markets should be in conformity with not only the letter but also the spirit of the laws and regulations in force in each member state, and also the principles of good conduct already applying to these markets, or recommended by this code.

2 Information should be available to the public which is fair, accurate, clear, adequate and which is given in good time. The information should be provided in such a way that its significance and intent can be easily understood. Any person, who by virtue of his profession or duties has the duty or the means of informing the public, is under a special obligation to ensure that it is kept properly informed, and that no particular class of persons attains a privileged position.

3 Equality of treatment should be guaranteed to all holders of securities of the same type issued by the same company, in particular, any act resulting directly or indirectly in the transfer of a holding conferring *de jure* or *de facto* control of a company whose securities are dealt in on the market, should have regard to the right of all shareholders to equal treatment.

4 When the securities of a company are dealt in on the market, the members of its supervisory board, its directors, managers, and persons exercising *de jure* or *de facto* control, should act in such manner as to ensure that the fundamental objective of this code of conduct is realised. They have a particular duty to avoid any action which would operate to the detriment of fair dealing in the securities concerned, or prejudice the rights of other shareholders.

5 Persons dealing regularly on the securities markets should act fairly in accordance with the code's objective, even if this could in certain cases result in their having to forgo short-term gain.

6 Financial intermediaries should endeavour to avoid all conflicts of interest, whether as between themselves and their clients or other persons with whom they have a fiduciary relationship, or as between these two last-mentioned categories of persons. If, however, such a conflict arises, they should not seek to gain a direct or indirect personal advantage from the situation, and should avoid any prejudice to their clients or other persons with whom they have a fiduciary relationship.

Supplementary provisions

1 All persons dealing regularly on the securities markets have a duty to promote investors' confidence in the fairness of the market by observance of the best standards of commercial probity and professional conduct.

2 Financial intermediaries have a special responsibility to observe the fundamental objective and the general principles of this code of conduct.

In particular, they should not connive at any breach by other persons of the provisions and principles referred to in the second paragraph of general principle 1, and they should not engage in manipulation which could distort the normal operation of the market.

3 No person should incite another person, whether or not an intermediary, to contravene the provisions and principles referred to in the second paragraph of general principle 1, nor exert pressure to obtain:

1 information which is not public and which cannot be divulged without contravening rules relating to such information, or

2 the carrying out of an irregular or dishonest transaction.

4 Financial intermediaries should seek out and recommend the best conditions for their clients for the execution of orders which are given to them, while observing the fundamental objective and general principles of the code.

They should execute the orders which they are given on an organised market, unless the principal has given express instructions to the contrary. However, if circumstances of the transaction or the nature of the securities make it difficult or even impossible to execute orders on an organised market, financial intermediaries may act as counterparties to their clients or offset orders outside the market, provided that they ensure that this does not prejudice their clients' interests, and provided that they are in a position to reply to any request on the part of the competent authorities as regards the justification for, the number of, and the conditions applying to, transactions carried out in this manner.

5 Financial intermediaries should refrain from encouraging sales or purchases with the sole object of generating commission.

6 Financial intermediaries should not disclose the identity of their principals except in cases where this is required by national regulations or the control authorities (and also in the investigation of crimes or other serious misdeeds).

7 Any attempt or manipulation by persons acting separately or in concert with others, which claims at or results in the rise or fall in the price of securities by fraudulent means, is contrary to the fundamental objective of this code.

Fraudulent means are considered in particular to be the publication or diffusion of information which is false, exaggerated or tendentious, and also the use of other devices aimed at disrupting the markets' normal operation.

Financial intermediaries and members of the supervisory board, the directors and managers of companies whose securities are dealt in on the securities markets, who become aware of any such attempt or manipulation should endeavour to take the necessary steps to thwart it. They should inform the competent authorities and the companies concerned without delay.

8 Financial intermediaries should endeavour to keep secret, even as between different departments or services of the same organisation, information which they acquire in the course of carrying out their duties which is not yet public and which is price-sensitive.

In particular financial intermediaries should not use such information in transactions which they carry out for their own account on the securities markets, nor in transactions upon which they advise their clients or carry out for their account.

9 Any person who comes into possession of information, in exercising his profession or carrying out his duties, which is not public and which relates to a company or to the market in its securities or to any event of general interest to the market, which is price-sensitive, should

refrain from carrying out, directly or indirectly, any transaction in which such information is used, and should refrain from giving the information to another person so that he may profit from it before the information becomes public.

10 Securities markets should be sufficiently open to prevent their being fragmented, whereby the same security can be dealt in at the same time on different markets at different prices.

11 When a security is dealt in on the market the public should be informed not only of the different prices at which transactions take place, but also of the volume of dealings, unless the organisation of the market makes it possible for the public to assess the liquidity of its investment by some other means.

12 Every company whose securities are dealt in on the market should publish periodically, and at least every six months, information which is clear, precise, complete and up-to-date concerning its business operations, results, and financial position. Any fact or important decision capable of having an appreciable effect on the price of securities should also be made public without delay.

13 When a fact or important decision, referred to in the preceding provision, cannot be made public without delay, for example because certain formalities have not yet been completed or because the company would be seriously prejudiced as a result, but the company nevertheless considers that there is a risk of leaks, the company should inform the competent authorities of the position. The latter should take the necessary steps to safeguard the markets' proper operation until the relevant fact or disclosure can be made public. In particular they may, if this step appears unavoidable, suspend transactions for the necessary period.

14 It is desirable that a public issue of securities should be preceded by the publication of a prospectus. The existence of the prospectus and the place or places where it may be obtained should be indicated in any publicity concerning such issue.

15 No investor or group of investors should be given more favourable treatment as regards information than other investors or the public. All investors should have free access to information.

16 On the occasion of each issue of securities of the same type that are or may be dealt in on several markets at the same time, the issuer should endeavour not to give more favourable treatment to one market than to another.

17 Any transaction resulting in the transfer of a holding conferring control in the sense referred to in general principle 3 should not be carried out in a surreptitious fashion without informing the other shareholders and the market control authorities.

It is desirable that all the shareholders of the company whose control has changed hands should be offered the opportunity of disposing of their securities on identical conditions, unless they have the benefit of alternative safeguards which can be regarded as equivalent.

18 Any acquisition, or attempted acquisition on the market, separately or by concerted action, of a holding conferring control in the sense referred to in general principle 3, without informing the public, is against the objective of the code.

4.6 Coordination of undertakings for collective investment in transferable securities

XI COUNCIL DIRECTIVE OF DECEMBER 20, 1985 ON THE COORDINATION OF LAWS, REGULATIONS AND ADMINISTRATIVE PROVISIONS RELATING TO UNDERTAKINGS FOR COLLECTIVE INVESTMENT IN TRANSFERABLE SECURITIES (UCITS)

(OJEC L 375 31.12.1985, directive 85/611/EEC)

XII COUNCIL RECOMMENDATION OF DECEMBER 20, 1985 CONCERNING THE SECOND SUBPARAGRAPH OF ARTICLE 25, PARAGRAPH 1 OF DIRECTIVE 85/611/EEC
(OJEC L 375 31.12.1985, recommendation 85/612/EEC)

The laws of the member states relating to undertakings for collective investment in transferable securities (UCITS) differ significantly from one state to another, particularly as regards the obligations and controls which are imposed on such undertakings. These differences distort the conditions of competition between those undertakings and do not ensure equivalent protection for unit-holders. The objective of this directive is to end this undesirable situation by determining basic rules concerning the authorisation, supervision, structure, activities and the information to be published. This directive can be considered as the first phase in a coordination process comprising several phases. In this first phase coordination will be confined, inter alia, to UCITS that are not of the closed-end type. Provisions for UCITS to which this directive does not apply give rise to different problems for which different provisions will be necessary. Coordination of such undertakings will take place at a later stage.
The directive is discussed in summary below.

Articles 1 to 3 give a number of general provisions:
a The member states shall apply this directive to undertakings for collective investment in transferable securities (UCITS) situated within their territories.
b For the purpose of this directive, and subject to the provisions below, UCITS shall be undertakings:
  - the sole object of which is the collective investment in transferable securities of capital raised from the public and which operate on the principle of risk-spreading, and
  - the units of which are, at the request of the holders, repurchased or redeemed, directly or indirectly, out of those undertakings' assets. Actions take by a UCITS to ensure that the stock exchange value of its units does not significantly vary from their net asset value shall be regarded as equivalent to such repurchase or redemption.
c The directive in question does not apply to:
  - UCITS of the closed-end type;
  - UCITS which raise capital without promoting the sale of their units to the public within the Community or any part of it;
  - UCITS the units of which, under the fund rules or the investment company's instruments of incorporation, may be sold only to the public in non-member countries;
  - categories of UCITS prescribed by the regulations of the member states in which such UCITS are situated, for which the rules are laid down in section V (articles 19-26) and in article 36 are inappropriate in view of their investment and borrowing policies.
d UCITS may be constituted according to law, either under the law of contract (as common funds managed by management companies) or trust law (as unit trusts) or under statute (as investment companies). For the purpose of this directive 'common funds' shall also include unit trusts.
e Investment companies the assets of which are invested through the intermediary of subsidiary companies mainly otherwise than in transferable securities shall not be subject to this directive.

The conditions for authorisation of UCITS are prescribed in article 4.

To carry on its activities a UCITS must be authorised by the competent authorities of the member state where it is situated. A unit trust shall be authorised only if the competent authorities have approved the management company, the fund rules and the choice of depositary. An investment company shall be authorised only if the competent authorities have approved both its instruments of incorporation and the choice of depositary.

Subsequently the obligations of UCITS are dealt with. The following categories are concerned:
- obligations regarding the structure of unit trusts;
- obligations regarding the structure of investment companies and their depositaries;
- obligations concerning the investment policies of UCITS;
- obligations concerning information to be supplied to unit holders;
- the general obligations of UCITS.

Article 25 paragraph 1 contains an important provision concerning the investment policy of UCITS. An investment company or a management company acting in connection with all of the unit trusts which it manages and which fall within the scope of this directive may not acquire shares carrying voting rights which would enable it to exercise significant influence over the management of an issuing body. Pending further coordination, the member states shall take account of existing rules defining the concept 'significant influence' under other member states' legislation.

In the recommendation supplemental to this directive the Council recommends that each time the concept of 'significant influence' is represented in another member state's legislation by a numerical limit, the member state's competent authorities should ensure, if so requested by that other member state, that such limits are observed by investment and management companies situated within its territory when they acquire shares carrying voting rights issued by a company established within the territory of a member state where such limits apply.

In articles 44-48 attention is given to the special provisions applicable to UCITS which market their units in member states other than those in which they are situated. Article 46 comprises the key aspects: If a UCITS proposes to market its units in a member state other than that in which it is situated, it must first inform the competent authorities and the authorities of that other member state accordingly. It must simultaneously send the latter authorities:
- an attestation by the competent authorities to the effect that it fulfils the conditions imposed by this directive,
- its fund rules or its instruments of incorporation,
- its prospectus,
- where appropriate, its latest annual report and any subsequent half-yearly report and
- details of the arrangements made for the marketing of its units in that other member state.

A UCITS may begin to market its units in that other member state two months after such communication unless the authorities of the member state concerned establish, in a reasoned decision taken before the expiry of that period of two months, that the arrangements made for the marketing of units do not comply with the provisions referred to in article 44, paragraph 1 and article 45.

Said article 44, paragraph 1 states that a UCITS which markets its units in another member state must comply with the laws, regulations and administrative provisions in force in that state which do not fall within the field governed in this directive. Under article 45 a UCITS must, with due regard for the laws, regulations and administrative provisions in the member state in which the shares will be marketed, take the necessary measures so that distributions to unit-holders, the repurchase or redemption of the units and the distribution of the information to be provided by the UCITS are ensured.

The authorities of the state in which a UCITS is situated shall be competent to supervise that UCITS. However, the authorities of the state in which a UCITS markets its units shall be competent to supervise compliance with the provisions referred to above.

The member states shall bring into force no later than October 1, 1989 the measures necessary for them to comply with this directive. Greece and Portugal shall be authorised to postpone the implementation of this directive until April 1, 1992 at the latest.

XIII COUNCIL DIRECTIVE OF MARCH 22, 1988 AMENDING, AS REGARDS THE INVESTMENT POLICIES OF CERTAIN UCITS, DIRECTIVE 85/611/EEC ON THE COORDINATION OF LAWS, REGULATIONS AND ADMINISTRATIVE PROVISIONS RELATING TO UNDERTAKINGS FOR COLLECTIVE INVESTMENT IN TRANSFERABLE SECURITIES (UCITS)

(OJEC L 100 19.4.1988, directive 88/220/EEC)

This directive further specifies the percentage of its own assets that a UCITS may invest in transferable securities from the same issuer.

V. INSURANCE COMPANIES

5.1 The insurance market in 1994

The internal market in 1994 or later in the 1990s (see XI and XXVII) for insurance companies is being achieved by three means: the liberalisation of insurance capital, free establishment of insurance companies and free provision of services by insurance companies. The movement of capital has to be liberalised by July 1, 1990 in most member states. Spain, Portugal, Greece and Ireland have the option to postpone this date for a number of years. This chapter discusses Community regulations concerning freedom of establishment and of provision of services by insurance companies. The legislation in this area is based inter alia on articles 52-58 (freedom of establishment and 59-66 (freedom to provide services) of the EEC Treaty.

In the discussion of the regulations concerning establishment and the provision of services a main division will be made into two categories. Firstly the category 'establishment and the provision of services in the narrow sense', dealing with the EEC provisions relating to the abolition of restrictions on the freedom of establishment and the freedom to provide services, will be discussed. Secondly the coordinating provisions will be dealt with. The objective of these provisions is not the abolition of the restrictions on freedom of establishment and to provide services, but the coordination of the regulations with which insurance undertakings must comply. The coordinating provisions therefore facilitate the exercise of the freedoms of establishment and the provision of services.

In the insurance legislation two *forms* of insurance are distinguished: non-life insurance (divided into a number of classes such as motor vehicle insurance, credit and suretyship insurance, legal expenses insurance, etc.) and life assurance. In addition, three insurance *techniques* are distinguished:

- Direct insurance.

  The insurance company with which the insurance is contracted covers in full the accepted risk.
- Re-insurance.

  The insurance is contracted with one insurance company, which then reinsures part of the accepted risk with other insurance companies. The former company remains fully liable to the insured person for the sum insured. In the case of payment to the insured person this insurance company can recover part of that amount from the other insurance companies with which it re-insured part of the risk.
- Co-insurance.

  The insurance agreement is simultaneously concluded with several insurance companies. The policy is signed by the various co-insurers and indicates the amount for which each co-insurer is liable.

To separate clearly the Community regulations relating to forms of insurance and insurance techniques, the directives concerning non-life insurance and life assurance always relate to direct insurance. The more complicated insurance techniques such as re-insurance and co-insurance are dealt with in separate directives.

5.2 Establishment and provision of services in the narrow sense

I GENERAL PROGRAMME ON THE ABOLITION OF RESTRICTIONS ON FREEDOM TO PROVIDE SERVICES
(OJEC 32/62 15.1.1962)

II GENERAL PROGRAMME ON THE ABOLITION OF RESTRICTIONS ON FREEDOM OF ESTABLISHMENT
(OJEC 36/62 15.1.1962)

Under articles 52 and 59 of the EEC Treaty the restrictions concerning the freedom of establishment and the freedom to provide services are to be abolished gradually (in a number of stages) during the transitional period until 1970. Article 54, paragraph 1 and article 63, paragraph 1, provide that the Council, in the context of the date of January 1, 1970, must draft programmes for the abolition of restrictions existing within the Community on the freedom of establishment and the freedom to provide services. This resulted in the two programmes referred to above.

As far as the services are concerned it can be remarked that the general programme in question makes a distinction between services within the meaning of article 60 of the EEC Treaty and those other than within the meaning of this article. Article 60 states that activities considered as services are those service activities normally charged for, in so far as the provisions relating to the freedom of movement of goods, capital and persons do not apply to such activities. As far as the liberalisation of services provided by banks and insurance companies involving capital movements, this provision is elaborated in article 61, paragraph 2. This article states that said liberalisation must be achieved in accordance with the gradual liberalisation of capital movements. In conformity with the latter Treaty provision the general programme on services stipulates that services involving capital movements must be liberalised in line with the liberalisation of capital movements. Services which do not involve capital movements are covered by the timetable for the abolition of restrictions by January 1, 1970. Both general programmes contain such a timetable, which divides the transitional period until January 1, 1970 into a number of stages. In this context article 54, paragraph 2 and article 63, paragraph 2, of the EEC Treaty provide that the Council can adopt directives in order to execute the general programmes or a stage thereof.

The Council has adopted two directives for the purpose of implementation of the programmes concerning insurance undertakings. One relates to reinsurance and retrocession (1964), the other relates to non-life insurance (1973). Both will be discussed below.

III COUNCIL DIRECTIVE OF FEBRUARY 25, 1964 ABOLISHING RESTRICTIONS ON FREEDOM OF ESTABLISHMENT AND THE FREEDOM TO PROVIDE SERVICES IN THE BUSINESS OF RE-INSURANCE AND RETROCESSION
(OJEC 878/64 4.4.1964, directive 64/225/EEC)

This directive liberalises all sectors of the re-insurance business, with respect both to establishment and to the provision of services. Where the business of re-insurance is performed by so-called mixed undertakings, which carry out direct insurance as well as re-insurance and retrocession, such mixed undertakings fall within the scope of this directive for the part of their activities relating to re-insurance and retrocession.

IV COUNCIL DIRECTIVE OF JULY 24, 1973 ABOLISHING RESTRICTIONS ON FREEDOM OF ESTABLISHMENT IN THE BUSINESS OF DIRECT INSURANCE OTHER THAN LIFE ASSURANCE

(OJEC L 228 16.8.1973, directive 73/240/EEC)

Under this directive member states will abolish restrictions which:
- prevent beneficiaries from establishing themselves in the host country under the same conditions and with the same rights as nationals of that country;
- exist by reason of administrative practices which result in treatment being applied to beneficiaries that is discriminatory by comparison with that applied to nationals.

In 1974, the European Court of Justice handed down two important judgements in the Reyners and Van Binsbergen cases, in which it held that the freedom of establishment and the freedom to provide services entrenched in the EEC Treaty had been directly enforceable since the end of the transitional period on December 21, 1969. As a result of these judgements, the Treaty provisions on the freedom of establishment (articles 52-58) and the provision of services (articles 59-66) became directly applicable. The directives, discussed above, abolishing the restrictions on re-insurance and non-life insurance became largely redundant as a result of these judgements. Only insurance services relating to capital movements are not covered by the direct applicability of the Treaty, since they are liberalised in accordance with the gradual liberalisation of capital movements.

In spite of the judgements of the Court, directives remain necessary. Their function now is no longer the elaboration of the treaty provisions on establishment and provision of services but rather to facilitate the exercise of the freedom of establishment and the freedom to provide services which have been directly applicable since the end of the transitional period. Coordination directives are very important for this purpose.

Coordination of the freedom of establishment was achieved by the first coordination directive on insurance other than life assurance of July 24, 1973 and by the first coordination directive on life assurance of March 5, 1979 (these two directives will be discussed below). The second Council directive on coordination of direct insurance other than life assurance was adopted on June 22, 1988 and concerns the freedom to provide services for large industrial, commercial and professional risks. The Council adopted the second life assurance directive on November 8, 1990. Complete liberalisation in the field of establishment and the provision of services by insurance companies is to be achieved by the third non-life insurance directive (amended proposal of February 24, 1992) and the third life assurance directive (proposal of February 25, 1991).

Recent progress concerning the freedom of insurance and life assurance undertakings to provide services was strongly advanced by two judgements of the European Court of Justice: Cassis de Dijon (February 20, 1979) and the four insurance judgements (December 4, 1986)

The first case concerns Rewe Zentral AG (a West German undertaking) versus the German government. Rewe Zentral wanted to import into West Germany Crème de Cassis, a liqueur which is also known as Cassis de Dijon. The West German government prohibited this since, by West German standards, the liqueur did not contain enough alcohol to be sold as a liqueur. The Court decided otherwise. The Germans did not have the right to prohibit the import of a liqueur which is freely available in the member state of origin (France) unless reasons of health, tax, fair competition or the protection of consumers could be advanced. The German government could not do so and had to allow importation. In fact the Cassis de Dijon judgement established the principle of mutual recognition: the French legislation relating to liqueur is equivalent to the German legislation; the French having recognised Cassis de Dijon as a liqueur. The principles of minimum harmonisation and supervision by the home country, together with the principle of mutual recognition thus established, form the three fundamental principles of the Single European Act of

1986. Pursuant to the above, the Commission attempted to have the Cassis de Dijon approach with its principle of mutual recognition applied to the freedom of provision of services by insurance undertakings. For this purpose the Commission filed legal procedures at the European Court against France, West Germany, Ireland and Denmark in connection with incorrect application by these four member states of the directive on Community co-insurance of May 30, 1978 (discussed below). The national laws of the said four states required foreign insurers to be established or authorised in the host member state in order to be allowed to provide services in the member state concerned. Freedom to provide services from the state where the insurer is established and authorised was not possible since the host member state did not recognise the insurance laws in the home member state as equivalent.

On December 4, 1986 the Court handed down the so-called four insurance judgements. The Court made a distinction between two cases. In the case of co-insurance the Court's opinion that the requirement to be established or authorised in the host state was inconsistent with Community law. In the case of co-insurance, the insurance of large industrial, commercial and professional risks are concerned, where the insured person or policy-holder is a sufficiently significant market party to be able to form an opinion of the quality and reliability of the foreign insurer. This is not the case with direct insurance. Here insurance for the general public is concerned, where that public is much less likely to be able to judge the quality and reliability of the foreign insurer. For this reason the Court is of the opinion that, in the case of such consumer insurance to cover mass risks, member states may bind foreign insurers to authorisation though not to a requirement of establishment, where this is necessary in order to protect the interests of consumers. The court did not give judgement about the intermediate case of direct insurance of industrial, commercial and professional risks. In view of the nature of direct insurance, a single insurer covers the total risk, while in the case of co-insurance the total risk is shared by several insurers. It is therefore plausible to assume that the total risk in the case of direct insurance of industrial, commercial and professional risks will be less than in the case of co-insurance of the same risks. Here lies the ambivalence of direct insurance of industrial, commercial and professional risks: the element of 'industrial, commercial and professional risks' seems to refer to co-insurance, while the element of 'direct insurance' refers to consumer insurance. In short the judgement of the Court concerning the four insurance judgements amounts to the following:

1	co-insurance + large industrial, commercial and professional risks	free provision of services across borders by foreign insurers
2	direct insurance + small industrial, commercial and professional risks	unclear whether the provision of services can be bound by a requirement for authorisation
3	direct insurance + mass risks	the provision of services can be bound by a requirement for authorisation

The above shows that there is a need for coordination directives in the field of insurance. The coordinating EC regulations relating to insurance will be dealt with in more detail below.

5.3 Coordination of non-life insurance

V FIRST COUNCIL DIRECTIVE OF JULY 24, 1973 ON THE COORDINATION OF LAWS, REGULATIONS AND ADMINISTRATIVE PROVISIONS RELATING TO THE TAKING-UP AND PURSUIT OF THE BUSINESS OF DIRECT INSURANCE OTHER THAN LIFE ASSURANCE

(OJEC L 228 16.8.1973, directive 73/239/EEC)

THE DIRECTIVE WAS RECTIFIED IN 1978

(OJEC L 5 7.1.1978)

This directive is also known as the first coordination directive for non-life insurance. The objective of the directive is, by means of coordination of the conditions for the taking-up and pursuit of the business of non-life insurance, to facilitate the effective exercise of the freedom of establishment, which, by virtue of the Reyners and Van Binsbergen judgements, is directly applicable. The exercise of the freedom to provide services does not fall within the scope of this directive. As we will see below, coordination relating to the freedom to provide services is achieved by the second coordination directive on non-life insurance of June 22, 1988 and by the proposed third non-life directive.

The first coordination directive foresees a need for subsequent coordination with regard to certain classes of insurance. This is due to the fact that the various national laws contain different rules regarding the simultaneous undertaking of health insurance, credit and suretyship insurance and insurance in respect of recourse against third parties and legal defence, whether with one another or with other classes of insurance. The problem is that continuance of this divergence after the abolition of the restrictions on the freedom of establishment would mean that obstacles to the freedom of establishment would continue to exist. Further coordination in these areas is therefore needed in order to resolve this problem. With regard to credit and suretyship insurance and with regard to recourse against third parties and legal defence insurance this coordination has been achieved through the adoption by the Council of two directives on June 22 1987 (to be discussed below). Health insurance is still at a very premature stage of Community legislation: as yet there has not even been a proposal for a directive; only draft documents are in circulation. Finally the first coordination directive has been supplemented with a directive relating to tourist assistance (December 10, 1984).

The first coordination directive on non-life insurance, to be discussed here, makes the taking-up of the business of direct insurance subject to authorisation. In addition to extensive provisions for the conditions for authorisation, the directive introduces provisions relating to the supervision of the financial position of authorised insurance undertakings. In this context three concepts are important, the technical reserve, the solvency margin and the minimum guarantee fund. Insurance undertakings are required to establish a technical reserve in order to meet their commitments. The solvency margin corresponds to the assets, free of all foreseeable liabilities, less any intangible items. It is required to withstand the uncertainties of the business. The solvency margin must bear a specific relationship to the undertakings' activities and shall be determined on the basis of either the annual amount of premiums or contributions, or of the annual burden of claims. This ensures that the requirements are determined according to objective standards, offering undertakings of equivalent size identical competitive conditions. To ensure that insurance undertakings possess adequate resources when they are set up and to prevent the solvency margin from falling below a minimum security level during the course of business, a minimum guarantee fund is required. The amount of this fund must be in relationship to size of the risk in the classes undertaken.

By virtue of article 1 this directive relates to the taking-up and pursuit of the self-employed activity of direct insurance carried on by insurance undertakings which are established in a member state or which wish to become established there in the classes of insurance defined in the annex to this directive.

ANNEX

A Classification of risks according to classes of insurance

1 *Accidents* (including industrial injury and occupational diseases)
- fixed pecuniary benefits
- benefits in the nature of indemnity
- combinations of the two
- injury to passengers

2 *Sickness*
- fixed pecuniary benefits
- benefits in the nature of indemnity
- combinations of the two

3 *Land vehicles* (other than railway rolling stock)
All damages to or loss of:
- land motor vehicles
- land vehicles other than motor vehicles

4 *Railway rolling stock*
All damage to or loss of railway rolling stock

5 *Aircraft*
All damage to or loss of aircraft

6 *Ships (sea, lake and river and canal vessels)*
All damage to or loss of:
- river and canal vessels
- lake vessels
- sea vessels

7 *Goods in transit* (including merchandise, baggage and all other goods)
All damage to or loss of goods in transit or baggage, irrespective of the form of transport

8 *Fire and natural forces*
All damage to or loss of property (other than property included in classes 3, 4, 5, 6 and 7) due to
- fire
- explosion
- storm
- natural forces other than storm
- nuclear energy
- land subsidence

9 *Other damages to property*
All damage to or loss of property (other than property included in classes 3, 4, 5, 6 and 7) due to hail or frost, and any event such as theft, other than those mentioned under 8

10 *Motor vehicle liability*
All liability arising out of the use of motor vehicles operating on the land (including carrier's liability)

11 *Aircraft liability*
All liability arising out of the use of aircraft (including carrier's liability)

12 *Liability for ships (sea, land and river and canal vessels)*
All liability arising out of the use of ships, vessels or boats on the sea, lakes, rivers or canals (including carrier's liability)

13 *General liability*
All liability other than those forms mentioned under 10, 11 and 12

14 *Credit*
- insolvency (general)
- export credit
- instalment credit
- mortgages
- agricultural credit

15 *Suretyship*
- suretyship (direct)
- suretyship (indirect)

16 *Miscellaneous financial loss*
- employment risks
- insufficiency of income (general)
- bad weather
- loss of benefits
- continuing general expenses
- unforeseen trading expenses
- loss of market value
- loss of rent or revenue
- indirect trading losses other than those mentioned above
- other financial loss (non-trading)
- other forms of financial loss

17 *Legal expenses*
Legal expenses and costs of litigation

The risks included in a class may not be included in any other class except in the cases referred to in point C.

B Description of authorisations granted for more than one class of insurance

Where the authorisation simultaneously covers:
a Classes Nos 1 and 2, it shall be named 'Accident and Health Insurance';
b Classes Nos 1 (fourth indent), 3,7 and 10, it shall be named 'Motor Insurance';
c Classes Nos 1 (fourth indent), 4, 6, 7 and 12, it shall be named 'Marine and Transport Insurance';
d Classes Nos 1 (fourth indent), 5, 7 and 11, it shall be named 'Aviation Insurance';
e Classes Nos 8 and 9, it shall be named 'Insurance against Fire and other Damage to Property';
f Classes Nos 10, 11, 12 and 13, it shall be named 'Liability Insurance';
g Classes Nos 14 and 15, it shall be named 'Credit and Suretyship Insurance';
h All classes, it shall be named at the choice of the member state in question, which shall notify the other member states and the Commission of its choice.

C Ancillary risks

An undertaking obtaining an authorisation for a principal risk belonging to one class or a group of classes may also insure risks included in another class without an authorisation being necessary for them if they:

- are connected with the principal risk,
- concern the object which is covered against the principal risk,
- are covered by the contract insuring the principal risk.

However, the risks included in classes 14 and 15 in point A of the annex may not be regarded as risks ancillary to other classes.

By virtue of article 2 the directive does not apply to:

1 The following kinds of insurance:
  a Life assurance, that is to say, the branch of insurance which comprises, in particular, assurance on survival to a stipulated age only, assurance on death only, assurance on survival to a stipulated age or an earlier death, life assurance with return of premiums, tontines, marriage assurance, and birth assurance;
  b Annuities;
  c Supplementary insurance carried on by life-assurance undertakings, that is to say, insurance against personal injury including incapacity for employment, insurance against death resulting from an accident, and insurance against disability resulting from an accident or sickness, where the various kinds of insurance are underwritten in addition to life assurance;
  d Insurance forming part of a statutory system of social security;
  e The type of insurance existing in Ireland and the United Kingdom known as 'permanent health insurance not subject to cancellation'.
2 The following operations:
  a Capital redemption operations, as defined by the law in each member state;
  b Operations of provident and mutual benefit institutions whose benefits vary according to the resources available and in which the contributions of the members are determined on a flat-rate basis;
  c Operations carried out by organisations not having a legal personality with the purpose of providing mutual cover for their members without there being any payment of premiums or constitution of technical services;
  d Pending further coordination, which shall be implemented within four years of notification of this directive, export credit insurance operations for the account of or with the support of the state.

Article 3 determines that the directive does not apply to mutual associations in so far as they fulfil all the following conditions:

- the articles of association must contain provisions for calling up additional contributions or reducing their benefits,
- their business does not cover liability risks - unless the latter constitute ancillary cover within the meaning of subparagraph C of the annex - or credit and suretyship risks,
- the annual contribution income for the activities covered by this directive must not exceed one million units of account,
- at least half of the contribution income from the activities covered by this directive must come from persons who are members of the mutual association.

This directive does not, moreover, apply to mutual associations which have concluded with other associations of this nature an agreement which provides for the full reinsurance of the insurance policies issued by them or under which the concessionary undertaking is to meet the liabilities arising under such policies in the place of the ceding undertaking. In such a case the concessionary undertaking shall be subject to the rules of this directive.

The directive continues with provisions relating to the conditions of admission, conditions for exercise of business and the withdrawal of authorisation. In broad outline these conditions correspond with the conditions for life assurance undertakings. For that reason these conditions will be discussed under XXV below (first coordination directive on life assurance).

VI COUNCIL DIRECTIVE OF JUNE 29, 1976 AMENDING DIRECTIVE 73/239/EEC ON THE COORDINATION OF LAWS, REGULATIONS AND ADMINISTRATIVE PROVISIONS RELATING TO THE TAKING UP AND PURSUIT OF THE BUSINESS OF DIRECT INSURANCE OTHER THAN LIFE ASSURANCE

(OJEC L 189 13.7.1976, directive 76/580/EEC)

Directive 73/239/EEC deals with amounts expressed in units of account used for the calculation of quantities such as the solvency margin and the minimum guarantee fund. In article 5 these units of account are defined as 'that unit which is defined in article 4 of the statute of the European Investment Bank'. This unit had the same value as the gold parity of the US dollar, fixed at 0.88867088 grammes of fine gold. However, because of this link to the US dollar, the conversion of these amounts into national currencies can lead to distortion of competition between undertakings whose head offices are situated in the various member states. By decision 75/250/EEC of April 21, 1975, the Council defined a European unit of account (EUA) which reflects the average development in the value of the currencies of the member states. The EUA can be considered as a weighted average of the national currencies, with the weights being calculated on the basis of economic indicators. The conversion rate for each currency against the EUA is determined automatically by reference to daily quotations on the exchange markets. The directive under review replaces the units of account referred to in directive 73/239/EEC by the European unit of account (EUA). Without further measures the introduction of the EUA would lead to a reduction in terms of national currency of the amounts expressed in the units of account in directive 73/239/EEC in some member states. For this reason the directive under review also provides that, until the first revision of the amounts expressed in directive 73/239/EEC in (European) units, the amounts expressed in national currency on the basis of the 'old' unit of account may not be lower than those converted on the basis of the new unit of account.

The European Monetary System (EMS) was established by resolution of the European Council on December 5, 1978. The European Currency Unit (ECU) plays an important part in the EMS. The ECU had the same value as the EUA. Since it is not functional to have two European units of account, the EUA was replaced by the ECU by Council regulation 3308/80 of December 16, 1980, for all Community decisions applicable at the moment of entry into force of the regulation.

VII COUNCIL DIRECTIVE OF DECEMBER 10, 1984 AMENDING, PARTICULARLY AS REGARDS TOURIST ASSISTANCE, THE FIRST DIRECTIVE (73/239/EEC) ON THE COORDINATION OF LAWS, REGULATIONS AND ADMINISTRATIVE PROVISIONS RELATING TO THE TAKING UP AND THE PURSUIT OF THE BUSINESS OF DIRECT INSURANCE OTHER THAN LIFE INSURANCE.

(OJEC L 339 27.12.1984, directive 84/641/EEC)

This directive has two functions:

- The inclusion, for supervisory reasons, of assistance operations, particularly tourist assistance operations, in the scope of the first directive.
- The inclusion of minor technical adaptations of a general tendency (not only concerning tourist assistance) into the first directive.

Article 1 of the first coordination directive is amended in such a way that the entire directive now applies to assistance activities as well. Assistance activities are defined as the assistance provided for persons who get into difficulties while travelling, while away from home or while away from their permanent residence. The class 'assistance' is added as class 18 in point A of the annex of the first directive (article 14 of the directive under review). Under article 15 any member state may, in its territory, make the provision of assistance to persons who get into difficulties in circumstances other than those referred to in article 1 subject to the arrangements introduced by the first directive. If a member state makes use of this possibility it shall, for the purposes of applying these arrangements, treat such activity as if it were listed in class 18 in point A of the annex to the first directive without prejudice to point C thereof relating to ancillary risks.

VIII COUNCIL DIRECTIVE OF JUNE 22, 1987 AMENDING, AS REGARDS CREDIT INSURANCE AND SURETYSHIP INSURANCE, FIRST DIRECTIVE 73/239/EEC ON THE COORDINATION OF LAWS, REGULATIONS AND ADMINISTRATIVE PROVISIONS RELATING TO THE TAKING-UP AND PURSUIT OF THE BUSINESS OF DIRECT INSURANCE OTHER THAN LIFE ASSURANCE

(OJEC L 185 4.7.1987, directive 87/343/EEC)

This directive amends the first coordination directive on non-life insurance with respect to export credit insurance (class 14), with respect to suretyship insurance (class 15) and with respect to other credit insurance (class 14).

Regarding *export credit insurance* the first coordination directive provides (article 2, paragraph 2d) that pending further coordination which was to be implemented within four years of notification of this directive, the directive does not apply to export credit insurance operations for the account of or with the support of the State. The directive under review of June 22, 1987 states that such operations should continue to be excluded from the scope of the first directive pending subsequent coordination (no period is mentioned). The reason for this is that the protection of insured persons normally provided by the first coordination directive is provided by the State itself where export credit operations are carried out for the account or with the guarantee of the State.

With respect to suretyship insurance and other credit insurance the first coordination directive states (article 7, paragraph 2c) that pending further coordination, which must be implemented within four years of notification of this (first) directive, the Federal Republic of Germany may maintain the provision prohibiting the simultaneous undertaking in its territory of health insurance, credit and suretyship insurance or insurance in respect of recourse against third parties and legal defence, either with one another or with other classes.

With respect to *suretyship insurance* the directive in question of June 22, 1987 provides for the total abolition of this specialisation requirement. This means that the simultaneous undertaking of suretyship insurance and other classes of insurances will become possible without supplementary financial guarantees. The reason for this is that the Council is of the opinion that the interests of insured persons are sufficiently safeguarded by the provisions of the first coordination directive. The specialisation requirement is also abolished in respect of credit insurance, though the directive of June 22, 1987 does now provide for supplementary guarantees, as follows:

- The establishment of an equalisation reserve for the purpose of offsetting any technical deficit or above-average claims ratio arising in that class for a financial year.

  The equalisation reserve must be calculated under the rules laid down by each member state, in accordance with one of the four methods set out in point D of the annex which shall be regarded as being equivalent. Member states may, however, exempt establishments from the obligation to set up an equalisation reserve for credit insurance business where the premiums or contributions receivable are less than 4% of the total premiums or contributions receivable by them and less than 2,500,000 ECU. It is also stipulated that the amount of the equalisation reserve must be disregarded for the purposes of calculating the solvency margin. The solvency margin is determined in relation to the average burden of claims. Due to the cyclical nature of the damages and losses covered by credit insurance, the latter is deemed equivalent to storm, hail and frost insurance, for the purpose of calculating the average burden of claims in the meaning of article 16, paragraph 2. This means that in the case of undertakings which primarily underwrite one or more of the risks of credit, storm, hail or frost the last seven financial years shall be taken as the reference period for the average burden of claims. If the insurance undertakings concerned do not primarily underwrite one or more of the risks of credit, storm, hail or frost, the solvency margin shall be determined on the basis of either the annual amount of premiums and contributions, or of the average burden of claims of the past three financial years.

- The increase of the amount of the minimum guarantee fund to 1.4 million ECU.

Member states are to take the measures necessary to comply with this directive by January 1, 1990.

ANNEX

D Methods of calculating the equalisation reserve for the credit insurance class

Method No 1

1 In respect of the risks included in the class of insurance in point A No 14 (hereafter referred to as 'credit insurance'), the undertaking shall set up an equalisation reserve to which shall be charged any technical deficit arising in that class for a financial year.
2 Such reserve shall in each financial year receive 75% of any technical surplus arising on credit insurance business, subject to a limit of 12% of the net premiums or contributions until the reserve has reached 150% of the highest annual amount of net premiums or contributions received during the previous five financial years.

Method No 2

1 In respect of the risks included in the class of insurance listed in point A No 14 (hereafter referred to as 'credit insurance'), the undertaking shall set up an equalisation reserve to which shall be charged any technical deficit arising in that class for a financial year.
2 The minimum amount of the equalisation reserve shall be 134% of the average of the premiums or contributions received annually during the previous five financial years after substraction of the cessions and addition of the reinsurance acceptances.
3 Such reserve shall in each of the successive financial years receive 75% of any technical surplus arising in that class until the reserve is at least equal to the minimum calculated in accordance with paragraph 2.
4 Member states may lay down special rules for the calculation of the amount of the reserve and/or the amount of the annual levy in excess of the minimum amounts laid down in this directive.

Method No 3

1 An equalisation reserve shall be formed for class 14 in point A (hereafter referred to as 'credit insurance'), for the purpose of offsetting any above-average claims ratio for a financial year in that class of insurance.
2 The equalisation reserve shall be calculated on the basis of the method set out below:

All calculations shall relate to income and expenditure for the insurer's own account.

An amount in respect of any claims shortfall for each financial year shall be placed to the equalisation reserve until it has reached, or is restored to, the required amount.

There shall be deemed to be a claims shortfall if the claims ratio for a financial year is lower than the average claims ratio for the reference period. The amount in respect of the claims shortfall shall be arrived at by multiplying the difference between the two ratios by the earned premiums for the financial year.

The required amount shall be equal to six times the standard deviation of the claims ratio in the reference period from the average claims ratio, multiplied by the earned premiums for the financial year.

Where the claims for any financial year are in excess, an amount in respect thereof shall be taken from the equalisation reserve. Claims shall be deemed to be in excess if the claims ratio for the financial year is higher than the average claims ratio. The amount in respect of the excess claims shall be arrived at by multiplying the difference between the two ratios by the earned premiums for the financial year.

Irrespective of claims experience, 3.5% of the required amount of the equalisation reserve shall be first placed to that reserve each financial year until its required amount has been reached or restored.

The length of the reference period shall not be less than 15 years and not more than 30 years. No equalisation reserve need be formed if no underwriting loss has been noted during the reference period.

The required amount of the equalisation reserve and the amount to be taken from it may be reduced if the average claims ratio for the reference period in conjunction with the expenses ratio show that the premiums include a safety margin.

Method No 4

1 An equalisation reserve shall be formed for class 14 in point A (hereafter referred to as 'credit insurance'), for the purpose of offsetting any above-average claims ratio for a financial year in that class of insurance.
2 The equalisation reserve shall be calculated on the basis of the method set out below:

All calculations shall relate to income and expenditure for the insurer's own account.

An amount in respect of any claims shortfall for each financial year shall be placed to the equalisation reserve until it has reached the maximum required amount.

There shall be deemed to be a claims shortfall if the claims ratio for a financial year is lower than the average claims ratio for the reference period. The amount in respect of the claims shortfall shall be arrived at by multiplying the difference between the two ratios by the earned premiums for the financial year.

The maximum required amount shall be six times the standard deviation of the claims ratio in the reference period from the average claims ratio, multiplied by the earned premiums for the financial year.

Where claims for any financial year are in excess, an amount in respect thereof shall be taken from the equalisation reserve until it has reached the minimum required amount. Claims shall be deemed to be in excess if the claims ratio for the financial year is higher than the average claims ratio. The amount in respect of the excess claims shall be arrived at by multiplying the difference between the two ratios by the earned premiums for the financial year.

The minimum required amount shall be equal to three times the standard deviation of the claims ratio in the reference period from the average claims ratio multiplied by the earned premiums for the financial year.

The length of the reference period shall not be less than 15 years and not more than 30 years. No equalisation reserve need be formed if no underwriting loss has been noted during the reference period.

Both required amounts of the equalisation reserve and the amount to be placed to it or the amount to be taken from it may be reduced if the average claims ratio for the reference period in conjunction with the expenses ratio show that the premiums include a safety margin and that safety margin is more than one-and-a-half times the standard deviation of the claims ratio in the reference period. In such a case the amounts in question shall be multiplied by the quotient of one-and-a-half times the standard deviation and the safety margin.

IX COUNCIL DIRECTIVE OF JUNE 22, 1987 ON THE COORDINATION OF LAWS, REGULATIONS AND ADMINISTRATIVE PROVISIONS RELATING TO LEGAL EXPENSES INSURANCE

(OJEC L 185 4.7.1987, directive 87/344/EEC)

The first coordination directive 73/239/EEC allows the Federal Republic of Germany to maintain, pending further coordination, the specialised exercise of the class of insurance in respect of recourse against third parties and legal defence. The directive under review achieves the envisaged coordination allowing member states the simultaneous undertaking in their territory of legal expenses insurance and other classes of insurance. The coordination relates to the possible conflict of interests between a person with legal expenses cover and his insurer arising from the fact that the latter is covering him in respect of any other class of insurance referred to in the annex to directive 73/239/EEC or is covering another person. The directive in question creates safeguards to prevent such conflicts of interests as far as possible. In addition, the directive provides for the free choice of a lawyer by the insured person and for an arbitration procedure.

Article 2

1 This directive applies to legal expenses insurance. Such consists in undertaking, against the payment of a premium, to bear the costs of legal proceedings and to provide other services directly linked to insurance cover, in particular with a view to:
- securing compensation for the loss, damage or injury suffered by the insured person, by settlement out of court or through civil or criminal proceedings,
- defending or representing the insured person in civil, criminal, administrative or other proceedings or in respect of any claim made against him.

2 The directive does not, however, apply to:
- legal expenses insurance where such insurance concerns disputes or risks arising out of, or in connection with, the use of sea-going vessels,
- the activity pursued by the insurer providing civil liability cover for the purpose of defending or representing the insured person in any inquiry or proceedings if that activity is at the same time pursued in the insurer's own interest under such cover,
- where a member state so chooses, the activity of legal expenses insurance undertaken by an assistance insurer where this activity is carried out in a member state other than the one in which the insured person normally resides, where it forms part of a contract covering solely the assistance provided for persons who fall into difficulties while travelling, while away from home or while away from their permanent residence. In this event the contract must clearly state that the cover in question is limited to the circumstances referred to in the foregoing sentence and is ancillary to assistance.

Article 3

1 Legal expenses cover shall be the subject of a contract separate from that drawn up for the other classes of insurance or shall be dealt with in a separate section of a single policy in which the nature of the legal expenses cover, and should the member state so request, the amount of the relevant premium are specified.

2 Each member state shall take the necessary measures to ensure that the undertakings established within its territory adopt, in accordance with the option imposed by the member state, or at their own choice, if the member state so agrees, at least one of the following solutions, which are alternatives:

a the undertaking shall ensure that no member of the staff who is concerned with the management of legal expenses claims or with legal advice in respect thereof carries on at the same time a similar activity
- if the undertaking is a composite one, for another class transacted by it,
- irrespective of whether the undertaking is a composite or a specialised one, in another having financial, commercial or administrative links with the first undertaking and carrying on one or more of the other classes of insurance set out in directive 73/239/EEC;

b the undertaking shall entrust the management of claims in respect of legal expenses insurance to an undertaking having separate legal personality. That undertaking shall be mentioned in the separate contract or separate section referred to in paragraph 1. If the undertaking having separate legal personality has links with an undertaking which carries on one or more of the other classes of insurance referred to in point A of directive 73/239/EEC, members of the staff of the undertaking who are concerned with the processing of claims or with legal advice connected with such processing may not pursue the same or a similar activity in the other undertaking at the same time. In addition, member states may impose the same requirements on the members of the management body;

c the undertaking shall, in the contract, afford the insured person the right to entrust the defence of his interests, from the moment that he has the right to claim from his insurer under the policy, to a lawyer of his choice or, to the extent that national law so permits, any other qualified person.

3 Whichever solution is adopted, the interest of persons having legal expenses cover shall be regarded as safeguarded in an equivalent manner under this directive.

Article 4

1 Any contract of legal expenses insurance shall expressly recognise that:

a where recourse is had to a lawyer or other person appropriately qualified according to national law in order to defend, represent or serve the interests of the insured person in any inquiry or proceedings, that insured person shall be free to choose such lawyer or other person;

b the insured person shall be free to choose a lawyer or, if he so prefers and to the extent that national law so permits, any other appropriately qualified person, to serve his interests whenever a conflict of interests arises.

2 Lawyer means any person entitled to pursue his professional activities under one of the denominations laid down in Council directive 77/249/EEC of March 22, 1977 to facilitate the effective exercise by lawyers of freedom to provide services (OJEC L 78 26.3.1977).

Article 5

1 Each member state may provide exemption from the application of article 4, paragraph 1 for legal expenses insurance if all the following conditions are fulfilled:

a the insurance is limited to cases arising from the use of road vehicles in the territory of the member state concerned;

b the insurance is connected to a contract to provide assistance in the event of accident or breakdown involving a road vehicle;

c neither the legal expenses insurer nor the assistance insurer carries out any class of liability insurance;

d measures are taken so that the legal counsel and representation of each of the parties to a dispute is effected by completely independent lawyers when these parties are insured for legal expenses by the same insurer.

2 The exemption granted by a member state to an undertaking pursuant to paragraph 1 shall not affect the application of article 3, paragraph 2.

Article 6

Member states shall adopt all appropriate measures to ensure that, without prejudice to any right of appeal to a judicial body which might be provided for by national law, an arbitration or other procedure offering comparable guarantees of objectivity is provided for whereby, in the event of a difference of opinion between legal expenses insurer and his insured, a decision can be taken on the attitude to be adopted in order to settle the dispute.

The insurance contract must mention the right of the insured person to have recourse to such a procedure.

Article 7

Whenever a conflict of interests arises or there is disagreement over the settlement of the dispute, the legal expenses insurer or, where appropriate, the claims settlement office shall inform the person insured of:

- the right referred to in article 4;
- the possibility of having recourse to the procedure referred to in article 6.

Article 8

The member states shall abolish all provisions which prohibit an insurer from carrying out within their territory legal expenses insurance and other classes of insurance at the same time.

Article 9

The second subparagraph of point C of the annex to directive 73/239/EEC shall be replaced by the following text:

'However, the risks included in classes 14, 15 and 17 in point A may not be regarded as risks ancillary to other classes.

Nonetheless, the risk included in class 17 (legal expenses insurance) may be regarded as an ancillary risk of class 18 where the conditions laid down in the first subparagraph are fulfilled, where the main risk relates solely to the assistance provided for persons who fall into difficulties while travelling, while away from home or while away from their permanent residence.

Legal expenses insurance may also be regarded as an ancillary risk under the conditions set out in the first subparagraph where it concerns disputes or risks arising out of, or in connection with, the use of sea-going vessels.'

Under article 10 the member states shall take the measures necessary to comply with this directive by January 1, 1990.

X SECOND COUNCIL DIRECTIVE OF JUNE 22, 1988 ON THE COORDINATION OF LAWS, REGULATIONS AND ADMINISTRATIVE PROVISIONS RELATING TO DIRECT INSURANCE OTHER THAN LIFE ASSURANCE AND LAYING DOWN PROVISIONS TO FACILITATE THE EFFECTIVE EXERCISE OF FREEDOM TO PROVIDE SERVICES AND AMENDING DIRECTIVE 73/239/EEC

(OJEC L 172 4.7.1988, directive 88/357/EEC)

The internal insurance market requires the possibility of policy-holders to have recourse not only to insurers established in their own country, but also to insurers which have their head office in the Community and are established in other member states. The first coordination directive on insurance other than life assurance of July 24, 1973 (73/239/EEC) achieved initial coordination in the area of freedom of establishment. The second coordination directive of June 22, 1988, discussed here, has a dual function. On the one hand it supplements the first directive by clarifying the powers and means of supervision vested in the supervisory authorities. On the other hand the directive introduces special provisions regarding the taking-up, pursuit and supervision of activity in the context of the provision of insurance services. The directive provides for a substantial freedom to provide services for large industrial, commercial and professional risks, since policy-holders who, by virtue of their status, their size or the nature of the risk to be insured, do not require special protection in the state in which the risk is situated should be granted complete freedom to avail themselves of the widest possible insurance market. For this reason the insurance of these large risks can be based on the approach of home country control. The provision of services relating to so-called mass risks is still subject to application of the supervisory rules of the country in which the insured risk is located (host country control). The influence of the four insurance judgements of the European Court of December 4, 1986 is clearly evident in the above.

XI PROPOSAL FOR A THIRD COUNCIL DIRECTIVE ON THE COORDINATION OF LAWS, REGULATIONS AND ADMINISTRATIVE PROVISIONS RELATING TO DIRECT INSURANCE OTHER THAN LIFE ASSURANCE AND AMENDING DIRECTIVES 73/239/EEC AND 88/357/EEC

(OJEC C 244 28.9.1990, proposal (90) 348)

THE PROPOSAL WAS AMENDED IN 1992

(OJEC C 93 13.4.1992, proposal (92) 63)

The aim of this proposed directive is to complete the internal market in direct insurance other than life assurance from the point of view both of the freedom of establishment and of the freedom to provide services. The second non-life coordination directive already grants complete freedom to policy-holders who, by virtue of their status, their size or the nature of the risks to be insured, do not require special protection in the member state in which a risk is situated. The proposal under review supplements the second non-life directive by enabling all policy-holders, irrespective of their status, their size or the nature of the risks to be insured, to have recourse to any insurer with a head office in the Community who carries on business there, under the freedom of establishment or the freedom to provide services, while guaranteeing them adequate protection. This complete freedom is to be achieved by bringing about such harmonisation as is essential, necessary and sufficient to achieve the mutual recognition of authorisations and prudential control systems, thereby making it possible to grant a single authorisation valid throughout the Community and apply the principle of supervision by the home member state. Home member states will henceforth be responsible for monitoring the financial health of insurance undertakings, including their state of solvency, the establishment of adequate technical provisions and the covering of those provisions by matching assets.

If adopted, the directive will have to be implemented on July 1, 1994. This will be later than the date of January 1, 1993 originally set by the internal market program.

5.4 Coordination of motor vehicle liability insurance

Motor vehicle insurance is one of the possible classes of non-life insurance (class 3 of the annex to the first coordination directive for non-life insurance of July 24, 1973).

Despite this, we will discuss motor vehicle insurance as a separate class of Community insurance legislation. The reason for this is that the legislation to be discussed aims to achieve coordination concerning the civil liability to which the use of a motor vehicle may lead, rather than a coordination of the exercise of the freedom of establishment and the freedom to provide services. As far as the coordination of the freedom of establishment and of the provision of services is concerned the Community insurance laws are therefore covered by the first and second directives on non-life insurance. Civil liability is covered by the legislation to be discussed below.

XII FIRST COUNCIL DIRECTIVE OF APRIL 24, 1972 ON THE APPROXIMATION OF THE LAWS OF THE MEMBER STATES RELATING TO INSURANCE AGAINST CIVIL LIABILITY IN RESPECT OF THE USE OF MOTOR VEHICLES, AND TO THE ENFORCEMENT OF THE OBLIGATION TO INSURE AGAINST SUCH LIABILITY

(OJEC L 103 2.5.1972, directive 72/166/EEC)

The aim of all frontier controls of compulsory insurance cover against civil liability in respect of the use of motor vehicles is to safeguard the interests of persons who may be the victims of accidents caused by such vehicles. As a result of disparities between national requirements these frontier controls impede the free movement of motor vehicles and persons within the Community.

The abolition of checks on green cards can be effected by means of an agreement between the national insurers' bureaux of the member states, whereby each national bureau would guarantee compensation in accordance with the provisions of national law in respect of any loss or injury giving entitlement to compensation caused in its territory by one of those vehicles, whether or not insured, and which are normally based in one member state and which entered via the member state in which the accident occurs. Such guarantee agreements between the national insurers' bureaux presuppose that all Community vehicles travelling in Community territory are covered by insurance. Through articles 3 and 4, the directive under review introduces compulsory insurance against said liability, the insurance to be valid throughout Community territory. The other articles contain coordinating provisions which enter into force after the guarantee agreement between the national bureaux has been achieved.

Under article 1 and for the purpose of this directive:

1 *vehicle* means any motor vehicle intended for travel on land and propelled by mechanical power, but not running on rails, and any trailer, whether or not coupled;
2 *injured party* means any person entitled to compensation in respect of any loss or injury caused by vehicles;
3 *national insurers' bureau* means a professional organisation which is constituted in accordance with recommendation No. 5 adopted on January 25, 1949, by the Road Transport Sub-committee of the Inland Transport Committee of the United Nations Economic Commission for Europe and which groups together insurance undertakings which, in a state, are authorised to conduct the business of motor vehicle insurance against civil liability;
4 *the territory of the state in which the vehicle is based:*
   - the territory of the state in which the motor vehicle is registered; or
   - in cases where no registration is required for a type of vehicle but the vehicle bears an insurance plate, or a distinguishing sign analogous to the registration plate, the territory of the state in which the insurance plate or the sign is issued; or

- in cases where neither registration plate nor insurance plate nor distinguishing sign is required for certain types of vehicle, the territory of the state in which the person who has custody of the vehicle is permanently resident;

5 *green card* means an international certificate of insurance issued on behalf of a national bureau in accordance with the recommendation No. 5 adopted on January 25, 1949, by the Road Transport Sub-committee of the Inland Transport Committee of the United Nations Economic Commission for Europe.

Article 2

1 Member states shall refrain from making checks on insurance against civil liability in respect of vehicles normally based in the territory of another member state.

Likewise, member states shall refrain from making such insurance checks on vehicles normally based in the territory of a third country entering their territory from the territory of another member state. Member states may, however, carry out random checks.

2 As regards vehicles normally based in the territory of a member state, the provisions of this directive, with the exception of articles 3 and 4, shall take effect:

- after an agreement has been concluded between the national insurers' bureaux under the terms of which each national bureau guarantees the settlement, in accordance with the provisions of national law on compulsory insurance, of claims in respect of accidents occurring in its territory, caused by vehicles normally based in the territory of another member state, whether or not such vehicles are insured;
- from the date fixed by the Commission, upon its having ascertained in close cooperation with the member states that such an agreement has been concluded;
- for the duration of that agreement.

Article 3

1 Each member state shall, subject to article 4, take all appropriate measures to ensure that civil liability in respect of the use of motor vehicles normally based in its territory is covered by insurance. The extent of the liability covered and the terms and conditions of the cover shall be determined on the basis of these measures.

2 Each member state shall take all appropriate measures to ensure that the contract of insurance also covers:

- according to the law in force in other member states, any loss or injury which is caused in the territory of those states;
- any loss or injury suffered by nationals of member states during a direct journey between two territories in which the treaty establishing the European Economic Community is in force, if there is no national insurers' bureau responsible for the territory which is being crossed; in that case the loss or injury shall be covered in accordance with the internal laws on compulsory insurance in force in the member state in whose territory the vehicle is normally based.

Article 4

A member state may act in derogation of article 3 in respect of:

a certain natural or legal persons, public or private; the list of such persons shall be drawn up by the member state concerned and communicated to the other member states and to the Commission.

A member state so derogating shall take the appropriate measures to ensure that compensation is paid in respect of any loss or injury caused in the territory of other member states by vehicles belonging to such persons. It shall in particular designate an authority or body in the country where the loss or injury occurs responsible for compensating injured parties in accordance with the laws of that state in cases where the procedure provided for in the first indent of article 2, paragraph 2, is not applicable. It shall notify the other member states and the Commission of the measures taken.

b certain types of vehicles or certain vehicles having a special plate; the list of such types or such vehicles shall be drawn up by the state concerned and communicated to the other member states and to the Commission.

In that case the other member states shall retain the right to require, on entry into their territory of such a vehicle, that the person having custody thereof be in possession of a valid green card or that he conclude a frontier insurance contract complying with the requirements of the member state concerned.

Article 5
Each member state shall ensure that, where an accident is caused in its territory by a vehicle normally based in the territory of another member state, the national insurers' bureau shall, without prejudice to the obligation referred to in the first indent of article 2, paragraph 2, obtain information:

- as to the territory in which the vehicle is normally based, and as to its registration mark, if any;
- in so far as possible, as to the details of the insurance of the vehicle, as they normally appear on the green card, which are in the possession of the person having custody of the vehicle, to the extent that these details are required by the member state in whose territory the vehicle is normally based.

Each member state shall also ensure that the bureau communicates this information to the national insurers' bureau of the state in whose territory the vehicle is normally based.

Article 6
Each member state shall take all appropriate measures to ensure that vehicles normally based in the territory of a third country or in the non-European territory of a member state entering the territory in which the treaty establishing the European Economic Community is in force shall not be used in its territory unless any loss or injury caused by those vehicles is covered, in accordance with the requirements of the laws of the various member states on compulsory insurance against civil liability in respect of the use of vehicles, throughout the territory in which the treaty establishing the European Economic Community is in force.

Article 7

1 Every vehicle normally based in the territory of a third country or in the non-European territory of a member state must, before entering the territory in which the treaty establishing the European Economic Community is in force, be provided either with a valid green card or with a certificate of frontier insurance establishing that the vehicle is insured in accordance with article 6.

2 However, vehicles normally based in a third country shall be treated as vehicles normally based in the Community if the national bureaux of all the member states severally guarantee, each in accordance with the provisions of its own national law on compulsory insurance, settlement of claims in respect of accidents occurring in their territory caused by such vehicles.

3 Upon having ascertained, in close cooperation with the member states, that the obligations referred to in the preceding paragraph have been assumed, the Commission shall fix the date from which and the types of vehicle for which member states shall no longer require production of the documents referred to in paragraph 1.

Under article 8, member states shall, not later than December 31, 1973, bring into force the measures necessary to comply with this directive.

XIII COUNCIL DIRECTIVE OF DECEMBER 19, 1972 AMENDING COUNCIL DIRECTIVE 72/166/EEC OF APRIL 24, 1972, ON THE APPROXIMATION OF THE LAWS OF THE MEMBER STATES RELATING TO INSURANCE AGAINST CIVIL LIABILITY IN RESPECT OF THE USE OF MOTOR VEHICLES AND TO THE ENFORCEMENT OF THE OBLIGATION TO INSURE AGAINST SUCH LIABILITY

(OJEC L 291 28.12.1972, directive 72/430/EEC)

THE DIRECTIVE WAS RECTIFIED IN 1973

(OJEC L 75 23.3.1973)

As a result of the entry of three new member states (United Kingdom, Ireland and Denmark) on January 1, 1973 the number of EC-member states increased from six to nine. For this reason the phrase '*six* national insurers' bureaux' in article 2, paragraph 2 of the directive 72/166/EEC, is replaced by '*nine* national bureaux'. This is done by the directive in question.

XIV FIRST COMMISSION DECISION OF FEBRUARY 6, 1974 RELATING TO THE APPLICATION OF COUNCIL DIRECTIVE 72/166/EEC

(OJEC L 87 30.3.1974, decision 74/166/EEC)

Directive 72/166/EEC calls for the conclusion of a guarantee agreement between the national insurers' bureaux of the member states. This agreement was achieved on December 12, 1973 and is of unlimited duration with twelve months' notice required for revocation. As a result of this agreement directive 72/166/EEC became fully applicable. The decision states that this will be the case as of May 15, 1974. From May 15, 1974 each member state shall therefore refrain from making checks on insurance against civil liability in respect of motor vehicles which are normally based in the European territory of another member state and which fall within the scope of the agreement of national insurers' bureaux of December 12, 1973.

XV SECOND COMMISSION DECISION OF FEBRUARY 6, 1974 RELATING TO THE APPLICATION OF COUNCIL DIRECTIVE 72/166/EEC

(OJEC L 87 30.3.1974, decision 74/167/EEC)

Under article 7, paragraph 2, of directive 72/166/EEC member states may remove checks on insurance against civil liability in respect of vehicles entering Community territory when such vehicles are normally based in third countries. In order to achieve this the member states must conclude guarantee agreements with the third countries concerned. This agreement was concluded on December 12, 1973 with the national insurers' bureaux of Sweden, Finland, Norway, Austria and Switzerland. Under this agreement the national insurers' bureaux of the member states guarantee the settlement of claims in respect of accidents occurring on their territory caused by vehicles normally based in the territory of these third countries. The second Commission decision discussed here states that from May 15, 1974 each member state shall refrain from making checks on insurance against civil liability in respect of vehicles which are normally based in the territory of the above third countries.

XVI COMMISSION RECOMMENDATION OF FEBRUARY 6, 1974 CONCERNING THE APPLICATION OF DIRECTIVE 72/166/EEC

(OJEC L 87 30.3.1974, recommendation 74/165/EEC)

By virtue of article 7, paragraph 1 of Council directive 72/166/EEC any vehicle normally based in the territory of a third country must be provided either with a valid green card or with a certificate of frontier insurance valid for the whole of the territory of the Community before entering that territory.

Since in the member states practice differs as to the duration of contracts of insurance against civil liability in respect of the use of motor vehicles in the form of frontier insurance, it is necessary to render uniform the practice followed in the member states as to the minimum duration of frontier insurance so as to prevent abuse, after the removal of checks at intra-community frontiers (e.g. a motor vehicle from a third country entering the Community in a member state which applies the shortest minimum required duration of frontier insurance and then proceeds to member states which apply a longer minimum duration). Of course this risk does not exist with respect to third countries mentioned in the second decision with whom the Community has concluded guarantee agreements. By way of this recommendation the Commission calls for member states to ensure that contracts of insurance against civil liability in respect of the use of motor vehicles concluded in the form of frontier insurance shall, not later than May 15, 1974, have a minimum duration of 15 days.

XVII THIRD COMMISSION DECISION OF DECEMBER 13, 1974 RELATING TO THE APPLICATION OF COUNCIL DIRECTIVE 72/166/EEC

(OJEC L 6 10.1.1975, decision 75/23/EEC)

On April 22, 1974 the national insurers' bureaux of the member states concluded a guarantee agreement with the national insurers' bureaux of Hungary, Czechoslovakia and the German Democratic Republic. The third decision, discused here, has the same function as the second decision. It provides that from January 1, 1975 each member state shall cease to carry out checks on insurance against civil liability in respect of vehicles which are normally based in the territory of said third countries in so far as such vehicles are covered by the terms of the agreements entered into on April 22 1974 between the respective national insurance bureaux of the member states and the like bureaux of said third countries.

XVIII FOURTH COMMISSION DECISION OF MAY 16, 1986 RELATING TO THE APPLICATION OF COUNCIL DIRECTIVE 72/166/EEC

(OJEC L 153 7.6.1986, decision 86/218/EEC)

The first decision on the application of directive 72/166/EEC provided for the removal of checks on insurance against civil liability between the nine member states.

This decision was based on the guarantee agreement of December 12, 1973. After the entry into the Community of Greece on January 1, 1981 the Greek national insurers' bureau did not become a party to this agreement. After the entry of Spain and Portugal (January 1, 1986) the insurers' bureaux of Spain and Portugal and the other member states, with the exception of Greece, on March 14, 1986 signed an addendum to the guarantee agreement of December 12, 1973 extending that agreement to the national bureaux of Spain and Portugal. This decision states that this will be effective as from June 1, 1986.

XIX FIFTH COMMISSION DECISION OF MAY 16, 1986 RELATING TO THE APPLICATION OF COUNCIL DIRECTIVE 72/166/EEC

(OJEC L 153 7.6.1986, decision 86/219/EEC)

The insurers' bureaux of Spain and Portugal, the bureaux of the other member states, with the exception of Greece, and the bureaux of Sweden, Finland, Norway, Austria and Switzerland on March 14, 1986 signed an addendum to the guarantee agreement of December 12, 1973 extending that agreement to include the bureaux of Spain and Portugal. This fifth decision stipulates that, as from June 1, 1986 Spain and Portugal shall refrain from making checks on insurance against civil liability in respect of vehicles which are normally based in the above-mentioned countries.

XX SIXTH COMMISSION DECISION OF MAY 16, 1986 RELATING TO THE APPLICATION OF COUNCIL DIRECTIVE 72/166/EEC

(OJEC L 153 7.6.1986, decision 86/220/EEC)

This is identical to the fifth decision, except that it relates in this case to a guarantee agreement of March 14, 1986 with other third countries, namely Hungary, Czechoslovakia and the German Democratic Republic. Checks on insurance against civil liability in respect of motor vehicles which are normally based in said countries are abolished from June 1, 1986.

XXI COMMISSION RECOMMENDATION OF JANUARY 8, 1981 ON ACCELERATED SETTLEMENT OF CLAIMS UNDER INSURANCE AGAINST CIVIL LIABILITY IN RESPECT OF THE USE OF MOTOR VEHICLES

(OJEC L 57 4.3.1981, recommendation 81/76/EEC)

The period elapsing between the occurrence of a road accident and the payment of compensation by the insurer of the person liable is sometimes extremely lengthy. Such lengthy periods are largely attributable to the slowness of the legal procedures for determining liability and fixing compensation. The object of this recommendation is to accelerate these procedures and states in article 1 that the member states shall take all the measures necessary to facilitate the communication to those concerned of police reports and other documents necessary for the payment of compensation by insurers covering against civil liability in respect of the use of motor vehicles.

XXII SECOND COUNCIL DIRECTIVE OF DECEMBER 30, 1983 ON THE APPROXIMATION OF THE LAWS OF THE MEMBER STATES RELATING TO INSURANCE AGAINST CIVIL LIABILITY IN RESPECT OF THE USE OF MOTOR VEHICLES

(OJEC L 8 11.1.1984, directive 84/5/EEC)

Article 3 of the first directive 72/166/EEC of April 24, 1972 requires each member state to take all appropriate measures to ensure that civil liability in respect of the use of vehicles normally based in its territory is covered by insurance. However, major disparities exist between the laws of the different member states concerning the extent of this obligation of insurance cover. This directive deals in more detail with this obligation of insurance cover.

Under article 1, paragraph 1, the insurance shall cover both damage to property and personal injuries. Without prejudice to any higher guarantees which member states may lay down, each member state shall require that the amounts for which such insurance is compulsory are at least:

- in the case of personal injury, 350 000 ECU where there is only one victim; where more than one victim is involved in a single claim, this amount shall be multiplied by the number of victims,
- in the case of damage to property 100 000 ECU per claim, whatever the number of victims.

Member states may, in place of the above minimum amounts, provide for a minimum amount of 500.000 ECU for personal injury where more than one victim is involved in a single claim, or in the case of personal injury and damage to property, a minimum overall amount of 600 000 ECU per claim whatever the number of victims or the nature of the damage.

It is also provided that each member state shall set up or authorise a body with the task of providing compensation, at least up to the limits of the insurance obligation for damage to property or personal injuries caused by a unidentified vehicle or a vehicle for which the insurance obligation provided for in paragraph 1 has not been satisfied. The obligations of such body are then defined specifically:

- Member states may exclude the payment of compensation by that body in respect of persons who voluntarily entered the vehicle which caused the damage or injury when the body can prove that they knew it was uninsured.
- Member states may limit or exclude the payment of compensation by that body in the event of damage to property by an unidentified vehicle.
- They may also authorise, in the case of damage to property caused by an uninsured vehicle an excess of not more than 500 ECU for which the victim may be responsible.

Under article 2, each member state shall take the necessary measures to ensure that any statutory provision or any contractual clause contained in an insurance policy issued in accordance with article 3, paragraph 1 of directive 72/166/EEC, which excludes from insurance the use or driving of vehicles by:

- persons who do not have express or implied authorisation thereto, or
- persons who do not hold a licence permitting them to drive the vehicle concerned, or
- persons who are in breach of the statutory technical requirements concerning the condition and safety of the vehicle concerned, shall, for the purposes of article 3 paragraph 1 of directive 72/166/EEC, be deemed to be void in respect of claims by third parties who have been victims of an accident.

The members of the family of the insured person, driver or any other person who is liable under civil law in the event of an accident, and whose liability is covered by the insurance referred to in article 1, paragraph 1, shall not be excluded from insurance in respect of their personal injuries by virtue of that relationship (article 3).

The philosophy behind article 4 is that the most suitable criterion for determining that a vehicle is normally based in a particular member state, is that it carries a registration plate of that country. For this reason article 4 replaces the phrase 'the territory of the state in which the vehicle is registered' (article 1, paragraph 4 of directive 72/166/EEC) with 'the territory of the state of which the vehicle bears a registration plate'.

XXIII THIRD COUNCIL DIRECTIVE OF MAY 14, 1990 ON THE APPROXIMATION OF THE LAWS OF THE MEMBER STATES RELATING TO INSURANCE AGAINST CIVIL LIABILITY IN RESPECT OF THE USE OF MOTOR VEHICLES
(OJEC L 129 19.5.1990, directive 90/232/EEC)

The first directive 72/166/EEC required each member state to take all appropriate measures to ensure that civil liability in respect of the use of motor vehicles normally based in its territory is covered by insurance. The second directive 84/5/EEC reduced considerably the disparities between the level and content of compulsory civil liability insurance. However, significant disparities still exist in the cover provided by such insurance. The object of the third directive discussed here is to reduce these disparities.

Article 1 provides that the insurance shall cover liability for personal injuries to all passengers, other than the driver, arising out of the use of a vehicle. This provision is necessary since in some member states there are still gaps in the cover provided to passengers of a vehicle by the compulsory insurance.

Under article 2, member states shall take the necessary steps to ensure that all compulsory insurance policies against civil liability arising out of the use of vehicles :

- cover, on the basis of a single premium, the entire territory of the Community, and
- guarantee, on the basis of the same single premium, in each member state, the cover required by its law or the cover required by the law of the member state where the vehicle is normally based when that cover is higher.

XXIV COUNCIL DIRECTIVE OF NOVEMBER 8, 1990 AMENDING, PARTICULARLY AS REGARDS MOTOR VEHICLE LIABILITY INSURANCE, DIRECTIVE 73/239/EEC AND DIRECTIVE 88/357/EEC WHICH CONCERN THE COORDINATION OF LAWS, REGULATIONS AND ADMINISTRATIVE PROVISIONS RELATING TO DIRECT INSURANCE OTHER THAN LIFE ASSURANCE

(OJEC L 330 29.11.1990, directive 90/618/EEC)

The second coordination directive on insurance contains provisions relating to the freedom to supply services. Certain risks, one of them concerning motor vehicle liability insurance, other than carrier's liability, were excluded from the scope of this directive. The directive under review does include the provisions relating to the freedom to provide services in the field of insurance against civil liability, other than carrier's liability, resulting from the use of motor vehicles.

The directive in question applies where an undertaking, through an establishment situated in a member state, covers a risk, other than carrier's liability, classified under class 10 of point A of the Annex to the first directive (motor vehicle liability) which is situated in another member state. The member state of provision of services shall require the undertaking to become a member of and participate in the financing of its national bureau and its national guarantee fund. The undertaking shall not, however, be required to make any payment or contribution to the bureau and fund of the member state of provision of services in respect of risks covered by way of provision of services other than one calculated on the same basis as for undertakings covering risks, other than carrier's liability, in class 10 through an establishment situated in that member state, by reference to its premium income from that class in that member state or the number of risks in that class covered there. The member state of provision of services shall require the undertaking to ensure that persons pursuing claims arising out of events occurring in its territory are not placed in a less favourable situation as a result of the fact that the undertaking is covering a risk, other than carrier's liability, in class 10 by way of provision of services rather than through an establishment situated in that state. For this purpose, the member state of provision of services shall require the undertaking to appoint a representative resident or established in its territory who shall collect all necessary information in relation to claims, and shall possess sufficient powers to represent the undertaking in relation to persons suffering damage who could pursue claims, including the payment of such claims, and to represent it or, where necessary, to have it represented before the courts and authorities of that member state in relation to these claims.

A second important aim of the directive under review is the introduction of the principle of national treatment with respect to non-life insurance undertakings from third (non-EC) countries. The scope of this principle is identical to the scope applicable to credit institutions and investment firms.

5.5 Coordination of life assurance

In the insurance laws two main forms of insurance can be distinguished: life assurance and non-life insurance. Non-life insurance, subdivided into classes such as motor vehicle insurance, credit and suretyship insurance, insurance against legal expenses etc., has been discussed above. Below we discuss Community regulations relating to life assurance.

XXV FIRST COUNCIL DIRECTIVE OF MARCH 5, 1979 ON THE COORDINATION OF LAWS, REGULATIONS AND ADMINISTRATIVE PROVISIONS RELATING TO THE TAKING UP AND PURSUIT OF THE BUSINESS OF DIRECT LIFE ASSURANCE *(OJEC L 63 13.3.1979, directive 79/267/EEC)*

This directive, also referred to as the first coordination directive on life assurance, is the counterpart of the first coordination directive on non-life insurance. The objective of this directive is to facilitate the effective exercise of the freedom of establishment (directly applicable, since the end of the transitional period on January 1, 1970 on the basis of the Reyners and Van Binsbergen judgements) through coordination of the conditions concerning the taking up and pursuit of the business of life insurance. The exercise of the freedom to provide services does not fall within the scope of this directive. A proposal for a second coordination directive on life assurance relating to the freedom of provision of services by life assurance undertakings was adopted by the Commission on December 23, 1988.

The structure of the directive under review is the same as that of the first coordination directive on non-life insurance:

Title I	:	General provisions concerning the classes to which the directive relates.
Title II	:	Rules applicable to undertakings whose head offices are situated within the Community (authorisation, technical reserves, solvency margins, minimum guarantee funds).
Title III	:	Rules applicable to agencies or branches established within the Community and belonging to undertakings whose head offices are situated outside the Community (authorisation, technical reserves, solvency margins, minimum guarantee funds).
Title IV	:	Transitional and other provisions

General provisions

By virtue of article 1 the first coordination directive on life assurance concerns the taking up and pursuit of the self-employed activity of direct insurance carried on by undertakings which are established in a member state or wish to become established there. The directive applies to the activities defined below:

1 The following kinds of insurance where they are on a contractual basis:
  a life assurance, that is to say, the class of insurance which comprises, in particular, assurance on survival to a stipulated age only, assurance on death only, assurance on survival to a stipulated age or on earlier death, life assurance with return of premiums, marriage assurance, birth assurance;
  b annuities;
  c supplementary insurance carried on by life assurance undertakings, that is to say, in particular, insurance against personal injury including incapacity for employment, insurance against death

resulting from an accident and insurance against disability resulting from an accident or sickness, where these various kinds of insurance are underwritten in addition to life assurance;
  d the type of insurance existing in Ireland and the United Kingdom known as permanent health insurance not subject to cancellation.
2 The following operations, where they are on a contractual basis, in so far as they are subject to supervision by the administrative authorities responsible for the supervision of private insurance and are authorised in the country concerned:
  a tontines whereby associations of subscribers are set up with a view to jointly capitalising their contributions and subsequently distributing the assets thus accumulated among the survivors or among the beneficiaries of the deceased;
  b capital redemption operations based on actuarial calculation whereby, in return for single or periodic payments agreed in advance, commitments of specified duration and amount are undertaken;
  c management of group pension funds, i.e. operations consisting, for the undertaking concerned, in managing the investments, and in particular the assets representing the reserves of bodies that effect payments on death or survival or in the event of discontinuance or curtailment of activity;
  d the operations referred to in c where they are accompanied by insurance covering either conservation of capital or payment of a minimum interest;
  e the operations carried out by insurance companies such as those referred to in chapter 1, title 4 of book IV of the French 'Code des assurances'.
3 Operations relating to the length of human life which are prescribed by or provided for in social insurance legislation, when they are effected or managed at their own risk by assurance undertakings in accordance with the laws of a member state.

By virtue of article 2, the directive does not concern:
1 subject to the application of article 1, paragraph 1c of this directive in respect of supplementary insurance, the classes designated in the annex to the first coordination directive (non-life insurance);
2 operations of provident and mutual-benefit institutions whose benefits may vary according to the resources available and which require each of their members to contribute at the appropriate flat rate;
3 operations carried out by organisations other than undertakings referred to in article 1, whose object is to provide benefits for unemployed or self-employed persons belonging to an undertaking or group of undertakings, or a trade or group of trades, in the event of death or survival or of discontinuance or curtailment of activity, whether or not the commitments arising from such operations are fully covered at all times by mathematical reserves;
4 subject to article 1, paragraph 3, insurance forming part of a statutory system of social security.

By virtue of article 3 the directive does not concern:
1 organisations which undertake to provide benefits solely in the event of death, where the amount of such benefits does not exceed the average funeral costs for a single death or where the benefits are provided in kind;
2 mutual associations, where:
  - the articles of association contain provisions for calling up additional contributions or reducing their benefits or claiming assistance from other persons who have undertaken to provide it, and
  - the annual contribution income for the activities covered by this directive does not exceed 500,000 units of account for three consecutive years.

Head office situated within the Community

Articles 6-14 concern the conditions of admission.

Article 6 requires each member state to make the taking up of the activities referred to in this directive in its territory subject to an official authorisation. This authorisation shall be sought from the competent authority of the member state in question by:

a any undertaking which establishes its head office in the territory of such state;

b any undertaking whose head office is situated in another member state and which opens an agency or branch in the territory of the member state in question;

c any undertaking which, having received the authorisation required under a or b above, extends its business in the territory of such state to other classes;

d any undertaking which, having obtained, in accordance with article 7, paragraph 1, an authorisation for a part of the national territory, extends its activity beyond such part.

Under article 7 authorisation shall be given for a particular class of insurance. Authorisation covers the entire class unless the applicant wishes to cover only part of the risks pertaining to such class. The following classes are mentioned in the annex to the directive:

I The assurance referred to in article 1, paragraph 1 a, b and c excluding those referred to in II and III.

II Marriage assurance, birth assurance.

III The assurance referred to in article 1, paragraph 1 a and b, which are linked to investment funds.

IV Permanent health insurance, referred to in article 1, paragraph 1 d.

V Tontines, referred to in article 1, paragraph 2 a.

VI Capital redemption operations, referred to in article 1, paragraph 2 b.

VII Management of group pension funds, referred to in article 1, paragraph 2 c and d.

VIII The operations referred to in article 1, paragraph 2 e.

IX The operations referred to in article 1, paragraph 3.

Each member state may grant an authorisation for two or more of the classes, where its national laws permit such classes to be carried out simultaneously.

Article 8 states that each member state shall require any undertaking setting up in its territory for which an authorisation is sought to adopt one of the forms which are listed exhaustively by country in the article.

Furthermore, these undertakings must submit a scheme of operations in accordance with article 9 and shall possess the minimum guarantee fund provided for in article 20, paragraph 2.

Under article 9, said scheme of operations must contain the following particulars or evidence of cover:

a the nature of the commitments which the undertaking proposes to cover; the general and special policy conditions which it proposes to use;

b the technical bases that the undertaking proposes to employ for each class of business, including the data needed to calculate premium rates and reserves referred to in article 17;

c the guiding principles as to reinsurance;

d the items constituting the minimum of the guarantee fund;

e estimates relating to the expenses of installing the administrative services and the organisation for securing business and the financial resources intended to cover them.

For the first three financial years it must also include:

f a forecast balance sheet;

g a plan setting out detailed estimates of income and expenditure in respect of direct business, reinsurance acceptances and reinsurance cessions;
h estimates relating to the financial resources intended to cover underwriting liabilities and the solvency margin.

An undertaking seeking authorisation to open an agency or branch in another member state than the one in which its head office is established is required to submit its memorandum and articles of association and a list of its directors and managers. In addition, a certificate must be produced attesting the classes of insurance which the undertaking is entitled to cover in its head office member state. (article 10).

The scheme of operations to be submitted shall be adjusted to this special case (article 11) and, in addition, shall be accompanied by the balance sheet and the profit and loss account of the undertaking for each of the past three years. Finally, the undertaking is required to designate a general representative having his permanent residence and abode in the host country and possessing sufficient powers to bind the undertaking in relation to third parties and to represent it in relations with the authorities and courts of the host country.

Any decision to refuse an authorisation shall be accompanied by the precise grounds for doing so and each member state shall make provision for a right to appeal to the court should there be any refusal (article 12).

Article 13 states that no undertaking may simultaneously carry on in a member state the activities referred to in the annex of the first coordination directive (non-life insurance) and those listed in article 1 of this directive. Undertakings which at the time of notification of this directive carry on simultaneously in a member state both these activities may continue to do so there provided that each activity is separately managed in accordance with article 14. Article 14 sets out to achieve a separation of financial interests. Profits from life assurance may not be used to cover the losses from non-life insurance and in addition the minimum financial obligations, in particular solvency margins, in respect of one or other of the two activities, namely an activity under this directive or under the first coordination directive (non-life insurance) may not be borne by the other activity. If one of the solvency margins is insufficient, the supervisory authorities shall apply to the deficient activity the measures provided for in the relevant directive, whatever the results in the other activity.

After having discussed the conditions of admission, we will now proceed to discuss the conditions for the pursuit of activities of insurance undertakings having their head office within the Community (articles 15-25). The provisions apply to authorised and admitted undertakings.

Article 15 provides that member states shall collaborate closely with one another in supervising the financial position of authorised undertakings.

The supervisory authorities of the member state in whose territory the head office of the undertaking is situated must verify the state of solvency of the undertaking with respect to its entire business. The supervisory authorities of the other member states shall provide the former with all the information necessary to enable such verification to be effected (article 16).

The solvency margin comprises the free assets held to enable the undertaking to cope with the instability of the business. It therefore consists of assets of the undertaking not held to cover any foreseeable liability. The latter purpose is served by the technical reserves (article 17). In contrast to consolidated supervision of the solvency margin, supervision of the technical reserves is exercised by each individual member state. The amount of the technical reserves, including mathematical reserves, shall be determined according to the rules fixed by the member state concerned, or, in the absence of such rules, according to the practices in such state. Technical reserves, including mathematical reserves, shall be required to be covered by equivalent and matching assets localised in each country where the activities are carried on. The term 'matching assets' implies the representation of underwriting liabilities expressed in a particular currency by assets expressed or realisable in the same currency. The regulations of the country where the activities are carried on shall determine the nature of such assets and the extent to which they may be used for the purpose of covering the technical reserves, and shall also determine the rules for valuing such assets.

Article 18 deals further with the solvency margin. This solvency margin consists of:

1 the assets of the undertaking, free of all foreseeable liabilities, less any intangible items; in particular the following shall be included:
  - the paid-up share capital or, in the case of a mutual concern, the paid-up amount of its fund,
  - one half of the unpaid-up share capital or fund once 25% of such capital or fund are paid up,
  - statutory reserves and free reserves not corresponding to underwriting liabilities,
  - any carry-forward of profits;

2 in so far as authorised under national law, profit reserves appearing in the balance sheet where they may be used to cover any losses which may arise and where they have not been made available for distribution to policy-holders;

3 upon application, with supporting evidence, by the undertaking to the supervisory authority of the member state in the territory of which its head office is situated and with the agreement of that authority:

  a an amount equal to 50% of the undertaking's future profits;
  the amount of the future profits shall be obtained by multiplying the estimated annual profit by a factor which represents the average period left to run on policies; the factor used may not exceed 10; the estimated annual profit shall be the arithmetical average of the profits made over the last five years in the activities listed in article 1.

  The bases for calculating the factor by which the estimated annual profit is to be multiplied and the items comprising the profits made shall be defined by common agreement by the competent authorities of the member states in collaboration with the Commission. Pending such agreement, those items shall be determined in accordance with the laws of the member state in the territory of which the undertaking (head office, agency or branch) carries on its activities.

  When the competent authorities have defined the concept of profits made, the Commission shall submit proposals for the harmonisation of this concept by means of a directive on the harmonisation of the annual accounts of insurance undertakings and providing for the coordination set out in article 1, paragraph 2 of directive 78/660/EEC.

  b where zillmerising is not practised or where, if practised, it is less than the loading for acquisition costs included in the premium, the difference between a non-zillmerised or partially zillmerised mathematical reserve and a mathematical reserve zillmerised at a rate equal to the loading for acquisition costs included in the premium; this figure may not, however, exceed 3.5% of the sum of the differences between the relevant capital sums of life assurance activities and the mathematical reserves for all policies for which zillmerising is possible; the difference shall be reduced by the amount of any undepreciated acquisition costs entered as an asset.

  c where approval is given by the supervisory authorities of the member states concerned in which the undertaking is carrying on its activities any hidden reserves resulting from the under-estimation of assets and over-estimation of liabilities other than mathematical reserves in so far as such hidden reserves are not of an exceptional nature.

Under article 19 the minimum solvency margin shall be determined as shown below according to the classes of insurance underwritten:

a For the kind of insurance referred to in article 1, paragraphs 1a and 1b other than assurances linked to investment funds and for the operations referred to in article 1, paragraph 3, it must be equal to the sum of the following two results:

- first result:
  a 4% fraction of mathematical reserves, relating to direct business gross of re-insurance cessions and to re-insurance acceptances shall be multiplied by the ratio, for the last financial year, of the total mathematical reserves net of re-insurance cessions to the gross of total mathematical reserves as specified above; that ratio may in no case be less than 85%;
- second result:
  for policies on which the capital at risk is not a negative figure, a 0.3% fraction of such capital underwritten by the undertaking shall be multiplied by the ratio, for the last financial year, of the total capital at risk retained as the undertaking's liability after re-insurance cessions and retrocessions to the total capital at risk gross of re-insurance; that ratio may in no case be less than 50%;

For temporary assurance on death of a maximum term of three years the above fraction shall be 0.1%; for such assurance of a term of more than three years but not more than five years the above fraction shall be 0.15%.

b For the supplementary insurance referred to in article 1, paragraph 1c, it shall be equal to the result of the following calculation:
- the premiums or contributions (inclusive of charges ancillary to premiums or contributions) due in respect of direct business in the last financial year in respect of all financial years shall be aggregated;
- to this aggregate shall be added the amount of premiums accepted for all reinsurance in the last financial year;
- from this sum shall then be deducted the total amount of premiums or contributions cancelled in the last financial year as well as the total amount of taxes and levies pertaining to the premiums or contributions entering into the aggregate.

The amount so obtained shall be divided into two portions, the first extending up to 10 million units of account and the second comprising the excess; 18% and 16% of these portions respectively shall be calculated and added together.

The result shall be obtained by multiplying the sum so calculated by the ratio existing in respect of the last financial year between the amount of claims remaining to be borne by the undertaking after deduction of transfers for reinsurance and the gross amount of claims; this ratio may in no case be less than 50%.

In the case of the association of underwriters known as Lloyd's, the calculation of the solvency margin shall be made on the basis of net premiums, which shall be multiplied with the flat-rate percentage fixed annually by the supervisory authority of the head-office member state. This flat-rate percentage must be calculated on the basis of the most recent statistical data on commissions paid. The details together with the relevant calculations shall be sent to the supervisory authorities of the countries in whose territory Lloyd's is established.

c For permanent health insurance not subject to cancellation referred to in article 1, paragraph 1d, and for capital redemption operations referred to in article 1, paragraph 2b, it shall be equal to a 4% fraction of the mathematical reserves calculated in compliance with the conditions set out in the first result (a) of this article.

d For tontines, referred to in article 1, paragraph 2a, it shall be equal to 1% of their assets.

e For assurances covered by article 1, paragraphs 1a and 1b, linked to investment funds and for the operations referred to in article 1, paragraphs 2c, 2d and 2e it shall be equal to:
- a 4% fraction of the mathematical reserves, calculated in compliance with the conditions set out in the first result (a) of this article in so far as the undertaking bears an investment risk, and a 1% fraction of the reserves calculated in the fashion, in so far as the undertaking bears no investment risk provided that the term of the contract exceeds five years and the allocation to cover management expenses set out in the contract is fixed for a period exceeding five years

plus

- a 0.3% fraction of the capital at risk calculated in compliance with the conditions set out in the first subparagraph of the second result of (a) of this article in so far as the undertaking covers a death risk.

The purpose of the minimum guarantee fund is to ensure that insurance undertakings already have sufficient means at the time of their establishment and to prevent the solvency margin of the undertaking from falling below a minimum safety margin during the pursuit of business. Article 20 provides that the minimum guarantee fund shall amount to one third of the minimum solvency margin as specified in article 19. The guarantee fund may not, however, be less than a minimum of 800,000 units of account and must consist of the items listed in article 18, paragraphs 1 and 2.

Under article 23 each member state requires every undertaking whose head office is situated in its territory to produce an annual account, covering all types of operation, of its financial situation and solvency. In addition, these undertakings are required to render periodically the returns, together with statistical documents, which are necessary for the purposes of supervision.

Article 24 deals with situations arising when an undertaking no longer complies with the requirements relating to the technical reserves, the solvency margin and the minimum guarantee fund:

1 If an undertaking does not comply with the provisions envisaged in article 17, the supervisory authority of the member state in whose territory it carries on its activity may prohibit the free disposal of assets located in that member state after having informed the supervisory authorities of the head-office member state of its intention.
2 For the purpose of restoring the financial situation of an undertaking whose solvency margin has fallen below the minimum required under article 19, the supervisory authority of the head-office member state shall require a plan for the restoration of a sound financial position to be submitted for its approval.
3 If the solvency margin falls below the guarantee fund as defined in article 20, or if the latter is no longer constituted as laid down in that article, the supervisory authorities of the head-office member state shall require the undertaking to submit a short-term finance scheme for its approval.
   It may also restrict or prohibit the free disposal of the assets of the undertaking.
4 The competent supervisory authorities may further take all measures necessary to safeguard the policy-holders' interests in the cases provided for in paragraphs 1 and 3.

Article 25 requires each member state to make it possible for an authorised undertaking to assign all or part of its portfolio of policies if the assignees possess the necessary solvency margin, due account being taken of the assignment.

The conditions for the taking-up and pursuit of the activities of insurance undertakings with head office in the Community have been discussed above. Article 26 deals finally with the possible withdrawal of authorisation of such undertakings.

1 The authorisation granted by the competent authority of the member state in whose territory the head office is situated may be withdrawn by such authority if the undertaking:
   a no longer fulfils the conditions of admission;
   b has been unable, within the time allowed, to take the measures contained in the restoration plan or financial scheme referred to in article 24;
   c fails seriously in its obligations under the national regulations.

   In the event of the withdrawal of the authorisation, the supervisory authority of the head-office member state shall notify such withdrawal to the supervisory authorities of other member states which have authorised the undertaking; they shall, thereupon, also withdraw their authorisation.

The supervisory authority of the head-office member state shall, in conjunction with such other authorities, take all the necessary measures to safeguard policy-holders' interests and, in particular, shall restrict the free disposal of the assets of the undertaking if such restriction has not been already imposed in accordance with the provisions of the second subparagraph of article 24, paragraph 1 and 3.

2 An authorisation granted to an agency or branch of an undertaking whose head office is situated in another member state may be withdrawn if the agency or branch:

a no longer fulfils the conditions for admission;

b fails seriously in its obligations under the regulations of the member state where it carries on its activity, with respect in particular to the establishment of reserves referred to in article 17.

Before withdrawing authorisation the supervisory authorities of the member state where the activity is carried on shall consult the supervisory authority of the member state where the head office is situated. If they deem it necessary to suspend the business of such agency or branch before consultation is concluded, they shall immediately advise the supervisory authority of the country where the head office is situated.

3 Any decision to withdraw authorisation or suspend business shall be supported by precise reasons and notified to the undertaking in question.

Each member state shall make provision for a right to apply to the courts against such a decision.

Rules applicable to agencies or branches established within the Community and belonging to undertakings whose head offices are outside the Community

Each member state shall make access to the activities referred to in article 1 by any undertaking whose head office is outside the Community subject to an official authorisation (article 27, paragraph 1). A member state may grant an authorisation if the undertaking fulfils at least the following conditions:

a it is entitled to undertake insurance activities covered by article 1 under its national law;

b it establishes an agency or branch in the territory of such member state;

c it undertakes to establish at the place of management of the agency or branch accounts specific to the activity which it carries on there and to keep there all the records relating to the business transacted;

d it designates a general representative, to be approved by the competent authorities;

e it possesses in the member state where it carries on its activities assets of an amount equal in value to at least one half of the minimum amount prescribed in article 20, paragraph 2a, in respect of the guarantee fund and deposits one fourth of the minimum amount as security;

f it undertakes to keep a solvency margin complying with article 29;

g it submits a scheme of operations in accordance with article 11, paragraphs 1 and 2.

Such undertakings are required to establish reserves, referred to in article 17, adequate to cover the underwriting liabilities assumed in the territory of the member state and such reserves shall be covered by means of assets which are equivalent to said reserves and, to the extent fixed by the member state in question, matching assets (article 28). The size of these reserves shall be determined according to the laws of the member state in which the agency or branch is situated.

Article 29 provides that each member state shall require of agencies or branches set up in its territory a solvency margin consisting of the items listed in article 18 and calculated in accordance with article 19. For the purpose of calculating this margin, account shall be taken only of the operations effected by the agency or branch concerned. The minimum guarantee fund is calculated in accordance with article 20. The assets representing the minimum solvency margin must be kept within the member state where activities are carried on up to the amount of the guarantee fund and the excess within the Community.

Under article 30 any undertaking which has requested or obtained authorisation from more than one member state may apply for the following advantages which may be granted only jointly:

a the solvency margin referred to in article 29 shall be calculated in relation to the entire business which it carries on within the Community; in such case, account shall be taken only of the operations effected by all agencies or branches established within the Community for the purpose of this calculation;

b the deposit required under article 27, paragraph 2e, shall be lodged in only one of those member states;

c the assets representing the guarantee fund shall be localised in any one of the member states in which it carries on its activities.

The advantages referred to above may only be granted if the competent authorities of all member states in which an application has been made agree to them. They shall take effect from the time when the selected supervisory authority informs the other supervisory authorities that it will supervise the state of solvency of the entire business of the agencies or branches within the Community.

Agencies and branches covered by this first coordination directive on life assurance may not simultaneously carry on in a member state the activities referred to in the annex to the first coordination directive on non-life insurance (article 31). Only if they manage each of these activities separately, may such agencies and branches which, at the time of notification of this directive, carry on both activities simultaneously in a member state, continue to do so.

Articles 23 and 24 relating to supervision of the technical reserve, the solvency margin and the minimum guarantee fund shall also apply to agencies and branches.

For the purpose of applying article 24, the supervisory authority which supervises the overall solvency of agencies and branches shall be treated in the same way as the supervisory authority of the head-office member state. In the case of withdrawal of authorisation by the authority referred to in article 30, paragraph 2, this authority shall notify the supervisory authorities of the other member states where the undertaking operates and the latter authorities shall take the appropriate measures. If the reason for the withdrawal is the inadequacy of the solvency margin, the supervisory authorities of the other member states concerned shall also withdraw their authorisations.

XXVI SECOND COUNCIL DIRECTIVE OF NOVEMBER 8, 1990 ON THE COORDINATION OF LAWS, REGULATIONS AND ADMINISTRATIVE PROVISIONS RELATING TO DIRECT LIFE ASSURANCE, LAYING DOWN PROVISIONS TO FACILITATE THE EFFECTIVE EXERCISE OF FREEDOM TO PROVIDE SERVICES AND AMENDING DIRECTIVE 79/267/EEC

(OJEC L 330 29.11.1990, directive 90/619/EEC)

The internal insurance market requires that it must be made possible for policy-holders to have recourse not only to assurers established in their own country, but also to assurers which have their head office in the Community and are established in other member states. The first coordination directive 79/267/EEC of March 5, 1979 achieved initial coordination in the field of freedom of establishment. The objectives of this second coordination directive are twofold. On the one hand it supplements the first coordination directive by clarifying the powers and means of supervision vested in the supervising authorities, and on the other hand it lays down specific provisions regarding the taking-up, pursuit and supervision of activity in the context of the freedom to provide services. The directive provides for a substantial freedom to provide services to life assurance buyers who take the initiative in seeking services cover. Policy-holders who, by virtue of the fact that they take the initiative in entering into a commitment in another state and thus place themselves under the protection of the legal system of that other state, do not require special protection in the state of the commitment (home country control rather than host country control) and should be granted complete freedom to avail themselves of the widest possible market in life assurance. On the other hand, the directive provides for application of the rules of, and supervision by, the country in which the service is provided (host country control) when it is the undertaking that takes the initiative in entering into a contractual relationship.

Another important aim of the directive under review is the introduction of the principle of national treatment with respect to life assurance undertakings from third (non-EC) countries. The scope of this principle is identical to the scope applicable to credit institutions, investment firms and non-life insurance undertakings.

XXVII PROPOSAL FOR A THIRD COUNCIL DIRECTIVE ON THE COORDINATION OF LAWS, REGULATIONS AND ADMINISTRATIVE PROVISIONS RELATING TO DIRECT LIFE ASSURANCE AND AMENDING DIRECTIVES 79/267/EEC AND 90/619/EEC

(OJEC C 99 16.4.1991, proposal (91) 57)

The aim of this proposed directive is to complete the internal market in direct life assurance from the point of view both of the freedom of establishment and of the freedom to provide services. The second life coordination directive already grants complete freedom to policy-holders who, by virtue of the fact that they take the initiative in entering into a commitment in another state and thus place themselves under the protection of that other state, do not require special protection in the state of the commitment. The proposal under review supplements the second life directive by enabling all policy-holders, irrespective of their status, their size or the nature of the risks to be insured, to have recourse to any insurer with a head office in the Community who carries on business there, under the right of establishment or the freedom to provide services, while guaranteeing them adequate protection. This complete freedom is to be achieved by bringing about such harmonisation as is essential, necessary and sufficient to achieve the mutual recognition of authorisations and prudential control systems, thereby making it possible to grant a single authorisation valid throughout the Community and to apply the principle of supervision by the home member state. Home member states will henceforth be responsible for monitoring the financial health of insurance undertakings, including their state of solvency, the establishment of adequate technical provisions and the covering of those provisions by matching assets.

The proposal does not mention a planned date of implementation after the proposal has been adopted by the Council. In any case this date will not be before July 1, 1994 which is the planned date of implementation of the third non-life insurance directive.

5.6 Coordination of co-insurance

XXVIII COUNCIL DIRECTIVE OF MAY 30, 1978 ON THE COORDINATION OF LAWS, REGULATIONS AND ADMINISTRATIVE PROVISIONS RELATING TO COMMUNITY CO-INSURANCE

(OJEC L 151 7.6.1978, directive 78/473/EEC)

The objective of this directive is to facilitate the effective exercise of Community co-insurance business by means of a minimum of coordination. This coordination covers only those co-insurance operations which are economically the most important, i.e. those which by reason of their nature or their size are eligible to be covered by international co-insurance.

By virtue of article 2 this directive applies only to those Community co-insurance operations which satisfy the following conditions:

a the risk, within the meaning of article 1, paragraph 1, is covered by a single contract at an overall premium and for the same period by two or more insurance undertakings, hereinafter referred to as co-insurers, each for its own part; one of these undertakings shall be the leading insurer;

b the risk is situated within the Community;

c for the purpose of covering this risk, the leading insurer is authorised in accordance with the conditions laid down in the first coordination directive, i.e. he is treated as if he were the insurer covering the whole risk;

d at least one of the co-insurers participates in the contract by means of a head office, agency or branch established in a member state other than that of the leading insurer;

e the leading insurer fully assumes the leader's role in co-insurance practice and in particular determines the terms and conditions of insurance and rating.

Those co-insurance operations which do not satisfy the conditions set out above or which cover risks other than those specified in article 1 shall remain subject to the national laws operative at the time when this directive comes into force.

The directive under review applies only to Community co-insurance transactions covering the following risks:

- Railway rolling stock.
  All damage to or loss of railway rolling stock.
- Aircraft.
  All damage to or loss of aircraft.
- Ships (sea, lake and river and canal vessels)
  All damage or loss of river and canal vessels, lake vessels and sea vessels.
- Goods in transit (including merchandise, baggage and all other goods).
  All damage to or loss of goods in transit or baggage, irrespective of the form of transport.
- Fire and natural forces.
  All damage to or loss of property (other than properties referred to above) due to fire, explosion, storm, natural forces other than storm, nuclear energy and land subsidence.
- Other damage to property.
  All damage to or loss of property (other than property referred to above) due to hail, frost and any event such as theft other than those mentioned under 'fire and natural forces'.
- Aircraft liability.
  All liability arising out of the use of aircraft, including carrier's liability.
- Liability for ships (sea, lake, river and canal vessels).
  All liability arising out of the use of ships, vessels or boats on the sea, rivers, lakes or canals, including carrier's liability.
- General liability.
  All liability other than those referred to above. Motor vehicle liability and damage caused by nuclear reactions or by drugs are also excluded.
- Miscellaneous financial loss.
  - employment risks;
  - insufficiency of income (general);
  - bad weather;
  - loss of benefits;
  - continuing general expenses;
  - unforeseen trading expenses;
  - loss of market value;
  - loss of rent or revenue;

- ° indirect trading losses other than those mentioned above;
- ° other financial loss (non-trading);
- ° other forms of financial loss.

Under article 4 the value of the technical reserves is determined by the different co-insurers according to the rules fixed by the member state where they are established, or in the absence of such rules, according to customary practice in that state.

The technical reserves shall be represented by matching assets, this means the representation of underwriting liabilities expressed in a particular currency by assets expressed or realisable in the same currency. Such assets shall be localised either in the member states in which the co-insurers are established or in the member state in which the leading insurer is established, whichever the insurer chooses.

Under article 5, the member states shall ensure that co-insurers established in their territory keep statistical data showing the extent of Community co-insurance operations and the countries concerned.

Article 6 states that the supervisory authorities of the member states shall cooperate closely in the implementation of this directive and shall provide each other with all the information necessary to this end.

In the event of an insurance undertaking being wound up, liabilities arising from participation in Community co-insurance contracts shall be met in the same way as those arising under that undertaking's other insurance contracts without distinction as to the nationality of the insured and of the beneficiaries (article 7).

This directive, adopted by the Council in 1978, did not answer the question whether the leading insurer must be established in the member state in which the insured risk is situated. In more general terms the question is whether a member state can require a foreign insurer to be either established or authorised in the host member state in order to be permitted to provide services in the concerned member state. The European Court handed down its verdicts in the four insurance judgements of December 4, 1986, which were discussed at the beginning of this study. In the case of co-insurance the Court was of the opinion that the requirement of establishment in, or authorisation by, the host country was incompatible with Community laws.

This is because co-insurance involves the insurance of large industrial, commercial or professional risks, where the policy-holder is considered to be a market party big enough to form an adequate opinion of the quality and reliability of the foreign insurer. This verdict supplements the directive on Community co-insurance.

Another problem arising out of the directive under review lies in the field of the nature and volume of the insured risks. The preamble to the directive states that the coordination covers only those co-insurance operations which are economically the most important, i.e. those which by reason of their nature or their size are liable to be covered by international co-insurance.

As far as the nature of the risks is concerned there is agreement that only industrial, commercial and professional risks fall within the scope of the directive. As regards the volume of the risks, both supervisors and insurance undertakings are not yet in agreement about the threshold values below which the insurance of the various risks does not fall within the scope of the directive.

5.7 Coordination of insurance agents and brokers

XXIX *COUNCIL DIRECTIVE OF DECEMBER 13, 1976 ON MEASURES TO FACILITATE THE EFFECTIVE EXERCISE OF FREEDOM OF ESTABLISHMENT AND FREEDOM TO PROVIDE SERVICES IN RESPECT OF THE ACTIVITIES OF INSURANCE AGENTS AND BROKERS AND, IN PARTICULAR, TRANSITIONAL MEASURES IN RESPECT OF THOSE ACTIVITIES*

(OJEC L 26 31.1.1977, directive 77/92/EEC)

Under the Treaty of Rome and confirmed by the Reyners and Van Binsbergen judgements of 1974, any discriminatory treatment on the basis of nationality with regard to establishment and to the provision of services has been prohibited since the end of the transitional period on January 1, 1970.

There is thus formal freedom with regard to the taking up and pursuit of the activities of insurance agents and brokers. But there are strict provisions making access to the profession conditional upon possession of formal evidence of qualifications. This anomaly can be resolved by the mutual recognition of diplomas, certificates and other evidence of formal qualifications and by the coordination of the provisions laid down by law, regulation or administrative provisions in member states. In 1976 there was not yet sufficient agreement to bring about such mutual recognition and coordination. This directive therefore confines itself to indicating transitional measures. The object of these measures is to allow as sufficient qualification for taking up the activities in question in host member states which have rules concerning the taking up of such activities, the fact that the activity has been pursued in the member state whence the person concerned comes for a reasonable and sufficiently recent period of time, in cases where previous training is not required, to ensure that the person concerned possesses professional knowledge equivalent to that required of the host member state's own nationals. The justification for this directive will disappear once the coordination of the conditions for the taking up and pursuit of the activities in question and the mutual recognition of diploma's, certificates and other formal qualifications have been achieved.

A summary of this directive is given below.

Article 1

1 Member states shall adopt the measures defined in this directive in respect of establishment or provision of services in their territories by natural persons and companies or firms covered by Title I of the general programmes (hereinafter referred to as 'beneficiaries') wishing to pursue in a self-employed capacity the activities as referred to in article 2.

2 This directive shall also apply to nationals of member states who, as provided in Regulation (EEC) No 1612/68, wish to pursue as paid employees the activities referred to in article 2.

Article 2

1 This directive applies to the following activities:

a professional activities of persons who, acting with complete freedom as to their choice of undertaking, bring together, with a view to the insurance or reinsurance of risks, persons seeking insurance or reinsurance undertakings, carry out work preparatory to the conclusion of contracts of insurance or reinsurance and, where appropriate, assist in the administration and performance of such contracts, in particular in the event of a claim;

b professional activities of persons instructed under one or more contracts or empowered to act in the name and on behalf of, or solely on behalf of, one or more insurance undertakings in introducing, proposing and carrying out work preparatory to the conclusion of, or in concluding, contracts of insurance, or in assisting in the administration and performance of such contracts, in particular in the event of a claim;

c activities of persons other than those referred to in (a) and (b) who acting on behalf of such persons, among other things carry out introductory work, introduce contracts or collect premiums, provided that no insurance commitments towards or on the part of the public are given as part of these operations.

2 This directive applies in particular to activities customarily described in the member states as follows:

a activities referred to in paragraph 1a:

- *Belgium*
  - Courtier d'assurance, verzekeringsmakelaar;
  - Courtier de réassurance, Herverzekeringsmakelaar;
- *in Denmark*
  - Juridiske og fysiske personer, som driver selvstændig virksomhed som formidler ved afsæthing af forsikringskontrakter;
- *in Germany*
  - Versicherungsmakler,
  - Rückversicherungsmakler;
- *in France*
  - Courtier d'assurance,
  - Courtier d'assurance maritime,
  - Courtier de réassurance;
- *in Ireland*
  - Insurance broker,
  - Reinsurance broker;
- *in Italy*
  - Mediatore di assicurazioni,
  - Mediatore di riassicurazioni;
- *in the Netherlands*
  - Makelaar,
  - Assurantiebezorger,
  - Erkend assurantieagent,
  - Verzekeringsagent;
- *in the United Kingdom*
  - Insurance broker;

b activities referred to in paragraph 1b;

- *in Belgium*
  - Agent d'assurance,
  - Verzekeringsagent;
- *in Denmark*
  - Forsikringsagent;
- *in Germany*
  - Versicherungsvertreter;
- *in France*
  - Agent général d'assurance;
- *in Ireland*
  - Agent;
- *in Italy*
  - Agente di assicurazioni;
- *in Luxembourg*
  - Agent principal d'assurance,

- Agent d'assurance;
- *in the Netherlands*
  - Gevolmachtigd agent,
  - Verzekeringsagent;
- *in the United Kingdom*
  - Agent;

c activities referred to in paragraph 1c:
- *in Belgium*
  - Sous-agent,
  - Sub-agent;
- *in Denmark*
  - Underagent;
- *in Germany*
  - Gelegenheitsvermittler,
  - Inkassant;
- *in France*
  - Mandataire,
  - Intermédiaire,
  - Sous-agent;
- *in Ireland*
  - Sub-agent;
- *in Italy*
  - Subagente;
- *in Luxembourg*
  - Sous-agent;
- *in the Netherlands*
  - Sub-agent;
- *in the United Kingdom*
  - Sub-agent.

Article 3

Member states in which the taking up or pursuit of any activity referred to in article 2 is subject to the fulfilment of certain qualifying conditions shall ensure that any beneficiary who applies therefor be provided, before he establishes himself or before he begins to pursue any activity on a temporary basis, with information as to the rules governing the profession which he proposes to pursue.

Article 4

Where in a member state the taking up or pursuit of any activity referred to in article 2, paragraph 1a and 1b, is subject to possession of general commercial or professional knowledge, that member state shall accept as sufficient evidence of such knowledge and ability the fact that one of the activities in question has been pursued in another member state for any of the following periods:

a four consecutive years in an independent capacity or in a managerial capacity; or

b two consecutive years in an independent capacity or in a managerial capacity, where the beneficiary proves that he has worked for at least three years with one or more insurance agents or brokers or with one or more insurance undertakings; or

c one year in an independent capacity or in a managerial capacity, where the beneficiary proves that for the activity in question he has received previous training attested by a certificate recognised by the state or regarded by a competent professional body as fully satisfying its requirements.

Article 5

1 If a member state makes the taking up or pursuit of any activity referred to in article 2, paragraph 1a, dependent on more stringent requirements than those which it lays down in respect of the activities referred to in article 2, paragraph 1b, it may in the case of the taking up or pursuit of the first-mentioned activity require this to have been pursued in another member state in the branch of the profession referred to in article 2, paragraph 1a for:

a four consecutive years in an independent capacity or in a managerial capacity; or

b two consecutive years in an independent capacity or in a managerial capacity, where the beneficiary proves that he has worked for at least three years with one or more insurance agents or brokers or with one or more insurance undertakings; or

c one year in an independent capacity or in a managerial capacity, where the beneficiary proves that for the activity in question he has received previous training attested by a certificate recognised by the state or regarded by a competent professional body as fully satisfying its requirements.

An activity pursued by the beneficiary in accordance with article 2, paragraph 1b, where it includes the exercise of a permanent authority from one or more insurance undertakings empowering the person concerned, in respect of certain or all transactions falling within the normal scope of the business of the undertaking or undertakings concerned, to enter in the name of such undertaking or undertakings into commitments binding upon it or them, shall be regarded as equivalent to the activity referred to in article 2, paragraph 1a.

2 however, in *the Netherlands*, the taking up or pursuit of the activities referred to in article 2, paragraph 1a, shall in addition be subject to the following conditions:

- where the beneficiary wishes to work as a 'makelaar', he must have carried on the activities concerned in a business where he was in charge of at least ten employees,
- where the beneficiary wishes to work as an 'assurantiebezorger', he must have carried on the activities concerned in a business where he was in charge of at least five employees,
- where the beneficiary wishes to work as an 'erkend assurantieagent', he must have carried on the activities concerned in a business where he was in charge of at least two employees.

Article 6

1 Where in a member state the taking up or pursuit of an activity referred to in article 2, paragraph 1c, is dependent on the possession of general, commercial or professional knowledge and ability, that member state shall accept as sufficient evidence of such knowledge and ability the fact that the activity in question has been pursued in another member state for either of the following periods:

a two consecutive years either in an independent capacity or working with one or more insurance agents or brokers or with one or more insurance undertakings; or

b one year under the conditions specified under paragraph a, where the beneficiary proves that for the capacity in question he has received previous training attested by a certificate recognised by the state or regarded by a competent professional body as fully satisfying its requirements.

2 The pursuit for at least one year of one of the activities referred to in article 2, paragraph 1a or 1b, and the receipt of the relevant training shall be regarded as satisfying the requirements laid down in paragraph 1.

Article 7

In the cases referred to in articles 4, 5 and 6, pursuit of the activity in question shall not have ceased more than ten years before the date when the application provided for in article 9, paragraph 1, is made. However, where a shorter period is laid down in a member state for its own nationals, that period must also be applied in respect of beneficiaries.

Article 8

1 A person shall be regarded as having pursued an activity in a managerial capacity within the meaning of articles 4 and 5, paragraph 1 where he has pursued the corresponding activity:

a as manager of an undertaking or manager of a branch of an undertaking; or

b as a deputy to the manager of an undertaking or as its authorised representative, where such post involved responsibility equivalent to that of the manager represented.

2 A person shall also be regarded as having pursued an activity in a managerial capacity within the meaning of article 4 where his duties in an insurance undertaking have involved the management of agents or the supervision of their work.

3 The work referred to in articles 4b and 5, paragraph 1b, must have entailed responsibility in respect of the acquisition, administration and performance of contracts of insurance.

Article 9

1 Proof that the conditions laid down in articles 4, 5, 6 and 7 are satisfied shall be established by a certificate, issued by the competent authority or body in the member state of origin or member state whence the person concerned comes, which the latter shall submit in support of his application to pursue one of the activities in question in the host member state.

2 Member states shall, within the time limit laid down in article 13, designate the authorities and bodies competent to issue the certificate referred to in paragraph 1 and shall forthwith inform the other member states and the Commission thereof.

3 Within the time limit laid down in article 13 every member state shall also inform the other member states and the Commission of the authorities and bodies to which an application to pursue in the host member state an activity referred to in article 2 and the documents in support thereof are to be submitted.

Article 10

1 Where a host member state requires of its own nationals wishing to take up or pursue any activity referred to in article 2 proof of good repute and proof that they have not previously been declared bankrupt, or proof of either one of these, it shall accept as sufficient evidence in respect of nationals of other member states the production of an extract from the 'judicial record' or, failing this, of an equivalent document issued by a competent judicial or administrative authority in the member state of origin or the member state whence the foreign national comes showing that these requirements have been met.

2 Where the member state of origin or the member state whence the foreign national concerned comes does not issue the document referred to in paragraph 1 it may be replaced by a declaration on oath,--or, in states where there is no provision for declaration on oath, by a solemn declaration-- made by the person concerned before a competent judicial or administrative body or, where appropriate, a notary in the member state of origin or the member state whence that person comes; such authority or notary shall issue a certificate attesting the authenticity of the declaration on oath or solemn declaration. The declaration in respect of no previous bankruptcy may also be made before a competent professional body in the said country.

3 Documents issued in accordance with paragraphs 1 and 2 must not be produced more than three months after their date of issue.

4 Member states shall, within the time limit laid down in article 13, designate the authorities and bodies competent to issue the documents referred to in paragraphs 1 and 2 of this article and shall forthwith inform the other member states and the Commission thereof.

Within the time limit laid down in article 13, each member state shall also inform the other member states and the Commission of the authorities or bodies to which the documents referred to in this article are to be submitted in support of an application to carry on in the host member state an activity referred to in article 2.

5 Where in the host member state proof of financial standing is required, that member state shall regard certificates issued by banks in the member state of origin or the member state whence the foreign national concerned comes as equivalent to certificates issued in its own territory.

Article 11

A host member state, where it requires its own nationals wishing to take up or to pursue one of the activities referred to in article 2 to take an oath or make a solemn declaration, and where the form of such oath or declaration cannot be used by nationals of other member states, shall ensure that an appropriate and equivalent form of oath or declaration is offered to the persons concerned.

Article 12

This directive shall remain applicable until the entry into force of provisions relating to the coordination of national rules concerning the taking up and pursuit of the activities in question.

Article 13

Member states shall bring into force the measures necessary to comply with this directive within eighteen months of its notification and shall forthwith inform the Commission thereof.

XXX COMMUNICATION FROM THE COMMISSION CONCERNING THE PROOFS, DECLARATIONS AND CERTIFICATES LAID DOWN IN THE COUNCIL DIRECTIVE OF DECEMBER 13, 1976 ON MEASURES TO FACILITATE THE EFFECTIVE EXERCISE OF FREEDOM OF ESTABLISHMENT AND FREEDOM TO PROVIDE SERVICES IN RESPECT OF THE ACTIVITIES OF INSURANCE AGENTS AND BROKERS AND, IN PARTICULAR, TRANSITIONAL MEASURES IN RESPECT OF THOSE ACTIVITIES.

(OJEC C 136 5.6.1981, communication 77/92/EEC)

Article 9, paragraph 2 of the directive of December 13, 1976, requires the member states to designate the authorities and bodies competent to issue the certificate concerning the professional knowledge of insurance agents and brokers from other member states. The communication in question offers a survey of said authorities and bodies.

XXXI COMMISSION RECOMMENDATION OF DECEMBER 18, 1991 ON INSURANCE INTERMEDIARIES

(OJEC L 19 28.1.1992, recommendation 92/48/EEC)

In this recommendation the Commission recommends to the member states that they ensure that insurance intermediaries established on their territory are subject to professional requirements and registration in accordance with the provisions contained in the annex to the recommendation. The professional requirements are related to the independence of insurance intermediaries and to their professional competence. Only registered persons shall be allowed to take up and pursue the activity of insurance intermediary.

5.8 Coordination of annual accounts and consolidated annual accounts

XXXII COUNCIL DIRECTIVE OF DECEMBER 19, 1991 ON THE ANNUAL ACCOUNTS AND CONSOLIDATED ANNUAL ACCOUNTS OF INSURANCE UNDERTAKINGS

(OJEC L 374 31.12.1991, directive 91/674/EEC)

The need for a separate directive on the annual accounts and consolidated annual accounts of insurance undertakings follows from the fact that insurance companies need not completely comply with the rules of Council directive 78/660/EEC on the annual accounts of certain types of companies and with the rules of Council directive 83/349/EEC on the consolidated annual accounts. For this reason, the directive under review first defines the articles in 78/660/EEC and 83/349/EEC applicable as well to insurance undertakings, after which the directive deals with derogations from the rules laid down in the two directives mentioned above.

Coordination in the field of the annual accounts and consolidated annual accounts of insurance companies serves the goal of improved comparability of these accounts across borders, which is in the interest of creditors, debtors, members and policy-holders of the Community insurance companies. In order to achieve this comparability, the directive settles a number of basic questions regarding the disclosure of certain transactions in the balance sheet and determines precisely the content of the various balance sheet items.

The planned date of implementation of the directive is January 1, 1994. However, member states may provide that the provisions of this directive shall first apply to annual accounts and consolidated annual accounts for financial years beginning on January 1, 1995 or during the calendar year 1995.

5.9 Remaining coordination

Two proposals representing other coordination efforts in the field of insurance are discussed below. They relate to coordination relating to insurance contracts and the compulsory winding-up of insurance undertakings.

XXXIII PROPOSAL FOR A COUNCIL DIRECTIVE ON THE COORDINATION OF LAWS, REGULATIONS AND ADMINISTRATIVE PROVISIONS RELATING TO INSURANCE CONTRACTS

(OJEC C 190 28.7.1979)

THE PROPOSAL WAS AMENDED IN 1980

(OJEC C 355 31.12.1980)

The objective of this draft directive is twofold. On the one hand assuring the policy-holder of protection on essential items in the contract, regardless of which national laws are applicable, and on the other hand the removal of the most important differences between the national laws and regulations in order to achieve fair competition.

XXXIV PROPOSAL FOR A COUNCIL DIRECTIVE ON THE COORDINATION OF LAWS, REGULATIONS AND ADMINISTRATIVE PROVISIONS RELATING TO THE COMPULSORY WINDING-UP OF DIRECT INSURANCE UNDERTAKINGS

(OJEC C 71 19.3.1987, proposal (86) 768)

THE PROPOSAL WAS AMENDED IN 1989

(OJEC C 253 6.10.1989, proposal (89) 394)

The proposal concerns the compulsory winding-up of insurance undertakings covered by the first coordination directive on non-life insurance and the first coordination directive on life assurance.

The objective of the proposal is, to achieve, by means of one single Community procedure, equal treatment for all insurance creditors, regardless of the member state in which they have concluded a contract with the insurer, in case of the winding-up of the insurer.

VI. PENSION FUNDS

I PROPOSAL FOR A COUNCIL DIRECTIVE RELATING TO THE FREEDOM OF MANAGEMENT AND INVESTMENT OF FUNDS HELD BY INSTITUTIONS FOR RETIREMENT PROVISION

(OJEC C 312 3.12.1991, proposal (91) 301)

With regard to the pension fund market, the Commission has identified three principal objectives which aim to implement effectively the Treaty giving freedom of services and capital movements for institutions for retirement provision. These objectives are:

- Freedom of cross-border investment management;
- Freedom of cross-border investment;
- Freedom of cross-border membership of such institutions.

Community legislation in these fields has become more important because of progress towards the single market in the area of life assurance. Particularly the adoption of the second life assurance directive which includes group life assurance contracts within its scope, has created a regulatory disadvantage for pension funds since these contracts are often used for the provision of pension benefits. In this way it will become possible for occupational pension benefits to be provided across national borders by means of life assurance contracts.

At this stage the Commission is of the opinion that the practical problems related to the objective of cross-border membership require further study before any additional legislation could be proposed. Therefore, the proposal under review only deals with the aspect of institutions for retirement provision as financial institutions, in other words with the first two of the three objectives outlined above. As the proposal does not cover the objective of cross-border membership, it does not require mutual recognition of the supervisory systems in different member states. The proposal merely aims to facilitate the exercise of freedoms for pension funds in respect of the investment of their assets and their choice of investment manager.

The freedom of cross-border investment management implies that institutions for retirement provision are free to select a provider of the service of investment management who is not established in their own member state. The same applies to the service of acting as a custodian or depositary for the assets of pension funds.

Concerning the freedom of cross-border investment the proposal lays down a number of principles for the prudent investment of assets of institutions for retirement provision. These principles are:

- The assets shall be invested in a manner appropriate to the nature and the duration of the corresponding liabilities and the level of their funding, taking account of the requirements of security, quality and profitability of the institution's portfolio as a whole;
- The assets shall be sufficiently diversified in such a way as to avoid major accumulations of risk in the portfolio as a whole;
- Investment in the sponsoring undertaking or undertakings shall be restricted to a prudent level.

The proposal not only lays down rules for prudent investment, but also restricts the possibilities for member states to apply rules which would limit the cross-border freedom of investment. In this respect the proposal states that member states shall not require institutions for retirement provision to invest in particular categories of assets or to localise their assets in a particular member state.

If adopted, the directive will have to be implemented on January 1, 1993.

FINANCIAL AND MONETARY POLICY STUDIES

*1. J.S.G. Wilson and C.F. Scheffer (eds.): *Multinational Enterprises.* Financial and Monitary Aspects. 1974 ISBN 90-286-0124-4

*2. H. Fournier and J.E. Wadsworth (eds.): *Floating Exchange Rates.* The Lessons of Recent Experience. 1976 ISBN 90-286-0565-7

*3. J.E. Wadsworth, J.S.G. Wilson and H. Fournier (eds.): *The Development of Financial Institutions in Europe, 1956–1976.* 1977 ISBN 90-286-0337-9

*4. J.E. Wadsworth and F.L. de Juvigny (eds.): *New Approaches in Monetary Policy.* 1979 ISBN 90-286-0848-6

*5. J.R. Sargent (ed.), R. Bertrand, J.S.G. Wilson and T.M. Rybczynski (ass. eds.): *Europe and the Dollar in the World-Wide Disequilibrium.* 1981 ISBN 90-286-0700-5

*6. D.E. Fair and F.L. de Juvigny (eds.): *Bank Management in a Changing Domestic and International Environment.* The Challenges of the Eighties. 1982 ISBN 90-247-2606-9

*7. D.E. Fair (ed.) in cooperation with R. Bertrand: *International Lending in a Fragile World Economy.* 1983 ISBN 90-247-2809-6

8. P. Salin (ed.): *Currency Competition and Monetary Union.* 1984 ISBN 90-247-2817-7

*9. D.E. Fair (ed.) in cooperation with F.L. de Juvigny: *Government Policies and the Working of Financial Systems in Industrialized Countries.* 1984 ISBN 90-247-3076-7

10. C. Goedhart, G.A. Kessler, J. Kymmell and F. de Roos (eds.): *Jelle Zijlstra, A Central Banker's View.* Selected Speeches and Articles. 1985 ISBN 90-247-3184-4

11. C. van Ewijk and J.J. Klant (eds.): *Monetary Conditions for Economic Recovery.* 1985 ISBN 90-247-3219-0

*12. D.E. Fair (ed.): *Shifting Frontiers in Financial Markets.* 1986 ISBN 90-247-3225-5

13. E.F. Toma and M. Toma (eds.): *Central Bankers, Bureaucratic Incentives, and Monetary Policy.* 1986 ISBN 90-247-3366-9

*14. D.E. Fair and C. de Boissieu (eds.): *International Monetary and Financial Integration.* The European Dimension. 1988 ISBN 90-247-3563-7

15. J. Cohen: *The Flow of Funds in Theory and Practice.* A Flow-Constrained Approach to Monetary Theory and Policy. 1987 ISBN 90-247-3601-3

16. W. Eizenga, E.F. Limburg and J.J. Polak (eds.): *The Quest for National and Global Economic Stability.* In Honor of Hendrikus Johannes Witteveen. 1988 ISBN 90-247-3653-6

*17. D.E. Fair and C. de Boissieu (eds.): *The International Adjustment Process.* New Perspectives, Recent Experience and Future Challenges for the Financial System. 1989 ISBN 0-7923-0013-0

18. J.J. Sijben (ed.): *Financing the World Economy in the Nineties.* 1989 ISBN 0-7923-0090-4

FINANCIAL AND MONETARY POLICY STUDIES

19. I. Rizzo: *The 'Hidden' Debt.* With a Foreword by A.T. Peacock. 1990 ISBN 0-7923-0610-4
*20. D.E. Fair and C. de Boissieu (eds.): *Financial Institutions in Europe under New Competitive Conditions.* 1990 ISBN 0-7923-0673-2
21. R. Yazdipour (ed.): *Advances in Small Business Finance.* 1991 ISBN 0-7923-1135-3
*22. D.E. Fair and C. de Boissieu (eds.): *Fiscal Policy, Taxation and the Financial System in an Increasingly Integrated Europe.* 1992 ISBN 0-7923-1451-4
23. W.C. Boeschoten: *Currency Use and Payment Patterns.* 1992 ISBN 0-7923-1710-6
24. H.A. Benink: *Financial Integration in Europe.* 1993 ISBN 0-7923-1849-8
25. G. Galeotti and M. Marrelli (eds.): *Design and Reform of Taxation Policy.* 1992 ISBN 0-7923-2016-6

*Published on behalf of the *Société Universitaire Européenne de Recherches Financières* (SUERF), consisting the lectures given at Colloquia, organized and directed by SUERF.

Kluwer Academic Publishers – Dordrecht / Boston / London

GPSR Compliance

The European Union's (EU) General Product Safety Regulation (GPSR) is a set of rules that requires consumer products to be safe and our obligations to ensure this.

If you have any concerns about our products, you can contact us on ProductSafety@springernature.com

In case Publisher is established outside the EU, the EU authorized representative is:

Springer Nature Customer Service Center GmbH
Europaplatz 3
69115 Heidelberg, Germany

Batch number: 10824484

Printed by Printforce, the Netherlands